BITTER ICE

BITTER ICE

A MEMOIR OF LOVE, FOOD, AND OBSESSION

Barbara Kent Lawrence

ROB WEISBACH BOOKS

WILLIAM MORROW AND COMPANY, INC. NEW YORK

Published by Rob Weisbach Books
An Imprint of William Morrow and Company, Inc.
1350 Avenue of the Americas, New York, N.Y. 10019

Library of Congress Cataloging-in-Publication Data
Lawrence, Barbara Kent.
Bitter Ice : a memoir of love, food, and obsession / Barbara Kent
Lawrence.—1st ed.
p.   cm.
ISBN 0-688-16215-0 (alk. paper)
1. Lawrence, Barbara Kent—Marriage. 2. Anorexia nervosa—
Patients—Family relationships.   I. Title.
RC552.A5L385   1999
616.85'262'0092—dc21
[B]   99-16615
CIP

Printed in the United States of America

First Edition

1 2 3 4 5 6 7 8 9 10

BOOK DESIGN BY BERNARD KLEIN

www.robweisbachbooks.com

To my friends and family, who welcomed me back

What
destruction am I
blessed by?
—A. R. Ammons

ACKNOWLEDGMENTS

I want to thank Professor Jay Simmons and my writing class at Boston University for being my first audience and helping me dare to tell this story; Candice Stover for her insightful encouragement. Peter Marcus for becoming my friend and guide in understanding that I needed to write; my agent Lane Zachary for believing that I could tell this story; and my editor Colin Dickerman for helping me do it. Thank you for all that I have learned from each of you, and for your constant support, like warm hands on my back.

My deep thanks to my children for their patience and love as I emerged from a self-spun chrysalis, and to my former husband for his understanding that I tell this story in part to understand my own complicity in the vulnerabilities we shared. I know he has made his own journey to recover and I admire him for his strength in doing so.

Acknowledgments

This is my best recollection of my life, and only that. I know that my friends and each member of my family would tell this story differently and I offer it to other people in the hope that they will find their own strengths.

PREFACE

I have used my own name in this book, because to hide behind a pseudonym would suggest that this story should not be told, but I have changed the names of almost everyone else because I want to give them anonymity.

I wrote this book because I needed to, for myself. Writing helped me understand, accept, and then forgive my own complicity in what was a profoundly dysfunctional relationship. I feel that the power of anorexia and bulimia grows in shame and secrecy. If in any way this book illuminates the shadows, for myself, my former husband, my children and other members of our families, and for any readers who may be in a similar situation, or have friends or family members who are—then I can justify the pain of making this story known.

Preface

Anorexia is a dangerous illness, reflecting, as some have suggested, elements in the culture of our time that have gone terribly awry. Writers, including Dr. Hilde Bruch, Dr. Ira Sacker, Peter J. Smith, Richard Gordon, and Stephen S. Hall, clearly make the case that anorexia and bulimia are increasing among boys and men and that it is no coincidence this is happening at this time in history—men are now subjected to the same cultural preoccupation with body image that has long afflicted women.

In an article, Peter J. Smith writes that "a few years ago, one in twenty of Dr. Sacker's patients was male. These days, Sacker estimates the ratio as one in twelve, adding that some patients who come in for treatment either for bulimia or anorexia are boys as young as five years old." Sacker states that "an increasing number of male and nonwhite adolescents and young adults are diagnosed as anorexic, and the disorder can remain entrenched long after a person reaches the age of thirty."

Too many women and men growing up at the end of the twentieth century are taking their pain out on their own bodies—for these illnesses are not just simply disorders in eating, but disorders in the person's sense of self. These are illnesses that mirror illness in our society, and we must look at them to dispel their power to hurt. In this book, I try to show the effects of these illnesses on a family, knowing that I was enabling the process of destruction because of my own vulnerabilites. There is no one to blame—the point is that we must acknowledge our own responsibility for our lives and make the best of them we can. I congratulate my former husband and his siblings, members of my own family, and myself for trying to do just that.

BITTER
ICE

1

CHRISTMAS AT THE FARM

December 1986

I heard the car and knew they were turning past the giant pink boulder that marked our driveway, bearing the name of the farm I had bought a few years before, sandblasted by the man who made headstones in Ellsworth. Though it was half a mile away, the cold air brought the sound down the hill and across the meadow, through the trees to where I stood and waited. I saw the gray Jetta as Stephen steered it up the curve of the hill. The frozen pond was on their left, sweeping to the pink granite that buttressed the trees against the mountain on the far shore; to their right, in the marsh, frozen cattails and grass pierced the snow. I stood on the rise of land where we had built our house, watching them coming home, my children, away at school, home now for Christmas. Up the frozen driveway, gravel spurting out from the tires, suddenly they were out of the car and we were hugging and laughing.

"Wow, you've grown, you look great."

"How are you? Where are Katadhin and Christofur?"

We carried blue canvas suitcases, duffel bags of laundry, and boxes of books into the house. Katadhin, Stephen's white cat, and Christofur, Katherine's sienna-brown cat, both Maine coons, made their entrances from behind the closet door, their tails arched like ostrich plumes, tufts of fur elongating their ears, thick ruffs around their throats, a regal pair. With theatrical precision they brushed their bodies and tails against chairs, over table legs, and against doorjambs until finally they reached my children, winding their bodies against their legs, and marking them in a ceremony of welcome.

"Where's Dad?"

"He's running, he should be back soon." I caught the apology in my throat, feeling both relieved and hurt for them that he was not there to greet them.

They dumped their bags in their rooms and came up the stairs to the large living room with its high cathedral ceiling and view over the pond, a height that made it feel like a tree house we shared with birds. We sat on the blue velvet couches and caught up on gossip. Though Stephen and Katherine went to the same school, there was lots to catch up on.

"You mean Sam is going out with Mrs. Wiggins?" Katherine asked Stephen. The new English teacher was at least a head taller than Sam and outweighed him. When his wife left him, his face had fallen into deeply lined arroyos, but now he smiled and my children were pleased.

"It is great, but it's just really weird to think of old people doing—sorry, Mom—well, doing anything, and I saw them holding hands after chapel," Katherine said, pausing. "The boys' cross-country did really well, but the girls were wimps and I don't know what Mr. Davis is going to do about it."

I thought about how separate their lives were from mine now. I lived in the past or the future. Only when my children were with me could I enjoy the present. I had thought so much about their return, hoped I could make their time with us fun and joyful, tried to make this *home* in ways my childhood homes never were. Because I hoped to disguise my own fears and pain from my children and from everyone else, I had enclosed myself in a little world, insular and insulated, isolating and isolated. I had pushed away old friends, members of my family who reached out to me, and avoided making new friends. I had walled myself up behind sandbags, hoping that my love for my children and my will would build a barricade strong enough to protect them. But when I sat in my small office at home, staring at the faces in frames that lined the walls, I realized I lived with the photographs of people I loved, not the people.

"Dad?"

"Yes. Hi, guys." We heard him sitting in the front hall, breathing hard, and I imagined him dripping sweat on the Mexican tiles, a haze of fog rising off his body as cold met the heat of the house.

We heard him strip off the wet clothes and carry them into the laundry, heard him open the dryer door that was now rimmed with rust and shove the clothes inside, walk to Stephen's bathroom, and slide into the icy water that already filled the tub. Finally we heard him splosh up the stairs to the living room, his slashed tennis shoes flapping with each step.

"Hey, great to have you home."

He offered a glancing hug and thin smile then went into the kitchen and opened the spigot on the plastic-lined 2.6-liter carton of Chardonnay in the icebox, filled a jelly glass, swigged the wine back into his throat, swallowed, and walked into the living room.

"I'll see you in a little while, got to take a sauna."

We heard him walk down the stairs and open the door. We heard the garage door open and close, and then the inner door of the gym. I knew we had an hour before he finished his sauna and took another bath. If I had been by myself, I would have eaten dinner in that time. If I had been by myself, I would have cooked a meal, timing it so that I could eat and clean up before he came back, because to eat with him anywhere near made me feel so nervous I choked on the food as I bolted it down.

"Would you like to eat now?" I asked my children.

"Oh, I'm not hungry, I'll just fix something later," Stephen replied.

"Me, too. I've got a lot to unpack," Katherine added. And they both got up and walked downstairs to their bedrooms.

We had an unacknowledged agreement, a conspiracy that meant none of us had to eat with him around. We had given up family dinners except on holidays. I could never get used to not eating together, a pattern so different from my own childhood, and I thought about the ways we had tried to make compromises, find alternatives.

I don't remember exactly when he—my husband, Tom—started eating ice. At first I really didn't notice because it was infrequent, but gradually it became constant and the crunching grated on my nerves. Ice was a substitute for food, and frozen water gave Tom the illusion both that he was eating and that he wasn't drinking the liquid he feared would make him bloat. At the office we shared, I turned around at my desk while he was sitting across the room from me, at his desk. I tried to avert my eyes, but I always saw him slip the melting ice, wrapped in a ragged dish towel, into his top drawer. While I was working, while I was on the phone, all day long he would pull ice cubes out and suck and crunch. I heard the crunching constantly, like an ice cutter cutting through the frozen Arctic, a thousand cicadas underfoot, squeezing Styrofoam—a sound like suicide as he substituted frozen water for food.

To rid himself of fluid, he spat. He spat into towels, new colorful tea towels, our bath towels, old or new, it didn't matter—baptizing them as his own. He left them in soggy heaps in his desk, thrown against the wall near the hamper, stashed in unexpected places, so that often when I was cleaning, my hand unwittingly wrapped around a grimy wet mass tucked in a drawer or thrown on a closet floor, even worse when it held chewed food.

He spat on the floor, in the office, too, but mostly at home, so that sometimes, if I forgot and walked around barefoot, my toes squished in the cool slime on the Mexican tile in the front hall or on the oak stairs. Sometimes I looked down in time and saw the silvery stain, like a slug's trail, across the blue-and-orange Oriental rug we bought in Jerusalem or the flowers of the Kashan in the front hall. The slate-blue carpet on the floor next to his side of the bed and the bed ruffle above it were stained reddish brown from spit, a stain I could not remove. Eating ice—spitting out the fluids that tried to nourish his body—he attempted to fool the cycle of living into a slow process of extended dying. Alcoholism, anorexia: an obsession is exactly that. An addiction warps not only the life of the one who is addicted but of everyone around him. He saw life through a monocle, his vision one-dimensional, focused on food, his body, purging, and his fear of bloating.

Tom never raised his hand against me, but he had beaten me down with relentless complaining and his desperate need for ritual, which made deviation from his patterns intolerable. Always the same schedule, never able to accommodate anyone else, not for business or friendship, not for his family. Always very early, a run followed by a plunge into a bathtub filled with ice and water, a sauna, another plunge, work from eight or so until two or three, then another run, a plunge, a sauna, another plunge, supper of a small bowl of food so covered in ketchup, mayonnaise, and mustard it was impossible to know, or even want to know, what it was, then another sauna and plunge. In bed by eight-thirty.

He wanted the bath to be very cold and would fill the tub with buckets of ice so it would feel like the brooks running from the mountains in the Adirondacks. "It feels so clean, so pure," he'd say. When we built the house we determined that each of us would have our own bathroom, which was less a luxury than a necessity. At first Tom just used his own bathroom, but then, when Stephen was away at school, he commandeered his as well. I asked Tom to stop because it was just one more room to clean, and he made things very dirty. But he replied that the water was colder in the downstairs bathroom and insisted that he use both. Then he started filling the kitchen sink with cold water and ice to sit while he was running so it would be ready when he returned. Sometimes when I came home, all the sinks and baths were full of ice and water except my own bathroom—which he never used.

The ice maker couldn't keep up with his demands, so he filled the Calphalon pots with water and put them in the freezer. The bottoms distended from the pressure, so the pots would roll over and were useless. Again, I begged him to stop, to buy cheap plastic containers in which to freeze water or just buy ice, but he couldn't stop, and he ruined most of the good pots I had bought for cooking.

Tom could no longer really run because he had injured his foot. He dressed in layers of sweatclothes to force his body to eliminate water as he stumbled down the road. Sometimes he became over-heated and his nose erupted in blood. The blood mixed with the sweat and dirt, spreading over his chin and neck and down his clothes. His turtleneck was stained pink, the blood dripped crimson over his maroon Groton sweatshirt, one he requested from our children for Christmas each year and wore until it was discolored from Clorox, threadbare and frayed at the edges. His once gray ski jacket was held by safety pins and duct tape—blotched with dirt and sweat. He had sliced his running shoes to accommodate his deformed foot, and then bound the flaps together with more duct tape. He wore a green wool ski cap over layers of other caps—an orange, a yellow—each stained and dirty. In winter, the frost collected on his beard and eyebrows, a frost created by ex-haling. Young men in trucks used to throw cans and apples at him as they drove past, and when he collapsed against our fence along the driveway or tried to do push-ups by the road, people stopped because they thought he was ill and needed help.

"Some people stopped to ask if I was all right," he would report to me. "I told them I was fine, just running." He could not see himself as he was seen.

When they were little, our children did not notice his strange-ness. It was not so pronounced then. Now, as I heard him coming back into the house from the sauna, I wondered how our adoles-cent children saw him. I was too scared to ask them, and they rarely mentioned it.

When we moved the last time, the old brown box full of Christ-mas decorations was thrown out by mistake. I lost my Christmas stocking, the fragile silvery-red Santa, and the old angel that had presided over my mother's tree. We lost the decorations from friends, ones I had bought to mark the years, ones my children had made. The loss emptied me and all I could do to fill it was to buy new decorations, birds like the ones that lived around us, to cover the branches of our tree. One Christmas we cut a tree off our property, but it seemed weak and thin. Then we had waited until the children were home for vacation, but by then all the full, thick trees had been sold—so this year I had bought a tree before they came home. We set it up in the stand in the living room, tied it with rope to the window handle so it wouldn't fall. The next evening we brought the decorations down from the attic in the red, green, and white box, each of us unwrapping the birds and handblown glass balls, the spun-glass butterflies and dragonflies.

"Oh, look, here is the Baltimore oriole we got at the bird-carving museum," Katherine said, smiling.

"And the eagle, like the one that sat on that tree and watched the carpenters building the house," I added.

"Hey, the glass spider made it through one more year," Stephen exclaimed as he carefully hung the ornament on a high branch.

A large dove of peace spread her white wings over the top of the tree. Tiny white lights sparkled, reflecting over delicate crystal icicles and snowflakes. Little wooden chickadees, woodpeckers, and blue jays, cardinals flashing red, mysterious woven straw Chinese birds, and a preening peacock with a bright flaring tail all perched on fragrant balsam branches. When we finished, the tree really was lovely. We spread a white sheet underneath and the cats climbed the lower branches and batted at the soft cloth birds that hung at the bottom of the tree for their amusement. We put out presents, not all the ones I had hidden away, but most, and I calculated again to make sure there was an equal number for each of my children.

We brought out the stockings, the ones I made to replace those we had lost. I had sewn the first ones with great care, appliquéing little scenes against the felt, trains chugging along wool tracks, animals and birds, butterflies in the jungle, incorporating things my children had loved. I had sewn a fancy bottle of wine against a flow of grapes on Tom's stocking, an unconscious irony at the time. The new ones were simpler. For Tom, a Princeton tiger peeked out of tall grass, and for my children, large trains, some with open-topped flatcars so I could hide a lottery ticket or a check, chugged along the tracks up the stocking. I had not felt able to decorate my own stocking, so it unfurled, a plain white felt flag of protest and surrender.

For months I had hidden away little games and odd jokes, everything from razor blades to jewelry, Silly Putty and perfume, peach silk scarves and the blue-and-red canisters of German bubbles that last a long time. I had wrapped each present in white tissue paper and bound it with colored tape and placed the presents in separate shopping bags marked with each person's name. I had planned and worked to make a "good" Christmas, in the only way I knew how to define that term, because I wanted, more than anything, to be a good mother.

Now it was time to pack each other's stockings. We sat in a circle in the living room, Tom on the straight-backed chair in front of the television, Stephen on the blue velvet loveseat, Katherine and I on the matching couch, and started with the tangerines, slipping them down the stocking so they waited in the toe.

"Hey, Mom, I think this is toothpaste. Now, could this be toothpaste?"

"Oh, lucky you, Stephen, I think you've got some deodorant," I teased.

They squeezed and shook every package, laughing about the pragmatic contents, guessing at the more mysterious ones, bewildered by some I had taken care to disguise.

"Now, Mom, what is this? It's so tiny and it doesn't make any noise when I shake it," Katherine said, holding the little package to her ear.

"Well, Kit, I think it's probably a package of nail files, but I can't remember," I replied, but through the wrapping I could see the gold ring with tourmalines from Maine that I had bought for my daughter because it reminded me of one I had when I was her age.

"Come on, Dad," they encouraged him, "you've got a ton of stuff here, I bet it's all that hot sauce you like or Dr. Bronner's soap."

Tom sat on the armless chair wearing his faded red-and-green madras pants, the pockets stained from bleeding pens. His orange Princeton rugby shirt was frayed and the color jarred with the pants and his mismatched red hunting socks. He looked like a rag doll, almost tolerable at home, but he wore these clothes to the office. I began to feel tense, watching him out of the sides of my eyes for a pout or clenching jaw, gauging from the redness of his face how much wine he had drunk in the kitchen.

We tried to wedge awkward shapes into the stockings, but the presents spilled out over the couch, and when we were finished Tom said he had to go to bed so he could run in the morning. The children asked him to play a game of Ping-Pong and he accepted after a little protest. After he went to bed we sat around and talked, and then Stephen and Katherine went to their own rooms. Before I walked down to the bedroom I still shared with Tom, I walked into the small kitchen, where I stood for a moment and thought about all the preparations I had made for Christmas Day.

In the evenings after work I had been preparing for Christmas dinner in the ways I had learned. I polished the silver that had lain in the brown cloth since Thanksgiving and before that since Christmas of last year. There was not so much of it now, because we sold what we didn't use or want, but I had my mother and stepfather's good flatware, the set with his initials, and the heavy-handled knives and forks balanced well in my hand. I polished the pearl-handled butter knives from Aunt Eleanor and Uncle Albert, and the handsome round silver tray with the embossed heraldic crest. I polished the elegant little gravy boat with my stepsister's mother's initials and thought about the adversities that had brought these artifacts to my table. I washed the ivory linen tablecloth my mother had bought when I was with her in Hong Kong and the four cleanest napkins in the big washtub. I wished I knew what to do to take out the stains of Christmases past, but I didn't dare use too much Clorox. Carefully I ironed the linen and folded it around tissue paper.

I arranged flowers, cleaned the house. I had bought the English crackers that Katherine loved and the glacéed apricots Stephen liked. I had cut the holly and pine boughs, gathered pinecones in the woods around our house, and bought two huge cones that came from California because their size amazed me. I had some special wooden train decorations for the table and red ribbons attached to a little favor for each of us to pull out of the centerpiece. Like a sorcerer's apprentice I had followed old rituals, hoping that by reenacting them I could create at least the illusion of beauty, love, and fulfillment. I didn't yet see that the feasts of my childhood had left me hungry and that old magic wouldn't exorcise the demons that were working against my family now.

Morning. Christmas morning. I startled awake, my dreams still swirling around me. I had always found more truth in myself in the early morning as I let the thoughts of night drift into the realities of day and before consciousness closed the gate of my mind and locked what I couldn't look at inside. Sometimes I dreamed that an enormous wave, a tsunami, swept down over us as we were swimming in the ocean, my children and my younger brother and sister, and somehow I had to rescue us all. Sometimes, when I woke, I pulled myself away from Kevin, an old boyfriend. His face and body had come back to haunt me and I felt him against me at night. Being with him in my mind was almost enough to keep me sane, and though I felt guilty about these dreams, they sustained me, and sometimes before I went to sleep, lying near one man, I conjured up the sounds and smells, the skin, muscles, hair, the hands, and mouth of another.

Sometimes at night I dreamed that I was a graduate student but I had to take an exam to pass the French requirement and my hands were sweating as I filled in the little bubbles on the form. When I awoke, at first I felt relieved. I had all the right things: I was a married woman, living in a beautiful house, running a successful business, with two wonderful children, each in a great school. But then slowly I remembered that I was chained to a man I did not love, to a man whose toxicity was making me ill, too.

I was learning to be scared by illness as I neared the age at which my parents had died: my mother at fifty-three and my father two months before her, at fifty-five. Sometimes I caught myself while sitting in front of the computer screen, my shoulders hunched so high they hugged my ears and a yoke of tension bracketing my neck. I forced my shoulders down, but in a few minutes the gnawing ache was back, a pain I could not get rid of.

Each fall the strain of living with Tom, trying to be a buffer between him and the world, trying to run our business and raise our children, caught up with me and I got sick—sometimes with a strange and frightening disease, one that found a way to stop my body because my mind wouldn't let me rest. One year my doctor thought I had lymphoma because my lymph system was so swollen, but it turned out be a reaction to black-fly bites. Another time it was rheumatoid arthritis or perhaps the start of very early menopause brought on by stress. One day I was able to run five miles and the next I was crippled by what the emergency-room attendant called "the worst case of water on the knees I have ever seen." I hobbled around, pulling myself up stairs with my hands, and then my wrists and hands began to swell and ache. I lay in bed at night staring at the ceiling, feeling betrayed by my body.

For this Christmas breakfast I heated a cranberry muffin and put it on one of the chipped plates with the pink border and ornate flowers in the center that had been Mummy's favorites. I poured a glass from the carton of orange juice and spooned vanilla yogurt into a little blue Chinese bowl. I made Irish Breakfast tea, stained deep as the Blackwater River that winds through County Cork, and I began to cook for dinner. All that week we had negotiated and bargained. I worked to plan the menu for a meal we could eat together that would not upset Tom, and yet would still feel like a celebration. I sneaked a few delicacies into the house—Godiva chocolates for after supper, a package of Boursin for before—but he found the cheese in the icebox and now the remainder looked like a gutted building.

I had negotiated for this Christmas dinner, trying as best I could to preserve some semblance of Christmas past, with its glowing perfection and surface warmth. I risked Tom's wrath and sourness, his lashing, cutting remarks and curt dismissal of my mind and body because it mattered so much to me to try to have a home for my children. I knew I drew my courage from my children and found the strength to defend them though I had not yet learned to defend myself. I was caught between my fear of hurting my children by leaving their father, and staying in a home where the very air seemed poisonous.

We negotiated. I gave up plum pudding; he allowed an avocado in the salad. He didn't want stuffing or gravy; I gave up muffins. He didn't want the wild rice we had gotten as a Christmas present, got upset if I pushed for two vegetables. I didn't even try to talk about dessert.

"It's just rich junk, that's what killed your parents. What are you trying to do to us? You always cook too much food. It's wasteful and disgusting. No one needs all that food."

I had cooked the things that could be set aside: boiled the water when he was running so he wouldn't see all the sugar dissolving, poured in two bags of cranberries like red pop beads, grated the orange rind. Let it simmer until the berries released their sour juice and mixed with the sugar, let it gurgle and splat like gas emerging through mud, then pulled it off the stove and stirred in the rind. Meringues—I could make them quickly, swirling the egg whites in the large copper mixing bowl, whisking in air to mound them with sugar and vanilla, baking them till just brown, like perfectly cooked marshmallows, then hiding them away in the upper cupboard. I sautéed the mushrooms, prunes, onions, sage, and garlic, melted the butter into the water and mixed it all into the bread crumbs, smelled the rich sweet steam like a delicious vaporizer. Then I wrestled with the turkey, the one our neighbors raised at their farm down the road. I tried to forget that I had looked at these birds fattening for the past two months. I washed and patted the milky-white breast, squeezed half an orange into the cavity and half as a kind of baptism over the breast and legs, rubbed butter into the skin like a rich emollient, stuffed and trussed, heaved the bird into the pan, breast down so the juices would flow into the meat.

"Good morning, Kit, Merry Christmas. Is Stephen up?" I asked.

"No, not yet. I think he was up late reading."

But a few minutes later we heard his door open and he came upstairs and they made their breakfasts. I had tried to get the things they liked; Honey Nut Cheerios, yogurt. I heard them pouring milk into bowls and the cereal. They talked as they sat at the table, then read yesterday's paper and the latest *Newsweek*. We talked a little while I worked on dinner, and while we waited for Tom to return.

When he came back from running and got cleaned up, we planned to open the stockings. But first he would go into his bathroom. His intestines were so constricted that they would not function without massive doses of powerful laxatives. For years he was an Ex-Lax junkie until he finally paid attention to medical warnings and started using a "gentle" herbal laxative. I don't know why it didn't occur to me to read the label until years after he started using this laxative—but it didn't. When I did I was shocked to learn that even this remedy was dangerous and that his system would break down under the stress of such purging.

I remember so many mornings listening to the explosions of his gut; the roar of cannon, thunder pealing through the ceiling. The children and I laughed in embarrassment and amazement because it was so impossibly loud, so invasive. The sounds and acrid-sweet smell permeated the house, filling our ears and noses with a pungency even Lysol couldn't interdict.

Sometimes I would be sitting on the couch reading or having breakfast at the table and he would come in the room, walk over near me, and then fart. The gas, an erupting mushroom cloud, would envelop me in its poison. At first I thought these episodes were accidental and I would forgive him, embarrassed for what I assumed was his embarrassment. But after too many times, when I felt like a prisoner forced to breathe the fetid air of the dungeon, I realized that this was exactly the point. This and his need to be totally accepted—no matter how outrageously he behaved.

For years I tried to identify the sickening smell that followed him during the day and filled our bedroom at night. I used to wake up at night when I slept next to him, my head and my heart drumming a tattoo. It was a thick sweet smell, but suffocating and sickly—I thought it was from the cheap white wine he drank from cardboard containers. Then I thought perhaps he had not cleaned himself when he went to the bathroom and it was the smell of shit. Finally, I realized it was the smell of his body feeding on itself, the slow destruction, cell by cell of a body desperate to survive but dying from starvation.

After my Christmas breakfast I walked alone through the woods. There were pileated woodpeckers in these woods, adzing their way through dead trees as if they were digging a canoe. I had found the yard where the deer bed on cold nights, circled around each other, the tracks of fisher, fox dens, and slides of otters. Sometimes Stephen and I went for a walk because he enjoyed finding these signs of life as I did. Sometimes I went with Katadhin, who tracked and pointed for me like a setter, finding a family of skunks, tunnels of voles, traces of hares and partridges, and stopping to sniff and mark the passage of other animals.

Later I dressed the table for dinner. It was twelve feet long, an antique English kitchen table with drawers, its soft surface pocked and scarred. I imagined the help sitting around it chopping onions and meat, then having their own dinner before they served up-stairs. I bought it because it fit the generous space of our large living-dining room, because I had inherited ten dining-room chairs, and because I had once hoped it would bring guests. But we rarely sat there, and even less often ate together.

We finished the preparations for dinner. Stephen washed and broke apart the heads of Boston and red lettuce and sliced the avocado and the tightly rolled endive. Katherine cut the French bread crossways, slipping herbed butter between the still-connected slices. Tom was running again. The kitchen of this large house was very small—perhaps because when we designed it, the children were young and we didn't think about fitting everyone in together as they grew, or perhaps because the kitchen is the heart of a house and I knew that ours had atrophied.

The turkey had been roasting all afternoon. Its rich smell dominated the house. Every twenty minutes we basted and admired it as it grew deep golden brown, the skin taut and crackled. Finally, it was time to take it from the oven to cool before Tom carved it open with the knife Stephen had sharpened. Tom came in and poured a glass of wine. I could see he was trying to be friendly and cheerful, but he frowned at the smells and sight of this relative abundance.

We sat at the table—nestled at one end. The empty expanse of the rest of the table was sometimes a mockery to me, but now I was glad we were by ourselves. We saw our children so infrequently and these moments were precious, so I tried to savor them. Tom poured wine into our glasses. The turkey was magnificent, tender and juicy, the stuffing soft and savory smelling, the gravy made with pan drippings and a little arrowroot; the cranberry sauce with orange peel filled a silver bowl. I had cooked wild rice with walnuts, and broccoli with hollandaise, and there was fresh green salad.

Tom served grudging portions, particularly to me. A thin slice of turkey with no crackling skin, a piece of broccoli, a tablespoon of stuffing. His face tightened, pain clamping his jaw and clawing at his eyes—as if he carved each slice of white turkey meat from his own body—yet he insisted on serving us. I had positioned the cranberry sauce and gravy out of his reach and deployed the serving dishes around the table, but like a general marshaling his troops, he ordered them in a row in front of his command post. He never offered us seconds, so we had to brave his salvos of anger to ask for more. The children were growing, so they could "get away" with it—but not me. I was caught by my children's need for me to stand up to him, which I could sometimes see in their eyes when I backed down before his demands, and my fear that his outbursts would upset them. I was scared to stand up to him because I was afraid he would break apart; I thought I was the stronger one and could bear hardships more easily.

He put almost nothing on his plate: a tight little circle of a piece of broccoli followed by a teaspoon of gravy over a mushroom and a morsel of turkey. Katherine said: "Dad, do you want some of the cranberry sauce, it's really good," but he snapped, "No. No cranberry sauce, no one needs so much sugar."

Stephen offered French bread fresh from the baker and butter with dill, but Tom pushed it away. "No one needs that fat."

He didn't want portobello mushrooms sautéed in butter and wine. He spurned the stuffing with nuts and prunes, chopped garlic, raisins and herbs, the crisp crackling brown turkey skin. He pursed his mouth and said self-righteously, "No one needs that junk."

"I want some more, Dad," Stephen said, and Tom obliged by slicing off a piece of turkey.

"Yes, I think I would like a little more," I added, hoping that by attaching my request to Stephen's it wouldn't offend Tom.

"Sure, Mom," Stephen said, picking up my plate and passing it to his father, so that Tom had to put something on it. But I watched as Tom clenched his jaw and I knew that we were pushing him into an uncomfortable place.

He made us feel as if we had no self-discipline, and were somehow dirty for eating and trying to enjoy this meal. He seemed to think self-abnegation could purify him, that his self-denial was some kind of religious ritual, cleansing him and freeing him from the dirty demands of the flesh. So he didn't eat. He sat pouting at one end of the long table, a scrawny Buddha sunk into his navel, playing with his hands, pressing the tips together, then pushing the palms till they met, tensing his lips in syncopation.

Sitting at the table, we tried to talk, searching for safe topics, topics we hoped would interest him and lure him into joining us. But finally we gave up and tried to keep a conversation going as if he were not there. But he was, and our conversation was stifled and trite, a ritual in itself that we wanted to get over with.

"Have you read the paper today?"

"Yes. Did you see the article about . . . ?"

"What is the most interesting book you read at school this term?"

"Well, I really like Chaim Potok's *The Chosen.*"

"How is your term paper going? "

"It's okay. I wish I had picked a different topic."

We struggled along, self-conscious under his glare, doing the best we could to support each other. I thought of the conversations around dining tables when I was a child, the talk between my brilliant stepfather and his friends, government officials and columnists, intellectual games played with passion and expertise, volley, parry, thrust.

While we tried to talk, Tom snaked his spoon across the table, dipping it furtively in the cranberry sauce, then the potatoes and gravy. Tentatively he sneaked a few spoonfuls, and then ran his forefinger around the rim—a child tasting leftover frosting in a bowl—finally dipping all his fingers in to scoop the potatoes out of the bowl and into his mouth. His hands were soon smeared with gravy and mashed potatoes, his face dotted with blobs of hollandaise, grease on his full lips, as if by not using the appropriate utensils or eating "properly," he was not really eating. We sat on either side of the table, Stephen, Katherine, and I, trying not to look at him, trying to pretend he was all right.

With relief we took the remains of dinner to the kitchen and Tom offered to clear the table. No, he didn't want any dessert and he couldn't understand how we could eat anything more after we had gorged ourselves. He had more wine. He had wine in the kitchen and at the table, and then he sat back down and watched, like a partially hooded hawk, blinking at tether. I brought out the meringues and a little piece of fruitcake for myself, because I was the only one who liked it. His eyes fixed on my spoon as I dipped it into the ice cream and scooped a few raspberries into my mouth in defiance. His eyes following as I chewed each bite. The meringue melted into a sullen clump in my mouth like Sheetrock dust, and it was hard to swallow.

We finished dessert. Again, he offered to clear the table. The children and I went to sit in the living room and waited because we knew what he was doing. If I went into the kitchen, I would find him, his hands sunk into the turkey like a frenzied gynecologist, tearing it to pieces, stuffing the meat in his mouth, clawing at the cranberry sauce, smearing it over his lips, pushing wads of potato into his mouth, swallowing as fast as he could so he would not choke on the food, as if getting this obscene act over with quickly made it more bearable, an act of self-hatred not pleasure.

I felt as if I were doing penance for some deep sin I could not remember or understand: ashamed and trapped and helpless. My parents were dead, his parents were dead. I had no close friends anymore—no one I could trust enough to talk to. I could not think of anyone who would help me.

When I was growing up, my father was a shadowy figure, falling away from me into the darkness. I had no image of a real father, a man I could call Daddy, and as an adult I duplicated my childhood and failed at what meant most to me: giving my children the best childhood I could. But maybe, after all, that is exactly what I did, in the only way I knew how.

2

CHRISTMAS AT THE FARM

December 1964

I drove my gray VW bug home from college in Vermont. It looked like a Nazi helmet, and I wished I'd had the courage to choose red instead of gray. I followed the dirt road, a furrow parting the drifts, the black silhouettes of trees shadowing the sunlit snow. I saw the herd of seventeen Hereford steers gaining weight in the field. Mummy had told me Rosier, our gnarled caretaker, called one night the previous week to say, "Ma'am, the wolves done it."

"Did what?" she had asked.

"Stole the laig."

"Leg to what, the piano?"

"No, ma'am, the steer."

But when Mummy drove from Washington to check, she found

20

the animal with a neat slit across the throat. So Rosier admitted it was the "wee sorts," people he had told us about when Mummy, whose name I shared, and my stepfather Desie first bought the farm, but whom we had never seen—people who were black and Indian and lived between the manicured farms in the thick webbed woods, curtained with creeper and bittersweet. Rosier told Mummy the wee sorts had killed what Mummy then laughingly called the "entire profit" of this gentleman's herd. How strange to have people living on the edges of our land with no home of their own, and more strange to feel like one of them.

I came to the edge of the property, where the driveway met the main road and saw the ivory-colored sign: PALMERSTONE. As I turned up the curve of the hill, I could feel tension tying knots inside me. I thought about what I had just learned in my anthropology class at college: that the Inca tied complex patterns of knots in ropes as mnemonic devices so that runners could re-member messages they carried to distant villages. I wished I knew how to untie my knots, how to rewrite the messages they carried inside me.

The frozen pond lay on the left, the house straight ahead, and to the right, the barn built in 1811 with wooden pegs. I saw the paddock and the horses, including Traveler, my sixteen-and-a-half-hand chestnut gelding, who raised his head in curiosity at my car, but hardly knew me. Started in 1624, the walls of the original house were a foot and a half thick, a refuge first from Indians and then from Yankees, and finished with two wings built after those dangers had passed. My mother and stepfather had added a tennis court and enjoyed planning an expansive master bedroom over a new and much larger living room.

I stumbled out of the car, stiff-jointed from the long drive, as they walked out the front door and stood under the portico, smil-ing. Toulie, the basset hound Mummy adopted from owners who had named him Toulouse-Lautrec, was loping about in the snow, but Gwen, my arthritic old beagle, hobbled over to the car, the first to greet me. Gwen had been waiting all this semester for me. Standing next to the car, looking up at me and wanting to jump in as she used to do, instead she picked up her paws, one after the other, in a little dance of welcome and rolled over so slowly on her back, exposing her belly swollen with age, and let me stroke her velvet doe ears again.

Gwen had been my friend since my first Christmas with Desie in 1948, when he brought her to me, carrying her up the stairs while I stared in disbelief—not daring to hope she was for me, a wiggly beagle puppy, all ears and tail, peeing her ecstasy across the black-and-white marble floor in the new house they had bought in New York. Desie had won my heart by giving me the puppy I wanted, insisting only that her name be Gwendolyn: his friend, also a new stepfather, missed the point entirely and gave his step-daughter an expensive carved jade temple dog. Gwen soon became my best friend, waiting every night for me as I walked up the stairs from dinner.

I turned away from her and walked to where they were standing, waiting for me. Mummy thin and elegant in a red Royal Stewart shirt from Abercrombie's and blue jeans, deep brown hair and eyes, fine English bones, beautiful at forty-four. I felt her collarbones jut against me and her hug was quick, her kiss a brush against my cheek. "Oh. Your hair is so long, you look like a hippie. Don't you want to go to Henri's Salon?" she greeted me.

Desie put out his arms to me. Seven years my mother's senior with gray hair at the temples, dimpled Irish smile, a Boston Brahmin transplanted by his father to New York, schooled at St. Mark's, Harvard, and Harvard Law School, he served his country without embarrassment at the CIA. Des, my ten-year-old half brother, a lively shrimp, bounced in excitement, and Joan, my twelve-year-old half sister who had always been beautiful, with thick blond hair and deep brown eyes, hugged me. My stepsister

Frankie, Desie's daughter, was in Barbados with her mother and stepfather for the holiday and I missed her already. She had become my friend and she took some of the pressure off me, as Mummy was always nice to her. My English grandmother, Grannie, was there, tall and handsome, taller than Mummy and not quite so beautiful. She used a rolling pin on her hips and thighs in an attempt to stay young and loved it when people thought I was her daughter.

"Good heavens!" Grannie echoed my mother. "You have had your ears pierced. You look like a Gypsy!"

I wanted to add that my friend Sheila, the first anorexic I knew—though we didn't than have a name for the fact that she ate only one hard-boiled egg a day—liked to pierce ears, holding half a raw potato behind the lobe and carefully driving a long needle through the flesh until she could force the gold stanchion through. But I spared them most of my college life, including this, because I knew they didn't like my friends or my changing view of the world, because it was hard for me to share what or who mattered to me, and because I knew it would only give them more to use against me.

"Here, let me take your bag," Desie offered, and he and my little brother looked for something to carry.

"I didn't have much time to pack after exams," I apologized. "There's really a lot of stuff. I can get it," I said, turning to block the car door as I looked at the debris in my car, seeing through their eyes the loose books jammed in between the seats and wedged around the spare tire, the dirty ashtray, a black hairbrush, a half-empty pack of unfiltered Camel cigarettes, pillowcases full of dirty laundry, and the green leather overnight bag Mummy gave me when I was in boarding school and in which I had grown red runner beans so vigorous they blocked out the light from the only window in the room. Now it held tubes of oil paint, a can of fixative, rags, and brushes.

Gwen sat in the hall while I carried my things into the house and up to the room I shared with my half sister, waiting for me at the foot of the steps because she could no longer climb them, following me with her eyes. I thought back to coming home from school each day, dressed in the drab uniform, a smoke-blue jumper, white shirt with innocent rounded collar, and stolid brown oxford shoes, a plain child with brown eyes and straight brown hair. I saw Gwen in my mind as I walked down the long hallway in their house in Georgetown, away from the dining room with its graceful mahogany table and heavy Georgian silver candlesticks. The walls there were robin's-egg blue and the Oriental export china gleamed from its perches. The deep brown floors glowed from buffing and I saw the little powder room with its exquisite and amusing wallpaper—Chinese men and women flirting behind parasols that spun in a rich blend of aqua, orange, salmon, peach, and purple. It delighted me that Mummy had found little hand towels in the colors of the wallpaper and I loved admiring how well they matched.

As I had walked down that hall as a child, I always wanted Desie and Mummy to call me back to the dining-room table. I wanted to sit with them and listen to them talk. I wanted to tell them about school and how in third grade, when there were boys in our class, they would drag me over to the side of the playground during recess where the teacher couldn't see us and pull down my pants. I wanted to tell Mummy and Desie that I didn't like this but that I didn't know what to do to protect myself—but I didn't dare, and besides, in fourth grade the boys went to their own school. I wanted to walk back to Desie and Mummy, instead of doing what I was expected to do—go to my room and work on my homework—and each night, by the time I reached the top step of the front stairs, I was crying. But each night Gwen was waiting there for me, her eyes following me up the stairs, her tail thumping slowly in cadence with my steps, and each night I sat on the top step and hugged her while she licked my tears away.

Every time I came back from college with hope, trying to feel at home, and each time I left I had to admit that this was not my home in some ways, because Desie was not my father. I always felt too aware of my voice, risen to a place that made me conscious of my words, as if I sent them out one by one as emissaries, hoping to find the right way to negotiate the narrow path through land mines that I knew were hidden just underneath our conversations: my friends, the war, my hair, the sexual revolution and my own evolution, my biological father, money. I knew the dangers when they exploded. Sometimes before I came home I wrote a script in my head. I tried to think of the things to say, to ask: "How is your work going?" But then Desie worked at CIA, so I couldn't expect him to tell me very much. "Mummy, what's going on at the Hearing and Speech Center?" "Joan, are you thinking of going to boarding school?" It all seemed trite, contrived, and constricted.

But now the smells, smells of this house, the farm, and the smells of Christmas, wrapped around me as I walked back down the stairs. I tried to separate them strand by strand. Dinner—maybe Maddie, our cook, had made a pie. I smelled evergreens—the tree, balsam? Garlands of cedar and pine outlined the oak mantel and twined down the heavy oak stairs that cascaded somewhat ostentatiously into the surprisingly small living room. The staircase ended in two ornate newel posts—modeled after some grand manor two hundred years ago and carved from trees cut from this land. The liqueur-sweet metal-and-cinnamon smell of Hoeppe's oil told me Desie and Des had been cleaning shotguns. And underneath it all, the smell of the old house itself, horsehair plaster, and polished wood, and when I opened the downstairs closet to put my coat away, the smell of rubber boots and wool and the ghost—this was where tradition said she lived, because she didn't like electricity and we didn't put a light there because it made a good story.

I loved being in this old house, feeling the voices of many people—the Civil War hero who killed his drunken brother-in-law on the front steps as he came stumbling in, gun drawn, looking for his terrified wife. Or was it the Civil War hero who was drunk? The voices of Carters, Fosters, and Turners, the only names in this Southern town to which we were newcomers, all woven together, Foster Turner, Turner Carter, Carter Foster, Turner Foster, in interminable connections between people living and dead. I loved finding arrowheads and bits of clay pipes in the newly plowed ground and thinking about Colonel Mosby, the Gray Ghost, who we knew hid out from Yankees in the icehouse at our neighbor's farm, so why not at ours, too?

I walked through the hall to the dining room, the smells intensifying, until I opened the swinging door to the kitchen and they burst around me. Maddie and her husband, Lester, our butler, welcomed me home with hugs and laughter. "Barbara, you sure are looking beautiful. Look at your hair, so long. I bet you've got those Northern boys twirling around your fingers."

"Oh, Maddie." I blushed.

"That's right, Barbara, sure is," Lester added, "sure is." Maddie, lean but warm like prune whip from the oven, was cooking dishes to last a few days because she and Lester would go home for their own Christmas. Lester was rubbing the silver with a yellow chamois cloth, his long ocher fingers frosted with polish. Nothing was as fancy here as it was in town, but there was still a bell on the table to ring so Lester knew when he was needed, and tall silver candlesticks and the flatware Mummy found at an auction.

"Lester, the silver looks so beautiful. Guess you haven't been doing much fishing lately with Des, but what about the wrestling? Have you been to the wrestling matches together?" I asked.

"Oh, yes, Miss Barbara. We love to see the wrasslin'. We saw a—"

"Lester, you hush up," Maddie interjected. "Barbara don't want to hear about those sweaty men beating each other up."

"Maddie," I asked, "what have you been cooking? It smells so good."

"Just a little fussin', just a little special fussin' to make a good Christmas for you all," she replied.

Pockets of smells rose from the stove: apples and cinnamon, and flaking pie crust and curls of lemon rind splined out for cocktails, mincemeat and cranberry sauce with grated orange peel, the beginnings of a beef-and-walnut stew or maybe Stroganoff. I saw baskets of orange tangerines and kumquats, purple grapes, dusky Bosc pears, and next to them, a tray of glacéed fruit arrayed in neat layers, like Roman soldiers drawn into a turtle formation. My eyes traveled over the silver tray with crackers and a crisp baguette that promised Brie, Jarlsberg, and Boursin before dinner. Then I saw the Christmas cake rising on a silver stand under a glass cover. "Maddie, wow! That's beautiful. How did you make it?"

"That's special marzipan icing and those little flowers, they are real, they're sugarcoated violets and buttercups that your mother and grandmother used to have when they were children. You better leave me alone now or you aren't going to have any dinner," and she turned back toward her stove.

Before dinner we gathered in the living room. The walls had been painted by a man who flew down from Philadelphia and hand-rubbed six coats of paint into the old walls in a blend of salmon and peach until they looked like worn sandstone at sunset. "How was your drive down from Vermont?" Grannie asked.

"Okay really," I replied. "It takes a while, but it was uneventful. What's going on at school?" I asked Des and Joan.

"We had the Christmas play. I was an angel and Des was a shepherd," Joan replied.

"Oh, I should have known," I added. "That's what I used to do at that school the whole semester. I loved it."

"Now, what is it you are taking at college this semester?" Desie asked.

I turned to look at him, thinking about the ways my life at college were changing my view about life at home. "I'm studying acculturation and culture change in one class and traditional societies in another. I think I'll take primitive economics next semester—it's the only kind I could understand," I joked. He laughed, and the moment passed. Then Lester announced dinner and we walked into the dining room, the oldest room in the house, nestled between the kitchen, which had once been a porch, and the living room. There were small windows looking out over the neighbor's pastures and cornfields and two corner cabinets with blue-and-white Dutch china, a fireplace with the original mantel, and floors of wide-board oak. Mummy sat at one end of the table, Desie at the other, Grannie on his right, I on his left, Joan and Des of either side of Mummy.

The dinner, lean beef Stroganoff with sliced mushrooms and onions, yellow egg noodles to absorb the rich sour-cream sauce, asparagus and hollandaise, warm French bread, salad with endives and avocados—lots of Château Lascombes, followed by homemade mango ice cream and the wonderful Scotch shortbread cookies that Desie's old nurse made and sent at Christmas—and then Grand Marnier and demitasse in the living room.

Here, at this table, I was an equal. Here, I ate the same food with the same silver and drank from the same crystal, and if I was careful I would not feel like a guest. Here, at dinner, everything was beautiful, rich, and abundant; I could confuse abundance with acceptance, nurturing, and love and feel full.

As we sat, Desie told a story about getting out of Burma after the war. "I heard about the bomb and I knew it was all over. I just started walking out of the jungle. I didn't get the orders to leave Burma, but I knew we would be going. I got credited with the fastest march to India—but it was just because we left a week early."

Mummy told us about a little boy at the Hearing and Speech Center who wasn't making progress because his parents were ashamed of his disability and never spoke to him.

"It's very odd really. Some of the little Negro children do better than the white children. I think it's because their families accept them and everyone plays with them." Grannie told us about her trip to England on the *Britannic* last year, and about how she was planning to go again next summer, as she did every year. I had thought about which stories to tell and which not to tell and finally settled on a few that seemed safe.

"Our archaeology class went to see Grandma Moses' house because it's an archaeological site. But it's so strange; her house is built of cinder block and painted bright pink. Inside there are cases and tables of artifacts they found when they plowed the fields around it, and some amazing paintings."

No more conversations about my hair and earrings. No conversation about the war or my dissolute friends. Mummy could tell my friends were disreputable because they had long hair, too. I wanted to point out that flappers had been considered dissolute because they *cut* their hair, but I had learned to bite my tongue and force platitudes out of my mouth. I had learned to skirt around my mother's fear and envy that I went to one of the best schools, and that she, daughter of an unassuming English barrister, felt she had never really gone to school at all. I was sad sometimes that she could not care about my world, as I did not seem to care about hers, sorry that she could not understand and appreciate what was best in me, and tried instead to turn my strengths to weaknesses. Whenever I attempted to talk about my life, about who and what mattered to me, she would stop me, saying, "You're so introspective, you just think about yourself. You are so selfish."

I wanted to answer her: "I am just confused and lonely. I don't know what I have done wrong to have a father who can't love me, but I apologize." I felt helpless and scared that it didn't please her that I loved her husband and wished that he were my real father. He was so brilliant and accomplished, so unlike my own father. I admired him and wished I could be more like him, but I feared I was my real father's child.

*   *   *

Once, when I had come home from boarding school, we sat at dinner in the house in Georgetown. Desie asked what I was studying, and excited by his interest and my own love of books, I answered, "Oh, we're reading English poetry with Mrs. Wordsworth—isn't that a perfect name for an English teacher? We just read Keats's odes 'To Autumn' and 'To a Nightingale.'"

And Desie had responded, drifting into the channels and eddies of his mind, "Isn't the second line of the third stanza in 'To Autumn' wonderful?" And then he continued to deliver brilliant commentary on a poem he had not read in twenty years. Spellbound, I listened to every word, until with a sharp crash, Mummy threw back her chair and it fell, legs quivering in the air as she rushed out of the dining room, clutching her napkin to her face and screaming: "I'm nothing, you don't even think I have a brain. I just sit here with these stupid little kids and you don't even talk to me."

And Joan and Des, their eyes round with fear and pain, looked at me, and Desie sighed and put his napkin down and went upstairs while I tried to make my little sister and brother feel better, asking them about their school or games or whatever I could think of to put light back in their eyes. Many years later, so many years later, I would realize that I had a mother who was beautiful but so vulnerable that she fought to hold center stage by denying entrance to those of us who were waiting in the wings.

But now we had had a good dinner—a great dinner—and it was time to sit together for a while and then go to bed. The next morning I went to find Alice, a stray cat, who in summer slept in a large bird's nest outside the kitchen window and during the winter in the barn, earning her keep by hunting the mice and rats that lived there, too. One day late in summer years ago, she brought her new litter out to play and I tried to pick up a kitten, but it ravaged my hand, spitting and clawing. Now I kept my distance, but I still loved sitting in the loft, waiting for the wild young cats to creep out from between the bales, gentling them with my voice, and when they learned to ignore me, watching them stalk, pounce, and wrestle in fur tangles, preparing for their own battles. The thick musty-sweet smell of hay tickled my nose, and I could feel it deep in my lungs. I listened to the horses clomping around in their stalls and smelled the leather and neat's-foot oil we used on their hooves. I had a book and lost myself in it and the peace of this barn for hours. History, biography, anthropology, how wonderful it felt to be in college and have an excuse to go off by myself for hours and call it "work."

That evening we pulled the huge thick-needled Christmas tree into the living room and lashed it to the window frames with clothesline so it wouldn't topple from the stand that seemed too small. Mummy had brought the box of decorations from the attic and we began the ritual of taking them out of their cardboard-and-tissue-paper nests. "Here's the angel," she said. "It looks a bit bedraggled. Will you fix it?" I loved taking the wings and smoothing them out, combing back the thinning rayon hair, making a new halo of gold foil to replace the one that had been torn, and finally giving it to Desie to put up on the highest branch. Mummy found the delicate, glass Santa Claus she had owned since her childhood. "Here it is, here is my favorite. Now I have to find a safe place for him. I don't want him to get hurt."

As I watched her my mind wandered back to one afternoon when I was about ten. I came back from school, dropped my book bag on the hall carpet, and stopped to look at the mail on the curved mahogany table in the front hall. There were many envelopes addressed to my brother and younger sister, all with the word "trustee" in the return address on the upper left corner. I knew these thick white envelopes were special and I sensed that they were what made the other children different from me. As I stood by the table fingering the envelopes, Mummy came down the stairs.

I looked up at her and she said, "What are you doing!" Her voice was a sharp prick into my thoughts.

"I'm just looking at the envelopes," I said, hoping that was all right. But then, though I sensed I was crossing onto treacherous ground, I said, "I was wondering why I don't get them, too."

She was standing level with me now, her eyes blazing. Suddenly she slapped me, her hand striking full force against my cheek. I was too shocked to cry and stood there absorbing the hurt while she turned on her heel and walked down the hallway.

But now we were almost finished decorating the tree and I tried to clear my head of the past. The tree glistened with ornaments and tinsel, some flung in tangled clumps, some carefully strung strand by strand. We put candy canes on the branches, and when we turned off the lamps the colored tree lights glowed in the room. It was time for Joan and Des to go to bed, and this time they didn't protest, because they knew if they never went to bed, it would never be Christmas morning.

The first Christmas morning after Mummy and Desie were married, I woke up at 2:30 A.M. when they were returning home from a party, and was sure it was time to open presents, but now I was on their side against my younger siblings and agreed to a more civilized hour to get up. At seven A.M. Desie bellowed *"Merry Christmas,"* his voice ringing through the house—the signal they had been waiting for. Des was first down the stairs, momentum rather than contact with the treads carrying him to the living-room floor. The tree lighted the room and there were presents—presents flowing away from the tree, over the floor, onto the rug, into the middle of the room. A river of presents, mysterious big ones, enticing little ones, a few very intriguing envelopes, some presents I could identify, some I couldn't. I had disguised Desie's gifts for Mummy; a broom turned into Marilyn Monroe with seductive yellow wool tresses and ambitious padding, a velvet pillow became a turtle, and the gold necklace hid in boxes within boxes.

Stockings came first and you couldn't open presents until after breakfast. Mummy had spent months shopping, finding funny jokes: windup alligators that scissored across the table; frogs that hopped and "ribbeted"; giraffes whose limbs, connected by elastic, collapsed as you tipped their platform back and forth; pocket games with little silver balls that wouldn't go where you wanted them to; a real Swiss Army knife for Des; Arpège for Grannie; flowered silk scarves and jewelry, lotions and potions, things useful and useless; balls of crepe paper with hidden favors; and finally for everyone, a tangerine in the toe. I loved my stocking—a great-aunt in England had made it for me when I was born. A gray cow jumped over a yellow moon and Humpty-Dumpty, with bow tie, white jacket with pearl buttons, and little blue shorts, perched on a wall of embroidered bricks. Across the top she had sewn my name, so I knew she really meant it for me. Des and Joan went through their store-bought stockings like marines on a search-and-destroy mission; then it was time for breakfast.

Desie made a huge Cheddar-cheese omelette, tipping the French pan from side to side to coat the bottom with the carefully cracked and beaten eggs, lifting the partially cooked membrane to let the raw egg flow to the heat, all the time coaching himself with mumbled comments. There was regular bacon and Canadian bacon thick and pink, shriveling brown at the edges, sausage, glistening with fat, freshly squeezed orange juice and scones with real English marmalade, and tongue. Grannie always brought a tongue because it was an English tradition.

I had learned that I was different on many occasions, in many places. When I was twelve we went to live in Japan because

Desie had been made head of field operations for the CIA in the Far East. He and Mummy gave a party for all the people who worked for him and I found myself stuck in an interminable conversation with a pudgy, red-faced man named Colonel Deaver. His eyes bulged out of his face like a frog's and his skin was oily, catching the light of the lanterns hung on the large tiled terrace that overlooked the gardens and carved marble pond with its circling orange-and-white carp. He asked me my name and I told him.

"Barbara Lawrence."

"Oh, you don't have Desie's name."

"No."

"Well, a name is the most important thing anyone can give you. A name tells you who you are and who loves you enough to give you his name."

On and on he went while I felt as if I was being slowly turned on a spit, but I couldn't leave this drunken man because I felt he was putting me in my proper place, telling me a truth I had to endure. So I listened, transfixed. What's in a name? Everything. And I had always had the wrong one.

Every time someone called Desie my father, I corrected them because I felt I had no right to call him that and was afraid he would be angry. Once I called him Daddy by mistake, just before he died, and blushed crimson, stammering my apology. I wish he had realized how painful this was for me and told me he didn't mind. But I had never told him how much it hurt me, and my father had had it written into the divorce decree that my name would not be changed if my mother remarried. My name was my punishment, telling me I was not good enough for the real name, the name that came with honor, history, and money. I knew the Williamson history, but not my own. I grew up with family portraits and family stories, but they were not of my family. It wasn't until a few years ago that I learned that my father's family included people who gave the nails to build Yale College, the last colonial governor of Connecticut, and even Yankee Doodle Dandy, who was not simply a mythical figure as I had once thought.

Finally it was time to open the presents in the living room, a ritual that seemed to go on for hours. Desie sat in his upholstered armchair, Mummy and Grannie were next to each other on the flowered couch. The chairs always seemed too small, but Mummy had once explained that the room was too small and larger furniture would have made it seem even more confining. I chose to sit on the floor near Des and Joan so that I could help distribute presents, which would take time away from opening my own. I was at an awkward age, in an awkward position in the family, and I didn't get as many presents; I wasn't young enough to be cute and get dolls, which I never wanted anyhow, or a red shining bike with a Klaxon horn, or bulky games. Perhaps I was not around enough then, but I always opened my presents slowly to finish at the same time as the rest of the family. Carefully I untied the ribbon and then rolled it up, peeled the Scotch tape from the neatly tucked folds of paper, pulled back the paper, and opened the box, parting the tissue with my fingers and slowly drawing out the new sweater. I killed time watching Joan and Des as they tore through wrapping paper and added their presents to the piles in front of them.

I tried to look busy, but somehow, no matter how I stalled, there was always a moment when I obviously had nothing to open and Mummy said in a voice that seemed almost mocking, though I don't think she intended it to be: "Oh, poor you. You didn't get so many presents this year."

I wanted to say, "Just like last year and the year before," but I was ashamed both of not being worthy or grateful enough for what I did have, so I answered: "Oh, but I have some wonderful things here. I love this sweater and bubble bath."

When I was very young, my real father, Collin, used to send presents for me at Christmas. I pictured him walking down the aisles of Saks Fifth Avenue or Abercrombie and Fitch, picking two of this and three of that. For one part of a day I felt so lucky, I had more presents than anyone. I took the pink tissue paper out and let it fall all over the floor, pulling out Nordic sweaters (there were three one Christmas) and bottles of perfumes, three silk squares—peach, rose, and beige—a necklace of twisting gold cages enclosing balls of turquoise, a huge Steiff lion that became my mascot, and a Stetson hat.

I loved my once-a-year feeling of having a father, but I could hear Mummy and Desie joking about him and I began to understand that once a year really wasn't much when you compared it with putting a roof over my head and clothes on my back and food in my mouth. I learned not to talk about my father to anyone and not to be excited if he sent me a present. I learned to be sarcastic about my father, the alcoholic. I learned the right words and thoughts to use so I would not betray anyone, except, perhaps, myself. But after a while he didn't send anything, so I didn't have to worry about offending anyone.

After we opened all the presents, Des had burrowed hopefully into the trash and in back of the enormous tree, but found nothing new. So we cleaned up the debris—red and green tissue paper, gold and silver foil, paper in carmine and magenta emblazoned with Renaissance angels piled next to Mickey Mouse striding across royal blue, and ribbon, red satin, cheap curling ribbon, crisp wide plaid, and thick navy-blue grosgrain ribbon, all swirled on the floor. We pushed ribbons and paper, tags and packing into garbage bags, but only after we each made a list of thank-you notes we must write, the payment for this orgy of delight. We made a game of wearing as many presents as we could—layers of silk shirts over cotton, new Lanz nightgown over denim skirt with three new sweaters and two new scarves in hilarious riot. Then we walked out to the enclosed porch and sprawled over the rattan furniture, positioned as we hit the cushions like marionettes with cut strings. We were full of food and presents, the symbols of love, so all must be well.

Mummy's hands draped over the arms of the chair, long thin hands, decorated with two rings, a jade-and-diamond one Desie bought her when we lived in Japan and a huge sapphire ring he had inherited. My mother had extraordinary hands, the skin taut and white, long fingers tapering to perfectly sculpted crimson nails, hard and tough. She spent a great deal of time taking care of them, doing her nails and having them done so that they became brilliant red exclamation points with which she gesticulated. My own were a "disgrace." I bit my nails and worried at them until they flaked off.

I wanted to be as graceful and adept as she was but perhaps I didn't have the natural gifts and she didn't teach me. When I was eighteen I "came out" as a debutante at the Washington Debutante Ball and in a party at the Sulgrave Club. Mummy and Desie found another set of parents who wanted to share the expense of a party, and though I disliked their daughter, I didn't protest because I knew it was something I had to do and because I liked the parties I attended that other people gave, particularly those far away from Washington. My party embarrassed me—the theme was "the Civil War"—camellias and moss festooned the ballroom, a horse and surrey decorated the entrance hall—at least we were spared Confederate flags. The guests were young men on the list of a woman who organized society parties. In protest, I invited few of my own friends.

My dresses for "the season" were beautiful, made by a gifted seamstress from material Desie brought home from trips to the Far East. I still have two: an orange shot-silk sari with thick gold embroidery, stitched into a long dress with a tight waist and flaring skirt with wide gold embroidered panel, and a deep pink brocade dress with matching stole. The dresses flattered my small waist and height and made me feel beautiful and elegant. Long white kid gloves with rows of pearl buttons covered my bitten nails and protected me from sweaty hands, my own and my partner's.

One evening, at a dance in Boston, a careless young man splattered champagne on my gloves, staining them with what looked like premature age spots. I was staying with Kevin, my boyfriend at the time, and his family so that we could go to the parties around Boston. The next morning I called Mummy from his house, asking for another pair of gloves—begging really, because I knew they were expensive, but also knowing she had many pairs. She mailed me a pair—but when I opened the box I found the gloves, yellowed and cracked, blotched with brown stains, and I wondered if she cared what I looked like only when her friends could see me. I was embarrassed when Kevin's mother found me crying and told me it was all right, I didn't need gloves. But I knew I did, I needed them to cover my bitten nails.

Maddie had set the Christmas table before she left and started the turkey early in the morning. I loved the immaculate ivory linen tablecloth with the intricate cutouts and embroidery that Mummy had bought when I was with her in Hong Kong, it seemed so incredibly complicated and beautiful and had been so carefully washed and ironed at Louise's Hand Laundry. Crystal glasses sparkled, waiting for Montrachet, the silver shone against the linen, and in the center of the long table holly and pine mounded with red ribbons, cones, and tall red candles. A red satin ribbon reached over to each place that promised a hidden present, and for each of us a red English cracker with gold seal waited by the forks for us to explode and find the treasures within.

Pop! "Pull that little paper thing—it looks like a straw. There, you've got it."

Pop! "What is your fortune?"

"Oh, darling, you look like Horatio Hornblower in that blue paper hat. So handsome." Mummy laughed.

There were loaves of warm sliced French bread with melted herb butter, thick brawny oyster soup with sherry, and a huge glistening brown turkey. The table was full with silver bowls of cranberry sauce with orange peel, boats of rich brown gravy with mushrooms and giblets, and the sideboard held silver serving trays with drifts of mashed potatoes and broccoli with more hollandaise. The salad bowl, carved from a huge section of oak, was full with Bibb lettuce, endive, and avocado, with home-made croutons, and dessert waited in the kitchen.

"Would you like Christmas cake?" Mummy asked Grannie.

"Oh, darling, I'm too full," Grannie replied, smoothing her jacket over her stomach.

"You have to have Christmas cake," Mummy insisted. "Or do you want a piece of the fruitcake Aunt Eleanor sent?"

There was plum pudding, flaming with brandy, doused with hard sauce, the fumes whishing through my nose, ice cream, vanilla spritzed with black seeds, and trays of cookies, glacéed fruit, cheese, and then, like a bad joke, a "savory," an English import that looked like a burned cheese brick.

We were full—and there was lots to play with, lots to do, and it bothered me when we sat in front of the television. I knew sometimes that Desie watched his favorite program, *I Spy*. I thought it was very funny that Desie, who was, in fact, a spy master himself, deputy director for plans at the CIA, watched *I Spy*. Perhaps he was getting new ideas. Perhaps the comedy was relief. I wondered if we would have watched television if Frankie had been with us, or if Desie would have wanted to talk with her instead. Desie got a Churchill cigar from the humidor and slowly cut the end off, a ritual I enjoyed because it gave him so much pleasure. We joked about Castro, delighted in the little show of power that allowed Desie's agents to liberate this symbolic treasure. I hadn't been able to tell Desie that I had given these cigars away, very carefully, to boyfriends I was trying to woo and once even tried one myself. Choking on the smoke that gripped my lungs after two puffs and coughing convulsively, I ended up burying it in its aluminum casket in our Georgetown garden beside a pink azalea.

Behind the screen of the canned laughter on the television, we strayed into conversation about the war.

"Don't believe what you read in the newspapers," Desie admonished me.

"But what can I believe?" I asked.

"Believe me," he replied.

I wished I could and wondered how a second-year student of anthropology saw that a two-thousand-year-old society wouldn't trade its heritage for beer and hamburgers, at least not unless it was completely pacified. But through my new friends and teachers at college, I was moving to a different side of the war and tried at home not to disappear over the horizon, clutching the perimeter of my known world although it became increasingly unfamiliar the longer I was away. Raised in a world where young women learned to be debutantes, to marry well and be decorative, first to go to parties and then to give them, to volunteer for charities as Mummy did so well. I did not want to follow her. I didn't feel entitled to that world because I didn't have the money or the pedigree, but also it seemed trivial and boring. Instead, I found refuge, meaning, and love in friends and books. But they didn't tell me where I fit, only showed me where I didn't. Now they were leading me to a different life, though the old one held me like the pit of quicksand I once fell into while walking on a marsh—the wet sand sucking me down while I scrabbled at the dune grass and clawed my way out, losing only my favorite shoes in the process.

In a year I would be marching against Desie and the war he helped plan. Lester had told me that he knew each week Mr. Williamson went to the White House because Lester had to be especially sure that Desie's shoes were highly polished, his suit pressed just so, and besides, Desie's driver had told him. Lester enjoyed the reflected status which made me realize there was yet another set of markers of stratification that line people off from each other like the layers of different-colored silt on the hardened shore, as clearly marked on the bottom as on the top. In 1963, for the first time I defied Mummy and Desie overtly and marched with other students at Georgetown University Summer School to the Lincoln Memorial, a speck of salt in what Josephine Baker called a sea of salt and pepper. Now, as I sat next to Desie on the couch, I knew I hovered on the edge of betrayal, torn between what I was learning and what I had learned, between the world I had known and the world I was beginning to know. I wondered how I could turn against this man who was as close to being my father as anyone would ever be. In some ways, I was grateful he died before either of us knew how wrong I thought he had been about this war. But if he had lived, I might not have needed to marry the year after he suffered a massive heart attack, falling on his tennis court and dying an hour later on the way to the hospital.

3

TIED IN KNOTS

August 1968

I had met Kevin in Washington when I was sixteen and he was seventeen. He was visiting Hayden, a mutual friend, who had called me to ask if I wanted to go to a party with them. I was thrilled. I had found it hard to find my place again in school, having left when our family went to live for a year in Japan and then another in the Philippines. I felt fat, nearsighted, clumsy, and ugly, and I was never asked out. Now I was invited to a party given by beautiful Sally Peck—Sally who was perfect, with sky-blue eyes and blond hair that curled around her face. She was everything I wasn't: petite, pert, and effervescently cheerful. Somehow she seemed always to know what to say and how to move in order to have a squadron of boys buzzing around her at Miss Shippen's dancing class. I was still quivering from being left standing on the dance floor at my school, when a boy, who had not chosen me as a partner, stopped dancing with me after thirty seconds, looked me in the eye, said, "I can't dance with you, you are too smart," and walked away. I wondered what I could have said to repel him so quickly.

Hayden, the son of a wealthy and successful man, was a lanky senior at St. Mark's. His mother had died when he was very young, and he was shy with girls, so I was flattered that he had called me. I thought hard about what to wear to Sally's party and finally put on a maroon wool dress that hugged my body and a pair of low black heels to disguise my height. I suffered over hiding pimples and attacked my limp brown hair with a curling iron until it arched in horns above my brow, which, unfortunately, made me look like a yak. When Hayden honked the car horn, I had been waiting nervously inside our front hall for twenty minutes, trying not to bite my fingernails, and sweating into the dark wool dress.

I walked down the steps, conscious of their eyes on me, trying not to trip or fall into the car. Hayden was driving, and after we said hi, he motioned to the backseat and said, "This is my friend Kevin."

I turned slightly but could not see him. When he said hello, in a strong, deep voice, something reverberated inside me, as if he had struck a chord in me I hadn't known was there—just his voice, just one word, but I fell in love with him in that instant.

There were about twenty people at the party—all classmates from the day school we had gone to and their friends, boys from St. Albans and Landon. I was one of the few who now went "away" to school and I had not seen them for a while. Margaret, known as Bubbles, was there, as well as Janet, who Mummy and Desie had said was the most beautiful girl in my class. I looked for someone to talk to, wanting to hide in a corner, and suddenly there was Kevin, asking me about myself, and where I went to school. I couldn't believe he wanted to talk to me, but we spent the entire evening together. I remember how the girls began to watch me and I realized they were a bit envious that this tall, blond, and so handsome stranger was paying attention to me. At one point he said proudly that he had just gotten his driver's license and passed six feet. He pulled out the license to prove it and suggested I stand next to him, measuring our bodies. We barely touched, but I could feel electric currents pulsating through me in places I hadn't thought about before. Somehow I talked easily with him, perhaps because I thought I would never see him again.

The next night Bubbles asked me to another party and again I was thrilled. I went by myself and very few people were there when I arrived, so I walked over to a couch and perched on the edge of the seat, talking aimlessly with a friend. Suddenly I felt the room change and out of the corner of my eye I saw Kevin walk in. I averted my eyes, hoping he would come to sit next to me, but when he did I said nothing, pretending I had not noticed he was there. I wanted more than anything in the world to turn to him and talk, to tell him I had thought of nothing and no one else since the night before. I wanted to tell him I had never felt before the way I did now, but instead I froze. I didn't say anything to him, and he never said a word to me. For two hours we sat on the couch, not speaking, ignoring each other, feigning in our shyness that we didn't know the other one was there, until finally he got up and left.

I thought about him continuously. He was the most marvelous person I had ever met and I wanted to see him again, but I didn't hear from him. When I got an invitation to a party to which I had to invite a date, somehow I dared ask him. I thought there was no hope he would come down from Worcester, Massachusetts, to a dinner dance in Washington, so I was ecstatic and terrified when he accepted. He came down on the train with Tom, a boy I knew slightly from dancing school who was his classmate at St. Mark's, lived in Washington, and had offered to let him stay for a couple of nights at his parents' house.

After Kevin picked me up I remember realizing that I had left my white gloves at home. I thought how nice it would be to feel his hands over mine, and his arm around me while we danced, but when we stood to dance for the first time our hands were so sweaty that they slid off each other. I was so nervous, so shy with him, that the whole evening I felt as if I were onstage, and so, I think, did he. We could hardly talk, and when he took me home I walked into the living room, passed the two large, welcoming couches because I thought it was too suggestive to sit on one of them, and turned instead to an armchair, giving him no choice but to sit down in another equally uncomfortable seat. We sat making very small talk for a little while and then he said he had to leave.

Again I thought of him constantly. When he was at Harvard and I was at Milton Academy, we kept running into each other, because as a senior I could go anywhere I wanted for church on Sunday mornings, and as often as possible I went with friends to Memorial Chapel at Harvard. Sometimes boys we knew would ask us to lunch in the huge wood-paneled dining room where freshmen ate. As I walked through the lines, trying to look cool, casual, and confident, I worried that I would see him and drop the tray. One time I saw him at a distance and he turned to pass me and say hello. Crossing the Yard, I was always aware that he might be nearby, and one Sunday, when we met some of his roommates outside their dorm, one of them raced up to their room, and a few minutes later there he was. I almost fainted. I couldn't think of anything to say, in fact I could hardly breathe. "Oh, hi. Good to see you," he said and then he was gone.

Late that winter I made up my mind to call and ask if he wanted to see me. When I did, he asked what I was doing right then, and before we could think ourselves out of meeting, we agreed to go out that night. He took me to Café Pamplona. I had never been to a café and it seemed mysterious and romantic. We met a friend of his and his girl there and then we went for a drive, Kevin and I sitting in the backseat. And then we were kissing and running our hands over each other's bodies in a way I had never done before and I felt so full of love and lust and confusion that I thought I would explode. But over the next eight years we never really broke through the fear and inability to speak—we saw each other, but always in a crazy pattern of wild loving and then, when I became too dependent, breaking apart, only to join again.

Mummy didn't like Kevin, but then she had never liked anyone I went out with. She might have been right. I was not good at picking men who would make me feel loved, and sometimes I think I chose men who would make her uncomfortable. When Kevin and I weren't seeing each other, I went out with Charlie, who was brilliant, a student at Yale who rarely went to class, could memorize any text in one reading, and loved country music and motorcycles and always had black grease under his fingernails. And then the brother of a friend at college who was younger than I was, and Ramsay, a friend who was hanging on the edge of the drug culture, but went to Harvard and lived near us in Georgetown, which made him more acceptable to Mummy. The only beau of mine she liked was Michael, the son of some affluent friends of hers. He asked me to marry him after a brief courtship, but then said, "Of course, you will quit college." "Why?" I asked. "Well, I can teach you everything you need to know," he answered. I could, at least, read that warning sign and I broke off our two-day-old engagement. I was so sure I was right that it didn't bother me that Mummy was disappointed.

Many times Mummy told me that I must marry a rich man because I didn't have any money. I realize now she probably was genuinely concerned, but her advice made me shy away from men who were wealthy because I felt awkward and self-conscious, worrying that I was attracted to them because they offered a kind of security I did not know. Perhaps she also worried about me because of things she had done in her own life, choices she had made, but I didn't see that then.

⋆   ⋆   ⋆

Mummy grew up in a middle-class family in England. No one in her family had been to college and no one had traveled outside the country except to go to war. Deeply settled in middle-class ways, with scones and cakes and high tea, gardens, rationing, treacle, and babies, they seemed to marvel at the butterfly that had escaped her chrysalis, although they were a bit suspicious of her as well, and resentful. She escaped on a scholarship, pushed by Grannie, who, in the black-and-white eight-by-ten glossy studio prints, is a doting stage mother, hovering over her child like a succubus. Mummy was a beautiful woman, blessed and cursed by having to gauge her worth by her reflection in the eyes of others. She was discovered by Fox Studios as a sixteen-year-old student after winning a scholarship to the Royal Academy of Dramatic Art and she made several movies in England and acted in plays.

When she was twenty, Ambassador Kennedy's oldest son, Joe, was an admirer, a stage-door Johnny who waited for Mummy outside the theaters. She spent time with him and his family, watching how the ambassador dubbed Joe the president, Jack the secretary of state, and so on down the male line. She told me the Kennedys sponsored her to come to the United States to raise money for Bundles for Britain. I imagine her, slender and graceful, smiling people into doing what she wanted them to do: "You need a plane? Yes, Mr. Piper will give you a Piper Cub. A radio? Yes, Abercrombie and Fitch has one for you. Anything for a good cause, and a beautiful brave Brit." Off they went. Two girls in a little plane, Mummy, who had just learned to fly, and her copilot, who knew something about navigating, but not, it turned out, quite enough.

They started in Washington, D.C., and decided to follow the train tracks to Baltimore but got confused when the tracks went underground. They followed the highway, trying to read the signs, a bit unnerving perhaps to drivers below, and finally gave up, landing in a chicken farm with an old black farmer who waved his arms furiously at them, trying to get them to go away and not scare his hens. But they landed, and charmed him into helping them. They proceeded around the country in this fashion, usually arriving too late for Mummy to give her fund-raising speech.

She met my father in November of 1941 at Hicks Air Force Base in Patterson, New Jersey. They were both beautiful and they fell in love or lust immediately. They got engaged on December 7, Pearl Harbor Day, and were married the following month; she was twenty-two, he was two years older. I've wondered sometimes if she was still mourning Joe Kennedy or just felt so adrift in the middle of a war and far from home that she succumbed to the first man who looked good to her. She hardly knew my father when she married him, and only later, Grannie told me, would she find out that he continued sleeping with other women after their marriage.

Mummy didn't tell me much about my father, Collin, but she did say that he drank a lot and that his mother, Little Grannie, was mostly to blame. Collin had married briefly when he was sixteen, a marriage Little Grannie had had annulled immediately. Mummy told me that when she and Collin came back from their honeymoon, she found Little Grannie had returned wedding presents she didn't like and completely decorated their apartment, choosing pieces that made it look like her own: heavy dark red velvet curtains denying the light; convoluted brass andirons that Mummy hated to polish; and dark heavily flowered chintz on the couch. Her friends told her how lucky she was to have such a generous and thoughtful mother-in-law, but she knew Little Grannie was a spider spinning a beautiful web. And she knew she needed her own mother as an ally.

Mummy left Collin when I was three and Grannie came over from England to live with us in a little apartment on Fifty-sixth Street. When Mummy went to Reno for six weeks to establish residency so she could get a divorce, Grannie stayed with me and tried to explain why Mummy was out west, and was sending me postcards of cowgirls and cowboys on horses. When Mummy came back she acted in plays that took her away for long stretches of time, but when she was in New York she often modeled in stores like Bonwit Teller and Elizabeth Arden. Sometimes she took me with her when she modeled and I sat on an upholstered bench at the side of the large showroom, admiring her as she swirled into the room, using the dress as a bullfighter uses his cape, to tempt and taunt the people watching her.

When she left Collin, she was twenty-six, young, and beautiful, and there were many men who came to take her out. I saw them as a parade: the man in the elegant tuxedo, the man with the white gloves because he had a bad case of poison ivy, the man who walked with a cane. She met Desie at a dinner party arranged by my godmother, who had decided that they would be a perfect match. She hadn't counted on Desie becoming enthralled with the partner on his left, who tamed large snakes, but later, after he and Mummy were engaged, he told her he was just pretending to be interested in the snake charmer, and that he had known right away that Mummy was the person he wanted to marry. The first image Desie's Brahmin father saw of her was a photograph in *Vogue* showing her lolling on a dark chaise longue with a rose in her mouth. I don't know how he reacted, but I do remember she said if she had continued acting, Desie couldn't be in the *Social Register*.

When she met Desie I was four. Of all the men who came to take her to dinner, I liked him best. One night as they were leaving they came to say good night to me. I sat regally in my bed and said to Desie, "Are you going to marry my mother?" I don't remember what he said; I do remember they both laughed suddenly in a high-pitched gasp and shortly afterward they were engaged.

After they were married, she had her clothes made in England and later in Hong Kong. Peal's made her shoes on lasts they kept of her elegant thin feet with the polished red nails. The English tailors loved to drape fine wool and silk against her just as Desie loved to bring home saris, brocades, and Japanese silks from his trips to the Far East, for her to hold up and parade before him. I remember a bolt of ivory Thai silk overshot with intricate gold-threaded patterns of frangipani that had been woven for the queen of Thailand but rejected for a minor flaw. The dressmaker made an evening dress for Mummy with a long train, and I thought she looked more beautiful than any queen.

In August, when I was seven, and we still lived in New York, a photographer took our photograph for the January issue of *Vogue* to help raise money for a charity. We stood in front of the polar-bear cages at the Central Park Zoo, watching the animals lethargically swimming the length of their tiny green-scummed pool, Mummy in a full-length mink coat, I in my tweed coat with the velvet collar. I was standing in my sturdy brown oxfords looking large-boned and hefty next to her fine-boned body poised against the bars of the cage. I always worried I looked too much like my father, reminding her of a time in her life she would have preferred to forget.

That fall Desie took a job with the CIA. We moved to Washington, and after renting a house for a year, they bought a town house in Georgetown. Mummy redesigned the closets, choosing little stands for her hats, thin taffeta-lined drawers for gloves that smelled like her perfume, and drawers with neat dividers for her silk-and-lace underwear. Often she would bring home clothes from Elizabeth Arden and other boutiques, modeling them for Desie as he sipped a bourbon and water after work. She would sweep down the staircase in a pale aqua floor-length dress trimmed with mink around the neck and ends of the wide sleeves, or layers of rose chiffon undulating in the breeze she made as she walked. He would admire, select or reject, and buy whatever appealed to him.

I thought Mummy was so talented, so beautiful, and so loved

by everyone else that I felt faded and dim in her shadow. I shied away from being feminine or sexual because it was easier if I didn't try to compete on her turf. Instead as I got older, I created a separate world of love, sex, and relationships with men that she never knew about or at least we never talked about. As my sister Joan once said, it was easier for us to get along with Mummy if we were twenty pounds overweight.

I thought Kevin was the most wonderful person I had ever known but I found it hard to tell him that. I was so afraid of losing him, so trapped by my own insecurities I couldn't be his friend. Sometimes when we walked down a street in Cambridge or at my college in Vermont, I thought people looking at us were wondering why such an extraordinarily handsome man wanted to be with such an ugly young woman. Now I realize I was ugly only in my own mind.

When I graduated from college, in December 1965, I moved to New York to be near Kevin, renting a small apartment about four blocks from where he lived. He had told me how happy he was that I was going to be close by, but he was very busy with his new job and there were many nights we didn't see each other. One evening he brought me flowers, red carnations with white speckles, and I was delighted. It had been an exciting day. I had been working as a caseworker for the department of welfare in the South Bronx and that day I had won the office pool we played using the check numbers as a poker hand. I had won over a hundred dollars and had splurged on our dinner, buying an expensive bottle of wine, a marbled slab of beef to roast, and artichokes. Kevin and I were going to Vermont for the rest of the weekend, but as I gaily talked about the trip he said he had found he couldn't go. My heart stopped. He said he'd forgotten he had accepted another invitation, and when I questioned him he added that it was to a dance with a woman he had seen casually before I moved to the city, someone who wasn't important to him. But I wondered why she was so important he had to leave me for her. After he left I grabbed the carnations he had brought and twisted them into shreds, the petals falling over the garbage can onto the floor. I cried for hours and wondered what he was doing. But after the weekend he was back and we made up, and continued to see each other, though never as often as I wanted, until in October he told me he had to stop seeing me, at least for awhile.

One morning in November I walked into the cavernous upper floor of the Mott Haven welfare center, the yellow fluorescent light glinting off green metal desks arrayed in platoons of five caseworkers, each with one supervisor. There were over two hundred of us and the spartan room swelled with the cacophony of ringing phones, file drawers being opened and shut, paper and feet shuffling. I blocked it out as I walked to my own desk, intent on dealing with Rita Alvarez, my least favorite client, who had once left me sweating on the stairs outside her sixth-floor walk-up as the mercury hit 106 degrees on the hottest day in New York in decades. I heard her inside, playing her radio and singing, laughing as she refused to answer her doorbell, though she had known I was coming that day to visit her.

I walked to my desk between Lane, a vicious and petty man who liked to leave his clients on hold or hang up on them if he knew they were at a pay phone, and Anne, my improbable friend—improbable only because we had met as two of over seven hundred trainees, were placed in the same training class, then in the same welfare center, and then transferred a year later to sit at desks next to each other. We had become good friends in part because we came from the same world of privilege and understood why we were caseworkers in Harlem and the South Bronx.

"Good morning."

Anne turned her freckled face to me, her eyes clear blue, framed by blond-streaked hair, upturned nose, and a square, firm jaw. But this morning there were crinkles at the corners of her eyes and she looked worried. I hoped there was nothing wrong between her and her fiancé.

"Hey, how are you? Everything okay?" I asked.

"I have to tell you something," she replied.

"What is it?" I wondered, concerned that her lower lip was trembling and her fingers were drumming on the desktop.

"I'm going to be in Kevin's wedding tomorrow. I wanted to tell you," she stammered.

"What?" I blurted. "What! I don't see . . . You don't mean *my* Kevin? You know Kevin?"

A fist the size of a medicine ball jammed into my gut. I blanched, and knew I was going to throw up. I stood up and rushed to the bathroom, hiding in one of the gray metal stalls, wedging myself into the angle of the metal panels—pushing my head against the corner—sobbing, "No, no, no."

Anne followed me. I saw her scuffed loafers outside the stall. I heard her voice—but only in small pieces, as if I could not comprehend sentences, only syllables and fragments.

"I couldn't tell you before. I wanted to," she said. "I listened to you tell me about Kevin. I listened to Ellen, my friend from home. I am going to be one of her bridesmaids. I didn't know—for so long, I didn't know you were talking about the same man."

I listened now, thinking, This is a bad dream—a crazy dream—how could she know Kevin?

"I talked to him. I begged him to tell you. Didn't he tell you?" Her voice was pleading, as if she had been hoping I knew so she wouldn't have to feel so guilty for not telling me before.

"No, no," I sobbed. "He just broke up with me again. Three weeks ago. Like the dozens of times over the past eight years. Said he needed to be away for a while. That there was someone he might see. That she wasn't so smart or good-looking. That she has money. He did say she believed in him. But, I thought he was—"

"I am so sorry. So sorry."

"But, Anne, I love him. I still love him."

"I am so sorry," she repeated.

She asked the supervisor if I could take the rest of the day off and got me a cab. I sat in the cab, watching the South Bronx turn into Manhattan, clenching my teeth until my jaws ached and the inside of my mouth was bruised, pressing my fingers together until my stubby nails had etched crescent moons in my palms.

I stood by the window in my apartment, looking at the cement five floors below. I saw him everywhere. On the couch, in the bed, standing next to me in the kitchen. I could not tear him out of me. I stared and stared out the window until I saw myself slammed against the cement, lifeless. I opened the window but the air slapped me in the face. And I thought, If I really love this man, I will go on with my life. I cannot wreck his. It was as simple as that, and the realization made me think perhaps I did love him, or at least myself, better than I thought I had. Two months after his wedding, he called me and I said, "I don't think I can talk to you," and slid the phone back into its cradle, sobbing convulsively. But I dreamed of him for years and years.

After Kevin, I went out with a kind man Anne introduced me to whose wife told him a week after their marriage that she had fallen in love with someone she had met the week before they married, and that she was going to leave him. We were both so wounded that we healed a bit with each other, but it wasn't love. He called me "Snookums," and I enjoyed having a nickname, even one so foolish. But as he indulged my love of cooking by buying ingredients and enjoying the dinners I made, he gained forty pounds and I felt repelled and guilty. He looked soft and almost effeminate, and I felt I was to blame, as if I had force-fed him like a goose destined to become foie gras.

One weekend we went to his parents' house in the country. Through the floorboards in my room I could hear his sister's high-pitched moan at the climax of making love with her husband and

I wondered if she really loved him or was faking. It made me realize that I was the one who was faking, and that the closer her brother tried to get to me, the less comfortable I felt. Pursuing was so much easier, because then I could always back off.

Several weeks after I told him I didn't want to see him anymore, I went to spend a weekend with an artist who lived in the Village in a loft splattered with paint. We enjoyed the differences in each other—but it was just a friendship—an acquaintanceship really. He had invited me to stay with his teacher and his teacher's wife who owned an old farm in Vermont. On Sunday they suggested we stay one more day, but I felt strangely pulled back to the city and took the train, arriving late that night. There was someone waiting for me outside my apartment, a thin man about my age holding a black briefcase. He said he was from the CIA and that he had been waiting for me for a day and a half and that I must call home.

As I dialed the phone number, my hands were shaking. Someone I didn't know answered and said he would get my mother. After a few moments, while I listened for clues in the hushed voices I could almost hear, she came to the phone and said, "I have awful news. Desie died playing tennis at the farm on Saturday. We didn't know where you were." Her voice was calm and controlled, but I knew she was acting.

"Can I come home?" I asked.

How strange this question seemed even then. Why was I asking for permission to come home when Desie had just died?

Mummy answered, "Of course." It was too late to go that night and I told her I would be on the first plane in the morning. I couldn't stand to be by myself, so I called the man I had just broken up with and asked if I could spend the night with him. With incredible kindness he told me to come right over, and so I spent the night on the second bed in his room, staring at the ceiling while he slept, comforted by the rhythm of his breathing.

The next day, on the shuttle to Washington, I stared out over the clouds. As the stewardess asked me if I wanted coffee, tea, or milk, I turned and saw Desie's face, the photograph he had on his CIA badge, the one that made him look like a Mafia hit man, stiff and wooden, staring at me from the obituary page of *The New York Times* the man seated next to me was holding. NATION'S NUMBER ONE SPY DIES ON TENNIS COURT, the headline read. I swallowed a sob and turned away.

When I got to Mummy and Desie's house, Mrs. Thomas, a woman I thought of as the archetypal mother and a close family friend, opened the door for me. I started to cry, but she said, "No, you must be strong for her. You mustn't cry." I sucked back my tears and shook myself to dispel the sadness, and then I walked up the stairs. Mummy was in the living room, standing with her close friend and lawyer, Charlie, as well as Joan, Des, Frankie, Mr. Thomas, and a few other friends. She was wearing a vivid brocade suit of green, blue, and purple. I had expected her to be in mourning, but she looked radiant as a peacock. I went over to hold her and she hugged me quickly, then backed away. "I am not going into mourning. We have to carry on. We just have to carry on." Her lower lip was trembling almost imperceptibly and her eyes looked as defenseless as a child's, but she had set a tone I had to follow. Perhaps she simply could not acknowledge how much she loved and missed Desie, how much losing him hurt her, when she was only forty-seven, and how scared she was.

Desie was brilliant, handsome, witty, debonair, sophisticated, and had a fascinating and controversial job. I have so many conflicting memories of our life with Desie—they tumble and whirl together in my head. I see him lying on the floor of the living room in the Georgetown house, wiggling through a pantomime in a game we often played—adverbs—acting out how to put on skis in the manner of the adverb "lugubriously." Joan, Desie, Mummy, and I are laughing hysterically, as we did when he droned the bass part of the only tune he could carry, "Little White Cloud"—"ugha-ugha-ugha." I see him wrapped in an old blanket sitting on the land he owned in Maine, telling us "Ugh in the Blanket" stories he made up. I wish I remembered the stories, but all I remember is our laughter.

Sometimes I didn't understand him, and he didn't seem to understand me. Once, when we were driving from Washington to the farm, he hit a rabbit and I was astounded that he didn't stop to see if it had been killed. Perhaps he was right, we never would have found it, but I thought we should have tried. Another time in the car, he turned to me and said, "You really are a very simple person, aren't you." It was a statement not a question. I doubt that any teenager feels simple; I know I did not. He made me feel as if he didn't want to understand me because I felt so complicated and incapable of dealing with all my complications. So I turned my face to the window and watched the rain streak the outside of the glass as my tears slid down the inside. I had learned to cry so silently that he never knew.

When I asked him for help in going to graduate school, something that mattered a great deal to me, he told me he would think about it. The next morning at breakfast, I walked into the dining room, my stomach cramping and my heart beating fast. My mouth was dry, but I took a swallow of orange juice and looked at him. He turned and said, "In answer to your question, no." Not, "no, I am sorry, I wish I could help," or "I admire what you want to do, but I have other priorities." No, no explanation, just "no." I wondered if he answered me that way because he had recently lost a lot of money and he felt embarrassed and ashamed that he could not help me, and I didn't want to push him into telling me that was the reason. I knew I must play the game through, so I sat down, picked up the newspaper, and ate my cereal; there was nothing to say and so I said nothing.

There were times I felt close to Desie; I had, after all, lived in his house since I was four years old. Mummy and Grannie reminded me many times that, except for a hundred dollars a month that Collin sent erratically, Desie paid for all the many luxuries I enjoyed: beautiful houses to live in, summers in Maine, fine food and clothes, and superb schools. I thought of him as responsible, important, brilliant, and successful—so unlike my own father. Desie protected me sometimes from Mummy's anger and fragility, and precisely because I was not his child, it may have been easier for him to be warmer and more open with me than with his own children. Though I was embarrassed by my dependence on his generosity, I appreciated his kindness to me. But I knew to keep my distance, not be demanding, not cause trouble, and not call him Daddy. When I called him by that name, on the last evening I saw him, just before he died, I blurted an apology to him that he didn't acknowledge—probably because he hadn't heard me, or perhaps because he didn't mind as I had for so long thought he would.

Then he was dead, suddenly, of a heart attack, playing tennis with Mummy and the ambassador from Great Britain and his wife. Just about to serve, then, flat on his face, with Mummy yelling to Lester, who bumbled out with an umbrella and held it over Desie's head to protect him from the July Virginia sun, offering his last act of service. Then there was no way to continue a conversation that should have taken us years; there was no way for me to know him as an adult.

After we buried him, my mother told us we had to meet in the living room with Charlie because he was going to read the will. I started to go with Joan and Des and Frankie, but Desie's sister, Aunt Eleanor, said, "Oh, you don't have to go, you aren't one of his children." Perhaps to spite her, but also because Mummy had asked me to join them, I went.

I sat in an armchair across from Mummy, who was sitting on

the white couch next to Charlie, who sat in another armchair. I could watch her, and when Charlie turned to her and said, "Well, actually, you are in the best shape you have ever been in." I knew he meant financially, but that she would twist his words and let them hurt her. I saw her mouth begin to tremble and I went over and sat next to her and put my arm on her shoulder.

"Oh, Charlie," she said, looking down at her hands, "I'm not in good shape, I'm not in good shape at all," and then she started to cry, but it was only for a few seconds.

Charlie began reading the will, and though I don't remember it well, I remember that in it Desie mentioned his children, and he left almost everything to Mummy.

I thought I should help organize his funeral because my sisters and brother had lost their father, and that I must be less hurt than they were. Mummy asked me to choose a casket at the funeral home in Georgetown, the one that had served the rich and famous in their grief for generations. The showroom was cavernous. The caskets were laid out in rows, with discreet tags and obscene prices: mahogany with aqua silk lining, or honeyed oak with red taffeta, brass hinged at waist height for a partial viewing. And my favorite, the aluminum tube, looking just like the cylinder that protected Churchill cigars—or perhaps a rocket. Are they going to fire him off into space? I asked myself, hiding in dark humor. I ordered the plainest pine casket they had because Mummy had told me to— because it was what he wanted. He had also told her once that he wanted a simple funeral. He wasn't going to have that in the Washington Cathedral, but at least I could get him the casket he wanted, though I had thought he prefer to be cremated.

At the graveyard in Georgetown, where I went to look for a plot, the director frowned when I told him the casket was pine. He looked at me with beady eyes, set close together, and I wondered if he also looked like an oily rat to his family and friends, and said, "Well, that means we are going to have to build a brick enclosure, health laws, you know. Do you think that type of coffin is fitting for someone in Mr. Williamson's position?"

I could no longer contain my anger and pain, and I replied, "His position is horizontal. The man is dead."

I tried not to cry at the funeral, tried to be helpful to my mother and sisters, and to my brother who was only fourteen. When Bishop Moore, a close friend of Charlie's, asked for suggestions for the readings, I responded, thinking about the irony of burying an agnostic in the cathedral, "What about the passage from Ecclesiastes, 'For every thing there is a season'?"

And I was pleased when Bishop Moore replied, "I've never used that, it seems a very good choice."

Even on a hot summer day, the Washington Cathedral was packed with people for Desie's funeral. As I stumbled down the steps to the limousine, I saw Frankie beginning to sob and she pulled me into the waiting car, the only honest outburst I remember. Three days afterward, when we were going as a family to dinner with friends, I collapsed from exhaustion walking up the stairs. Too tired to move I lay there for a few moments, resting my face against the roughness of the beige wool carpet, but then I knew I must get up and go to dinner.

In November of that year I answered the phone and heard a voice saying, "Hi, this is Tom Russell. I don't know if you remember me but your sister Joan is a friend of my brother's. He suggested I give you a call."

"Oh, Tom, you old drunk," I replied, surprised and pleased to hear from someone from "home," remembering his red face at dancing school and later at debutante parties and wanting to create some connection with a joke. I remembered his blond hair and laughing blue eyes. I remembered he was tall and athletic, that he was in Kevin's class at boarding school, but I hardly knew him.

"Do you want to go for a drink sometime?"

"Sure."

"What about tomorrow? I live near you on York Avenue and there is a place called Ollie's Bar I like a lot. I'll come get you at seven."

I wore my dangling peacock feather earrings, a blue-and-green Thai silk shirt, and an emerald-green burlap skirt. I thought I looked interesting—a bit daring—not like your regular run-of-the-mill debutante. My hair was long and brown and I wore dark stockings and shoes to disguise my thick, shapeless legs.

We went to Ollie's that night and many times again. They served enormous hamburgers with tomatoes, ketchup, and onions on crusty French bread or crunchy rolls, and cheap red wine. The first night we sat at the crowded bar and I felt like a grown-up. It was fun and reassuring to be with someone I had known since I was a child—someone who understood Washington gossip and the pressures of life growing up there. Slowly we became friends, talking about old romances, his affair with a woman in Paris whom he still seemed to love, and mine with Kevin. We talked about our parents, and siblings, growing up in Washington, and our current attempts to find the loves of our lives. I was relieved that he never touched me—I was sick of warding off unwelcome advances in exchange for dinner or drinks. We looked at the society of our parents and their friends in very similar ways, and after we were married, people came to say we even looked alike, that we looked like sister and brother.

One day many months later Anne and I were talking about our love lives. Hers was definitely in better shape, or so it seemed then, than mine. I was going out with a number of men—a dark, olive-skinned man with a motorcycle who whisked me down city streets in defiance of death or mutilation, another tall impecunious artist who made me feel drearily bourgeois, a musician with curly brown hair who tried to lure me to his pallet on the floor saying he knew we would fit together so well, a much older man who attacked me in a taxi after trying to get me drunk at the Algonquin Club. But there was no one I wanted to see more than once or twice and I couldn't be with Kevin.

So we talked about men and Anne asked, "What's wrong with Tom? What about him?"

It was a completely new thought. I had seen him only as a convenient friend, someone safe and easy to be with. As I sat there quietly looking at my hands, I tried thinking of him as a "beau." I tried to see him as someone to "go out with," perhaps to marry. I heard my grandmother saying, again and again, that she wanted to be a great-grandmother. I heard my mother telling me about other young women getting engaged to suitable young men. I felt vulnerable, tired, scared, and, at twenty-five, almost old. And so I said, "Nothing, nothing is wrong with him."

Suddenly it all seemed clear. Of course, Tom was the right man. Anne approved. He came from the same world, he was bright and funny, athletic, from a "good family," yet he didn't seem to Buy the Act—he wasn't stuffy or hung up on doing the proper things. He had studied for the ministry, been in the marines, was going to desert but got a special dispensation because of his family's military background and his father's nervous breakdown. He was writing a book—he had been a junior editor at a publishing house in New York—and he was studying for a master's degree that would help him join the Foreign Service. I would love to be in the Foreign Service, I thought, I would love to live overseas and I would love to be a diplomat's wife. He seemed just right.

Once Anne had suggested I go after Tom, I did, laughing at his jokes, smiling, holding him just a little longer when we said good night. As my attitude toward him changed, so did his toward me. But the first night we touched each other's body on his bed, a foldout couch with a broken spring he had rescued from the street, I thought how thin he was and wondered if touching him would ever make me feel the way I had felt making love with Kevin.

We courted at antiwar rallies, football games, and bars. Tom's godfather had given him a long raccoon coat he had bought when he was in college. It was a perfect coat for sitting in cold stadiums and watching football games as its voluminous interior could easily encompass flasks of bourbon and milk punch. We sat huddled together, often with his friend Charlie, drinking surreptitiously, cheering and yelling.

I had dreamed of being rescued by my white knight on a white horse. I wanted my own dream, but one that was also acceptable to my mother, yet I didn't want her life of endless social obligations, unfocused volunteer work, and bridge games. I thought in being with Tom I could have what I wanted from each of our dreams—a life that was "socially acceptable," an intellectual partner, and a like-minded adventurer to have children with, who would protect and love us. Mostly, I just reacted to the pressure of being twenty-five in a society where young women were supposed to marry well and live happily ever after. And I missed Desie very much. He had defended me sometimes even against my mother, because he understood better than she the culture in which I was growing up. Sometimes I felt as if I wasn't supposed to feel so hurt by losing him, because, as my mother and younger sister told me at different times, "You still have a father." But I hadn't seen Collin in many years, and felt that I had never had a father and never would.

One week we went with Tom's family to ski at Johnny-See-Saw's, an informal resort that his father and mother had been to many times before she died the same year as Desie, in 1967. I saw photographs yellowing in frames that showed Tom's parents, lolling back in the snow, smiling at each other. Tom's brothers and sisters were there, and his father, though not his father's fiancée Danielle. I wanted so much to like them and to have them like me. Tom's father was very kind to me and I thought he liked me because he kept asking if I had everything I wanted. Tom's sister

Melinda talked incessantly, always about herself, and complained that the boys were mean to her, and they were. They constantly put her down, teasing her with little bloodletting nicks. "Melinda, you've put on some weight. The skiing is going to be good for you, run some of that fat off you."

At first I took her side. At night, as we lay in the bunkbeds, she would talk about growing up. "The boys were always mean to me. I don't think they meant to be mean, but sometimes it really hurts, especially when they say I am fat. I had trouble in school and when they tease me about it, it really hurts. Mummy was so perfect. She could do anything. But sometimes she was impatient." And then later, "And sometimes she drank too much."

As I lay there in the dark listening to her voice drifting up, I could only respond in trite phrases. "Oh, that's hard," "I'm so sorry." At first I was sympathetic, but when I heard the same stories again and again, I began to understand how she could so irritate her brothers that they lashed out at her. She had little sense of when to let go, and I was thankful to be so exhausted from a day of skiing that sleep carried me away.

I began to feel like one of the family as we got used to being to-gether that weekend. We drank too much, not something I was used to, but which was fun in a mindless and mind-dimming way. I noticed that when Tom drank, his nose got very red and his face flushed, but I didn't read it then as a sign that he drank too much. There is a picture of us looking like puppies tangled together in a laughing mass on the floor of the living room at the end of one such evening. On another night we all walked up a mountain to see the stars and found the snowmaking machines showering the trail with flakes. We walked closer and closer, Tom and I together, then Melinda and Tom's brothers Jonathan and Michael strung along behind us. The closer we got to the snow machine the more magical it seemed—moonlight shone through the flakes, which in-tensified as we drew closer, so that it seemed we were in a blizzard, surrounded and embraced by the snow—until Tom and I were held together and the others seemed far away, though in the distance I could hear Melinda admonishing her brothers to leave us alone. I remember knowing we were going to kiss in the blowing artificial snow, haloed by the moon, in a beautifully choreographed romantic moment, but I felt as if I were playing a role for an appreciative, though small, audience.

A few months later I decided to give a surprise party for Tom's birthday on May 7. I didn't have enough room in my apartment for all the people I wanted to invite and I thought it would be fun to have a party in Central Park. I laughed when I found I had to apply for a parade permit because I was expecting more than twenty-five guests. I knew that in early May there would be few flowers gracing our picnic spot, so I bought lots of paper flowers in wild colors. I asked guests to bring something to eat and talked with the man at the liquor store about the wine and beer. I ordered a huge and expensive cake and delighted in the little subterfuges I resorted to in order to keep Tom from knowing about the party. We had been getting along pretty well, but I could feel tension between us that I didn't understand. Perhaps, I thought, it's just that I'm worrying about him finding out about the party. But there seemed to be something else I couldn't identify. His voice sounded tight and he didn't seem eager to see me.

The night before the party he turned to me and said, "I found the invitations on your clipboard, in with your notes from class." I was studying for a master's degree at night and I wondered what he was doing going through my notes, but I answered, "Oh, no, that's too bad." He continued, saying that he thought we should break up, that he was getting in too deep, and that he didn't want to see me except as a friend, but that he would come to the party and pretend it was a surprise because he knew I had gone to a lot of trouble and lots of his friends were coming. I felt disappointed, tired out by the prospect of getting to know someone else, but I didn't protest. Perhaps I was relieved. I couldn't think of anything else to do. It was a civil enough arrangement and it seemed important not to disappoint our friends. I appreciated Tom's attempt to be kind to me, not forcing me to go through the embarrassment of calling people to tell them I had to cancel the party, and so I agreed.

The next evening, with the help of some friends, I stabbed the sticks of brightly colored paper flowers into the ground in a rough circle demarcating our assigned place for the party, hauled the wine and beer, ice and condiments, plates, brightly flowered paper napkins, plastic glasses, and cutlery to the park and then waited for everyone else, including Tom, to show up. Several uninvited guests hovered around the fringes hoping for handouts, but we were protected by a policeman on horseback discreetly watching from behind a clump of trees. Tom arrived and I felt awkward, as if I were pulling him into a place he didn't want to be, but everyone made a big fuss over him, which he seemed to enjoy. When the evening grew too cool, we adjourned the party to my apartment, squeezing into the living room and flowing over into the kitchen and bedrooms. We had a joyous time, particularly given that Tom and I had broken up the night before.

The excitement of giving the party had helped me cover up my feelings, but in truth, I wasn't touched as deeply by Tom's rejection as I had been when Kevin had left me. Two days later I found a note under my door, written in Tom's tiny, almost indecipherable hand, that said he cared about me and wanted to keep seeing me. I was surprised—surprised that he had slipped the note under the door instead of calling, surprised by the tininess and illegibility of his handwriting.

On Memorial Day weekend, we drove to his family's house in Keene Valley in the Adirondacks. He seemed nervous, and at one point missed a turn he should have taken, and berated himself. The house was a large Victorian set in a valley on the side of a mountain and overlooking a range of other mountains. Tom told me his father had bought the house as a surprise for his mother, a place for her to take the children for the summer while he sweated through the heat of Washington. But Tom said she had never liked it—that she felt isolated and lonely and that when the black flies bit her, her face swelled up. I wondered how her husband could make such a big purchase, one that would change their lives, without first consulting his wife.

That night Tom built a fire in the fireplace in the library, a small room filled with a strange assortment of furniture, including an untuned piano, two faded green upholstered armchairs, a baronial carved wooden straight-backed chair, a Victorian love seat, a few unmatched Windsor chairs, and canvas-backed folding seats. The walls were covered with trail maps of the mountains in the Adirondacks—including the forty-two peaks over four thousand feet, with thick lines in green or red marking where Tom and members of his family had hiked. The house was full of artifacts of activities the family enjoyed together: golf clubs, fly rods in canvas and leather cases, binoculars, Tom's father's journals, old sheet music, and lots of books. I was puzzled by signs of parsimony, such as the mismatched wallpaper in some of the bedrooms and incomplete sets of china, but Tom explained to me that his mother was just frugal and enjoyed finding bargains.

Because she died shortly before Desie, I never knew Tom's mother, though my own mother had known her "socially" in Washington. I saw her only in photographs, a large-nosed woman, with what seemed to be rough, uneven skin. To me, she did not seem attractive, though perhaps her dated clothing and tightly furled hair were partly to blame. Instead, she looked stern and dour. I was surprised to learn from Tom that his father loved his mother very much, worshiped her almost. I was not surprised to learn that she ran the family real estate business better than her husband had, during the time when he served in the navy in the war, because Tom said she was highly intelligent, and frustrated by the narrow possibilities open to her as a proper Washington wife.

One weekend when I visited Mummy, I asked her about Tom's mother. "I didn't really know her, my friend Irene did because she is married to Tom's uncle. I don't think she went out much. I don't think they had much money. I met her on fund-raising boards, but she was very quiet. I've heard she drank too much. But I didn't know her."

Tom thought his mother might have better enjoyed living after women's liberation because she didn't seem able to break the bonds of convention and do what she wanted to or was capable of doing. Sitting in a booth at Ollie's Bar, we faced each other and he told me both his mother and her sister were alcoholics, the sister a lesbian who wore manly clothing and had recovered through AA. Tom said, "I brought home an A in Spanish, I got a ninety-eight on the test, and my mother asked why I didn't get a hundred. Her father had said the same thing to her. He had wanted sons but got daughters, and nothing she did was ever enough for him." Another time he joked that his mother took baths in three inches of cold water and didn't like spending money. I thought she sounded odd and I was glad that I didn't have to deal with her. "She would get so drunk at night," he told me, "that she woke us all up in the middle of the night, yelling and screaming that we had to clean our rooms. She was horrible to Melinda. They would get into the most awful fights. She used to threaten me that they didn't have the money to pay for my school and I was going to have to leave so Melinda could get the attention she needed. Dad would come home and just go in his room and shut the door, saying, 'Tommy, you take care of it.' "

"God, it sounds awful," I said sympathetically. "I never knew my father really, but I know he drank a lot." It seemed familiar ground.

★   ★   ★

When Tom took me to his father's summer house for the first time, it was cold and there was no central heating. Tom brought a mattress down from a second-floor bedroom and put it in front of the fire and we huddled under thick green comforters Tom's mother had sewn, made of multiple blankets, covered in green-flowered gingham, drinking red wine, talking and watching the fire burning.

Coached by my friends, Barbie and her husband, Bob, who was a psychiatrist, I had stopped having sex with Tom. "Don't give it all away," they had said. Now, as we lay together in front of the fire and Tom wanted to make love, I told him again that I wouldn't.

"What if we were married?" he asked.

"Well, then it would be different," I answered. He said he had been thinking about that and then he asked me to marry him. When I said yes, I felt enormous relief and excitement surge through me. I thought how wonderful it would be to get married, and that finally I was worthy enough that someone I could seriously consider had asked me. Most of all I felt grateful to him, and when we made love, though we were inexperienced with each other, I was almost swept away by the promise of the future.

The next day he added that he had been thinking about the guests and had made a list of all the people he wanted to invite to our wedding. He hoped we would get married there under the large pine tree overlooking the mountains in late August. "It will be perfect," he said. "It will be cool and beautiful here—much better than sweating through August in Washington—and besides, your family doesn't have a summer place anymore. I don't want to have a huge Washington wedding." Mummy had sold the farm right after Desie died, and Tom was right, we didn't have a place for a summer wedding.

I was surprised, but flattered. He had been thinking about our marriage a lot and seemed so clear and pleased with his plans. I was tired of worrying about how I was going to pay to finish graduate school and about finding a job after I graduated. I had five hundred dollars in my savings account and I was twenty-five years old. It was reassuring to hear Tom making decisions and I thought my white knight had finally shown up. I didn't know what I wanted, hadn't thought about my wedding, and I didn't want to lose him.

I thought about Anne and Allen's wedding, about how her mother had taken over and Anne and Allen seemed like dolls at someone else's party. Perhaps I also wanted to hurt my mother by not giving her a chance to put on a big wedding or perhaps I feared she wouldn't want to bother. I felt a little like an appendage to Tom's plans, but I didn't dare disagree with him for fear of losing him, and so I told him that getting married in August in his father's summer house in the Adirondacks, a place I had only been to that one day, under a pine tree, was exactly what I wanted, too.

Tom's father and stepmother were coming up the next day from Washington, so we decided to wait to tell them until they arrived. I wanted to tell my younger sister first because I felt closest to her of my siblings at that time, so I called her from a pay phone in Lake Placid where we were shopping. Telling her made the news seem real to me and I was happy that she seemed excited for me. The next day at dinner, we told Tom's father and stepmother that we wanted to get married that summer at their house in the Adirondacks.

I remember his father's eyes as he turned to me and I wish I had acted on what I saw—his eyes were so full of gratitude and relief that he looked like a little child. I read in those eyes that he was amazed that I was going to marry Tom and so pleased that it scared me. But I didn't know what to do with the thought and it passed through my mind, though I stowed it away. Years later I would see the same look on the face of a man from whom we were buying an expensive piece of property—and I thought, My God, he is relieved to be getting rid of this. We shouldn't buy this land." But we did, and lost a lot of money when we tried to sell it a few years afterward.

The next day, I finally called my mother. I had been reluctant to tell her because I didn't know how to say I wouldn't be getting married in Washington, where she could have a party and invite her friends. I knew I was hurting her, and though I felt guilt and confusion at doing so, I had to admit to myself, even then, that I wanted to hurt her because she had, sometimes, hurt me. I called her and said simply that Tom and I had decided to get married, and before she had time to talk about when and where I said that we had decided to get married in the Adirondacks that August because Washington would be so hot. "Oh," she replied. "Oh, well," and then paused and added, "but you must let me give you an engagement party in Washington."

The first afternoon of the Memorial Day weekend we drove to a dirt road that wound up the foot of the mountains from a club Tom's family had been members of for many years. I had thought we would walk together, but Tom started to run and yelled out over his back, "Watch out for bears," then rounded the curve out of sight. I was disappointed but I enjoyed my time alone, and I accepted that running was vital to him; in fact, I admired his athleticism. Often we swam in the pools of the Ausable River or Johns Brook, and once I took a snorkeling mask and watched the trout swimming below where fisherman cast their flies.

The last day of the long weekend he told me he was going on a serious climb but one of his friends would take me on a smaller mountain. I arrived wearing my blue jeans and tennis shoes. Tom's friend arrived in lederhosen and climbing boots. I asked what we were going to climb. She replied, "A little mountain called Giant."

Unfortunate name, I thought. "Someone's joke?" I asked hopefully.

We started climbing and I was soon winded, stumbling over a river of stones, a slide that had cascaded down the mountain a few years before. She bounded like a gazelle—her knees unobstructed while mine were trapped in cloying cloth.

Finally we stopped and she said, "Over there, you can see the top of the mountain." I had thought I was already *on* the top of the mountain and couldn't find another until it occurred to me to look much higher and farther away.

"There, over there." She pointed to a peak in the far distance.

"Oh . . . Wonderful," I replied, trying to sound strong and eager.

A little farther along, the skies opened and thunder and lightning saved me. "Oh, so sad, we have to go back."

But by then I realized she was an old girlfriend exacting her revenge, and I felt triumphant that I had won the prize.

Tom and I laughed later as I told him how grateful I was to have been rescued by the storm. It made a good story, and he was proud, I think, of having two women dueling over him. But I was uncomfortable telling him how I really felt. I was hurt that he had let an old girlfriend introduce me to the mountains he loved so much and had thought so little about what it would be like for me to hike with her, as I wasn't used to climbing, and smoked.

After getting engaged, Tom and I went back to the city. I had left the department of social services in January to go to school full-time for a semester, using the five thousand dollars Desie had promised to give me annually shortly before he died so un-expectedly, and which Mummy had given me about six months later. I had finished my courses and was about to start writing a master's thesis in sociology on young unwed mothers. I had met several of these young women, many of them still children themselves, while I worked at the department of social services, and was convinced the babies filled a huge emotional void in their lives. Sex and a relationship with a man seemed secondary to them. But as Tom and I talked about getting married in August and the excitement of being engaged took over, we decided to move to the Adirondacks and live in his father's house for the summer. I changed my research topic to one I could work on anywhere using the *Congressional Record:* "Social Darwinism and the Rat Extermination Act," an unlikely subject but one that would travel well.

The only argument we had was whether or not to keep Tom's apartment on York Avenue. I thought we needed a place to come back to after the summer, and I was sharing a large apartment with Joan and a friend of hers but the lease ended in June. Tom said it would be easy to pick up another apartment. "We can live in Dad's house for the summer. It will be perfect. We won't waste money paying rent." It seemed foolish to pay two months' rent on his apartment, but I was scared not to have a place to return to in the fall. However, I wanted to trust Tom's decision and defer to him, the man I was going to marry, so we put our few belongings into storage and Tom's ancient car and drove to the Adirondacks for the summer.

In late June, Mummy gave an engagement party for us in Washington. We didn't want to go, but I knew I had to let her have this party. Our first night in Washington Tom gave me an engagement ring his father had given him for me, a deep blue sapphire surrounded by eight sizable diamonds. It was beautiful—seemed solid, traditional, respectable, and elegant. I remember lying in bed at my mother's house, looking at the ring sitting on the beside table and thinking, "This is going to be all right. The ring is perfect. We are going to be all right." I knew I didn't feel swept away, I didn't feel "in love" the way I had with Kevin, but I thought I had found a companion. The ring had belonged to Tom's mother, enlarged when she lay dying to accommodate her swollen finger, and would now be made smaller for me. There was a slight crack in the sapphire, but the color was such a rich deep blue that the fracture line was barely perceptible.

The night before the party my mother and I went to Tom's father and stepmother's large Georgetown house for dinner. Set on a hill with at least an acre of land, the grounds now boasted a new tennis court, and his father and stepmother had renovated the entire house. It was an impressive, capacious house, filled with antique furniture, good paintings, and Chinese porcelains. I hoped my mother noticed that Tom's father seemed to have done very well for himself. After dinner Tom and I sat on the needlepoint-covered bench in front of the fire sort of playing at being the young lovers while Mummy and Mr. Russell talked "business." At one point I heard her say to him, "I don't think we should give them any money, do you?"

"Oh, of course not," he replied, anxious to agree with her. It made me angry that she should interfere that way. She didn't have to give us anything, but I wondered why, when each of her other children had inherited trust funds, she needed to deny me whatever Tom's father might have given us. It seemed unfair, and I wondered if someone had suggested the idea to her, because it seemed so intrusive to me. Later I realized she might have said it in hopes that Tom would get a job to support us.

For the party, Mummy had rented a pink tent to cover the garden of the Georgetown row house and invited her friends. She had asked me what flowers I wanted and I told her peonies were my favorites for that time of year. The house was full, with Joan and Des there as well as a friend of Mummy's, and there was no bed for me to sleep in. "I'm sorry," she had said, "you'll have to sleep on the couch in the garden room. I think it will be long enough. You won't mind, will you?"

I don't feel much like a guest of honor, I thought, but I laughed and answered, "No, of course, that's fine." The night before the party and the night of the party I tried to sleep, but the couch was too short for my long body and the room so luxuriantly decorated with bouquets of opulent pink peonies gathered in the corners and festooned around the tent and in huge vases that both nights I woke gasping as the flowers sucked the oxygen out of the air. By the second morning I felt exhausted and eager to get back to the Adirondacks with Tom.

The afternoon of the party Mummy asked me to come to her bedroom. I sat on the celadon-green silk-covered chaise longue, while she sat on her large bed. "I've been thinking about what I should do for you. I'm going to give you a thousand dollars to buy a wedding dress and trousseau," she said. I didn't know what to say. It seemed a grand sum to me, and I liked being allowed to spend it as I wanted to. Then she said, "Are you sure this is what you want to do? My friend Irene, his aunt, says she's worried, that you could do much better." Again, I felt my voice constrict. I had never talked easily or honestly with her and I couldn't start now. I felt defensive and I pulled back from her, though I think she really was trying to make me consider important questions.

"I don't think his aunt likes him," I replied. Mummy stood up and walked over to a window.

"Irene has known Tom since she married his uncle. She says he has tried many things but they haven't worked out. He has had lots of chances but he doesn't carry them through. She said he was at Harvard seminary and then dropped out and went into the marine corps for six months." Then she turned and looked at me, saying, "Do you know about that?"

"Yes, Mummy, he told me all about that," I answered. "He went to seminary because he really didn't know what he wanted to do, but he felt called to the church. Then he realized he wasn't and felt he should serve his country. But then he realized he didn't support the war." I tried to look her in the eye, but I felt as if I were reciting a speech and I looked down at the floor, counting the birds in the needlepoint rug she had made for Desie that lay at the end of the bed. "When he tried to get out," I continued, "well, there was a problem with his father, but it's okay now and he has worked very hard on the book."

"But Irene said he went back to the seminary after he got out of the marine corps," she countered.

I could feel myself starting to flush. "I know," I mumbled.

"And she also said he worked for Scribner's, but he quit," she added. "Irene said his family worried he would never settle down, never accomplish anything, never make any money." I could feel the blood rushing up my body and I was worried my blush would betray how upset I felt.

There it is again, the money issue, I thought. I turned away from her, blocking her words because I didn't want to think about money, and I felt she was judging Tom by her shallow standards.

"What is his book like?" she asked me.

"Oh, it's wonderful, " I replied with enthusiasm and relief. "It's really well written and there's an editor at Scribner's, a man Tom worked with there, who says he really likes it. It is a story about Tom's adolescence, sort of like *Catcher in the Rye*." That seemed to placate her and we never talked again about Tom's prospects. Instead we moved to neutral ground: where I would register for presents, how many invitations we would send, whom I would choose as bridesmaids.

I wrote all the thank-you notes that summer. I didn't understand why we were getting so many presents because we had limited the invitations to one hundred and twenty-five. Finally, I asked Mummy about it and she said she had ordered another five hundred because she had so many friends, but that we were not to worry, with the wedding so far away from Washington, none of them would come. I wrote thank-you notes to people I didn't know for presents I hadn't seen and just after we were married I mailed them all.

Mummy had told me I must be conservative about spending

money and had to follow a strict budget. She was worried about money because Desie had died just short of his twentieth year at the CIA, and as a result, she was eligible for only a small pension. It unsettled me to hear her talk about pensions and Social Security because she and Desie had always seemed to take money for granted—at least until he lost his money to his old friend who was supposed to manage it for him while he worked in government. The subject of money had always been off-limits, not discussed.

Before I was married, a man who worked for Desie and was a friend of Frankie's once asked me to go skiing with him and a group of friends. I told him I would love to but I didn't have the money. He looked surprised and said, "But your father has lots of money, what do you mean?" I told him Desie was my stepfather, not my father, and that I was paying my way through graduate school by working for the department of welfare in Harlem and the South Bronx as a caseworker. I told him I loved school and my work but that I didn't make enough money to go on a vacation. He asked, "How old were you when your mother married Desie?"

I answered, "I was four," adding, "You know I asked him to marry her," to divert him from a conversation that was beginning to feel dangerous.

But he continued: "And how long is it since you saw your father?"

I told him, though I could feel a protective curtain pulling down in front of me. "The last time was about six or seven years ago for dinner," I replied. "It was sort of grim, he was drunk. I hadn't seen him for a long time before that."

He seemed shocked that in a family of wealth, three children were rich and one was not, but I knew I should be grateful for what I was given, partly because Mummy and Grannie had told me so many times that I must be. Now, planning my wedding, I knew I must be very careful not to spend very much money, and that Mummy would give a "real" wedding someday for my younger sister.

No one offered me the use of the Williamson family wedding dress and I was scared that if I asked I would be told that I couldn't wear it. Instead, I bought a Mexican wedding dress for one hundred and twenty-five dollars because it was inexpensive. Mummy didn't go with me to choose the dress, or any of the bridesmaids' dresses, or make any of the other plans for the wedding; since I had done my best to distance myself from her, however, I shouldn't have expected her to. I thought apple-green skirts with white Mexican blouses and different cummerbunds in vivid blue, pink, and purple would look cheerful, be affordable, and that my bridesmaids could use them again later. Mummy told me that Aunt Eleanor had offered do the photography and I decided we could collect flowers like Queen Anne's lace from the field for our bouquets. Getting married under the big pine tree in the garden meant we didn't have to pay for a church, and Tom's friend Bob would marry us. Mrs. Tweadie, a local woman, would make the maple wedding cake and the club would cater. Then Mummy's friends Mr. and Mrs. Jefferson donated all the champagne—so I thought I had done well in keeping down expenses.

Mummy was resigned, perhaps even relieved, that we were getting married far from Washington and wanted a very simple wedding, but she and Tom's father still argued through us about details, and each seemed to feel put-upon—she for trying to "do" a wedding so far away, he for having the wedding so close to home. To Tom and me, it seemed they both enjoyed being in the middle of things and complaining, and we joked and laughed about them. Making the plans together gave us a chance to see our similarities, though I ignored our differences. I loved parties and if I had not been afraid of disappointing Tom, or of standing up to my mother, I think I would have liked a large wedding, gathering together all my friends. Instead we enjoyed defying what was expected of us, not feeling swallowed up in the Washington social scene, not caring about "high" society.

I had found my place in my family by compromising and subjugating my own needs to those, as I perceived them, of everyone else. Because I hadn't learned as a child that I would be loved even if I disagreed or behaved badly, I was incapable as an adult of disagreeing with Tom, who I thought was offering me sanctuary. At first I was afraid of disagreeing with him because I thought that if I did, he would leave me, but over the years of our marriage we fell into a pattern in which my fear of upsetting him allowed him to control me.

Mummy had been most upset by our decision to marry under the huge white pine tree in front of Tom's father's camp. She had started going to church regularly after Desie died, and her relationship to God, previously sporadic and incomprehensible to me, now seemed to matter more to her. When I called her from New York to tell her, she had replied, "Isn't there a church there you can be married in? I don't understand why you want to get married under a tree."

I could hear the anxiety in her voice, almost pleading with me, but I answered her, "Mummy, I haven't been to a church since I had to go at Milton Academy, and then I always went to whatever service was quickest. God just isn't important to me. I don't believe in God. Religion is just the opiate of the people," I said mockingly, "and I don't need it."

"You may look back and regret that you weren't married in a church," she replied.

"Well, I don't believe in God," I reiterated, my resolve hardening as we spoke, because I could hear the echo of my conversation with Tom.

"Didn't Tom go to seminary? What does he think about this?" she asked.

"It was his idea," I answered.

In late July, I took the bus to Portland, Maine, because my friend Abigail was getting married at her family's summer place in Small Point, on the ocean. While I was in Portland, I walked around the old part of the city and passed a pawnshop. I saw wedding rings in the window and on an odd whim went in and bought two. I liked that they were solid and substantial, fourteen-carat gold and very inexpensive, and the woman's ring looked like the one Desie had given my mother. It seems a strange thing to have done, but I think I wanted the security of having the rings, and Tom and I were so broke that it seemed a sensible way to have nice ones. I wondered who had owned them and why they had pawned their wedding rings, but pushed the thoughts out on my mind.

When I left after the wedding, the bus that was to take me to the ferry across Lake Champlain was late and I knew I didn't have time to catch the ferry if I walked. Two men in a car, who had just picked up a friend at the bus stop, offered me a ride. I was scared to get in the car with them, and when the man sitting next to the window got out to let me sit between himself and the driver, I told him I would prefer sitting next to the window, thinking I could jump out more easily. As I tried to balance the risks of accepting a lift from people I didn't know with missing the ferry and keeping Tom waiting, I moved the engagement ring around my finger so that they couldn't see the stones, only the band, thinking that if the men thought I was married I would be safer. As I did so, I felt a circle of security settle around me; I belonged to someone, I belonged to a man who cared enough about me to marry me. During the short ride to the ferry I talked about how my husband was going to meet me on the other side of the lake, and thought as they left me off just in time to catch the boat that I was smart and lucky, but it seems more likely they never intended any harm in the first place.

Tom and I spent over a month living together in his father's house. As summer people returned to the valley, his father insisted I move to live with a friend from school whose family had a house in the same valley. "Why?" we wondered. "We don't want to upset the neighbors," he answered, and we laughed that the raccoons and deer, our only close neighbors, would be upset.

We lived in a swirl of plans for the wedding, enjoying our time off with no responsibilities. We worked on the garden, sifting rocks that turned up endlessly, planting peas, and then lettuce, corn, tomatoes. I loved to garden, and enjoyed working on land that had been part of Tom's family since he was a child. We climbed several of the mountains, starting with a small mountain that was in our backyard, though Tom would race ahead of me and then come back to walk with me for a short time before running up the mountain again.

At first it seemed strange that he liked to stuff rocks into his backpack to carry up and down a mountain, and to wear layers of sweaters, sweatpants, and sweatshirts. Standing next to the old soapstone sink in the large kitchen one day, I watched as he took his dried sweatclothes from the pile in the laundry basket. "I don't understand," I said. "I don't see why you have to wear so much of that stuff. You must be boiling."

"Yeah, I am," he replied, "but that's the point. It's the only way I can really work up a sweat. I have what's called Reynaud's phenomenon, and it killed my mother."

"That's awful," I said, adding apprehensively, "what does that mean for you?"

"It's a very strange thing—not a disease. In women it leads to skleroderma—that's what killed her—or lupus, but only in a first-born daughter, which she was." I felt better and he added, "I just have the symptoms of Reynaud's, which means my hands get really cold and I don't sweat easily." I was sympathetic and proud of him for dealing with such a strange and frightening illness. It scared me to think that he had the same condition that led to the disease that

killed his mother, and so I didn't question the time he spent exercising once a day to purge the water from his body.

He loved his ritual of running and sweating, forcing what he
saw as the accumulated poisons from his body and then plunging
himself in the cold mountain streams off the trails, or in the series
of rock pools that caught cascading water and formed natural bath-
tubs where he could immerse completely. This ceremony of "baptism" was sacrosanct for him, a time of purification.

He looked so rugged and strong when he climbed that I
didn't worry about what he was wearing. He knew the mountains as well as he knew a tennis court, and I loved his confidence and competence on each. I began to enjoy climbing and
seeing sudden expansive views over the jagged peaks of the
mountains cresting like waves to the horizon, blues and greens. I
was amazed that he always knew where we were, so that even if
we bushwhacked through deep woods, we were never lost. To
me the mountains, Noon Mark, Sawteeth, Indian Head, and
Nipple Top, named for their obvious characteristics, always
looked new and I couldn't recognize them from different angles.
I had almost no sense of direction and feared being lost, but
Tom always knew where we were and climbing with him made
me feel safe.

The night before the wedding I wore a deep pink-and-blue
floor-length chiffon dress that Mummy had intercepted when a
friend was giving it to the thrift shop. I loved swirling around in
it and felt beautiful. I remembered my New York friend Nancy
couldn't attend because she had just broken up with her friend
Bruce, and instead Bruce, a strangely affected man with a European
accent, showed up alone. He had insisted on referring to Nancy
as Amanda. No wonder she left him, I thought. He is so incredibly
controlling, and I wondered what had compelled him to come to
my wedding without her when I had met him only once before.
An hour before the party a slow leak appeared in the ceiling just

over my head. Maria, the Spanish woman who had cooked and cleaned and run Tom's parents' household for many years, went upstairs to check and found Bruce passed out in the overflowing tub. Maria screeched, "Zee man ees naked, zee man ees naked, he drunk, I theenk." Someone hauled Bruce out of the bathtub and eventually got him to the party, where he proceeded to take photographs; his present to us was to be a picture of everything and everyone. This turned out to be fortunate because the photographs Aunt Eleanor took were blurred—taken with a shaky hand and eyes that couldn't focus, or perhaps were focusing on her own increasingly lubricated vision.

Tom's father and stepmother held the dinner in the expansive living room of their summer house, a room with dark paneling; ornate, carved mahogany furniture; and peeling, waterstained, but beautiful wallpaper original to the house. The living-room couches had been replaced with ten round tables seating eight, and a long head table facing the rest of the room. I loved having so many people there I cared about.

The next day there was a picnic lunch and Tom came over and we talked, though he was not supposed to see his bride. He was limping from a groin injury he had suffered about three weeks earlier, though doctors had told him they found nothing wrong with him. They could not find a physical cause—no pulled muscles, no tears or strains—and so they told him the pain must be psychological. Tom had told me the doctors asked, "You are getting married? You have a groin injury? Well now, what does that mean? Is there anything worrying you?"

We had laughed about their concerns though secretly I worried that the doctors might be right. Now Tom seemed in a lot of pain and suddenly, when I looked at him that day, he seemed frail and tense to me. When he walked he grimaced with each step, and if he sat down it was hard for him to raise himself up again. I remember wondering if I was doing the right thing, but then I asked myself, What bride has not thought that? and I pushed the fears out of my head.

That afternoon we gathered for the ceremony. Friends and relatives stood on the lawn in front of the back porch. I wore a borrowed mantilla of intricate lace that had belonged to President Polk's bride, loaned to us by a friend of my mother's, and my white cotton Mexican wedding dress. I took Des's arm and we stepped onto the porch, and walked down the steps to the informal aisle we had made by strewing pine and balsam boughs. I was glad I had not invited my father, because I wanted to leave him behind, to enter my new life without him. As we followed my bridesmaids, my friends Nan, Anne, my sisters Frankie and Joan, Tom's sister Melinda, I was like a child going onstage, hoping I wouldn't trip and that I would say my lines correctly. When I saw Tom standing to the right of the tree, his hair slicked back, smiling, he looked so thin and weak to me that I almost didn't recognize him, and thought I was seeing him for the first time. I felt a shudder of doubt twitch through me and I wondered why I was marrying him. I thought about turning away and walking back into the house. I looked at the people, our audience, and I knew I could only keep walking ahead. Des gave me away and I stood next to Tom, who was standing next to his two brothers in front of Bob, the minister. After we took our vows we knelt for Bob's blessing; Tom could not stand up because of the pain in his groin and so his brothers and I had to lift him to his feet.

There are pictures of us pushing cake into each other's mouth, and of me smoking my last cigarette, though I didn't know then that I wouldn't smoke again. There are pictures of us walking through showers of rice to the car, and of my mother smiling in the receiving line. I had promised her beautiful weather, but it was ninety-six degrees and we were all sweating. It was a plain wedding, but our friends enjoyed themselves, I think, and though our parents argued, they got through it. Sometimes, over the years, when we looked at the photographs, we remarked that none of our friends who had been married when they came to our wedding were still married, and we congratulated ourselves for still being together.

After making a show of leaving our wedding dinner we drove off in the Brown Bomber, the wood-sided station wagon Tom's family kept at their summer place, which now, in addition to its neon-pink-and-blue CLEAN FOR GENE sign, boasted a trail of cans roped together that battered each other down the driveway. We went swimming with friends at the rock pools on John's Brook and then came back to join the party. It seemed silly to leave when the people who cared most about us had driven so far to be with us, and in another small defiance of tradition I wanted to stay at the party instead of leaving, as brides and grooms were supposed to. I wanted to show everyone and par-ticularly myself that there was nothing really new in our status as a married couple, to make it seem an easy, even ordinary rite of passage. So we had put bathing suits on under our "going-away clothes," and when I took off my pink wool dress and jacket, rice spilled out over the rocks.

The first night of our marriage we stayed in the little guest cottage owned by Tom's father's friends down the road from where we were married. When we walked into the camp I thought it was kind of these neighbors to let us stay the night, and that I was being "good" about not going on a real honeymoon. In the dark cabin, while we got ready to go to bed, we took turns using the bathroom, undressing apart from each other. Tom complained that his groin really hurt and he was sick throughout the night, throwing up from something he had eaten, he said. I worried that our guests might have gotten sick, too, and was relieved when I found that no one else had become ill. Though the crab crepes, shrimp, and huge maple cake made by Mrs. Tweadie looked in-viting, I had hardly eaten anything because I was excited and tense.

That night we were both so exhausted that we hardly touched. Dealing with the wedding and our parents had worn me out, and any disappointment I felt in not having a romantic night was eased by thinking that we knew each other well enough that we didn't have to make love. In fact, I felt relieved, though that, too, should have troubled me.

4

Unironed Sheets

August 1968

I was excited about moving to New York City as a "married woman," eager to help find us an apartment. Tom had assured me many times during the summer that we would pick one up easily when we moved back to the city. I loved his confidence that everything would work out, but looking for our own place proved disappointing and difficult.

The first week in New York we stayed with Bonnie and Charlie in their elegant apartment; Bonnie's family was very wealthy and Charlie had a job, and their apartment seemed spacious and "grown up" to me. Tom said Charlie and Bonnie wouldn't mind our being there, it would save us money, and we would rent a place quickly. We slept on their couch, bumping into each other on the way to the bathroom and trying to accommodate ourselves to their schedules until it became clear that it was time to move. By then Frankie was going away for ten days and we used her apartment until she came back, and at about that time Tom's friend Alex left town for a few weeks and we moved to his apartment on Ninety-ninth Street between Second and Third Avenues.

Alex's father and mother had disowned him when he became an aspiring painter after graduating from Harvard. He lived in a small apartment in Harlem, a part of town I knew from when I was a caseworker for the department of social services. I wondered if 100th Street had been cleaned up in the two years since I had last been there, when it had had the highest number of murders and rapes in the city and the largest percentage of population working as prostitutes or drug dealers. Tom told me Alex had warned him not to marry me because I would be too concerned with money and "society." The criticism stung me, though I thought it unfair and that Alex hardly knew me. Around Alex I felt particularly conscious of my suspect upper-class origins, so like his own, and eager to show I was just as anxious to end the war, racism, and classism.

At the front of Alex's brownstone were three steps and a stoop spattered with pigeon droppings. On the steps there was a bottle of Red Rose wine, the pint size winos favor, Kleenex, rained into clumps in the corner, and a faded and frayed Marlboro box. Everything in the front hall was brown, floors with small hexagonal deep brown tiles and tiles that were once intended to contrast but were now simply a more variegated brown, stained and layered over many years with the detritus of feet. The walls were painted like Indian pudding with an oily sheen of polished dirt crusted over the surface. The ceiling was dull beige, shadowed by the light of a single hanging bulb. I had been in halls like this many times when I was visiting my welfare clients.

Alex lived in two rooms. The kitchen had a small bed against one wall, the white living room was surprisingly sunny, and Alex's paintings glowed on the walls. The dishes hadn't been done in a while and the apartment smelled of old clothes and dirt. Alex was a bachelor, and I guessed if we were going to be living there for a week or two I had better get to work. The first night we joked that the bed was too small for one person, impossible for two. The cloying smell of the sheets kept waking me up and I wanted to turn over but didn't because I was afraid I would wake Tom up. Instead I turned when he did so as not to disturb him.

The next morning I took the sheets to be washed and ironed and I tackled the dirty dishes, soaking and scrubbing until my hands and the Brillo pads were used up. While I was washing the pots, I boiled water for hot chocolate I had seen in a brown tin on one of the shelves. The pots were very dirty, particularly the frying pans. I thought about Mummy saying that if you scrubbed hard you could always get them clean, but these were caked with cooked grease and rust. I got the tin that promised fine German hot chocolate, loosened the lid, and then with one hand started scrubbing again. With the other I took off the top, quickly dipped two big spoonfuls of the powdered mixture into a newly clean mug, poured in hot water, two teaspoons of sugar, and stirred. I took the first sip and it was delicious, sweet and rich. I felt what I thought were little pieces of chocolate but when I crunched one I gagged on what turned out to be the shell of a small beetle whose acrid guts spilled into my mouth. I stared in shock as its companions circled my mug, little brown beetles with pale white stripes down their backs. As I watched them go around and around the cup, I wondered what I was doing there and I felt scared that I had made a mistake in following Tom, in trusting that he knew what he was doing.

We kept looking for a place to live. The newspapers offered lots of apartments, though few in our price range, but at first we were excited about our prospects.

"Wow—sunny frplcd lv rm hrdwd flrs, 2 bdrms," Tom read.

"Oh, I like this, grdn apt, gorgeous rhododendrons. Hey, at least you get two whole words," I exclaimed.

We fantasized about the wonderful place we would find. I thought about having friends over and planning "little dinner parties" with our new French china with the teal blue and gold circling bands, the Orrefors crystal, and the silver that was waiting in storage at my mother's. We called the numbers in the ads but nobody answered. Sometimes we got busy signals, and very rarely a voice that grunted "taken already" before slamming the receiver against our eardrums.

I was never able to get the sweet dirt smell out of the sheets, but by the time Alex returned we were used to the neighborhood and I felt warily safe as long as I didn't go out late by myself. I remembered the way I used to walk when I was a caseworker, constantly sweeping my eyes over the streets and alleys, always listening in the back of my mind for sounds of anger or fear, watching shadows on the sidewalk to see how close people were behind me, and, if there were no shadows, turning around, always checking stoops and alleys.

In many ways I enjoyed being married. In the first weeks of our marriage we watched the horror of the 1968 Democratic National Convention, shocked by the ferocity of the confrontation between police and demonstrators protesting the war. As we sat on the couch in the borrowed apartment, I hid my face from the violence I was seeing on the screen, and felt safe being with someone who shared my distrust of the people who were running the war. I felt as if I were growing up and entering the adult world, one I did not like very much. With Tom I was learning to stand up for what I thought was right, and it gave me confidence to think that in each other Tom and I had found an ally.

Tom had a marvelous memory and gift with words. I loved the way he brought new bits of information into a conversation, that he had read so much and could quote Kant, Kierkegaard, and philosophers who were only names to me, not ideas. I loved that he was always reading. He was fascinated by all sorts of things, some of which, like sports scores from decades before, did not interest me, but many, such as the works of writers I had never heard of, I found compelling—I felt doors on new worlds of knowledge opening before me, and sometimes my own more practical and pragmatic approach to life seemed dull in comparison. I didn't hunger for Tom the way I had hungered for Kevin. I didn't want to touch him and be touched, but I also didn't feel as controlled by the wanting or emptiness I had felt in myself when I was with Kevin. It was easier not to feel so overpowered, as if Tom and I were friends rather than lovers.

I thought it was wonderful that he was writing a book, perhaps the most important thing anyone could do. I loved the risk and the hope of discovery and chance of sharing the acclaim, by association, for the intellectual excellence and artistic ability that I was sure were in our future. I wanted to help make this possible, so I was trying hard to be a good wife. I was trying to keep our temporary home clean, do the cooking, write my thesis, and find a job. But I was giving up pieces of myself in my attempts to be accommodating. I had been taught to accede to a man's wishes, and I did. I gave up eating the sweet desserts I loved because Tom told me they were unhealthy and because he ate sparingly, I gave up cigarettes because he said they were even worse and he didn't want the smell of smoke in the apartment, most important, I gave up some of my dreams: a nice apartment, friends to ask over, a job that mattered to me. I was so scared of losing Tom, as I had lost my father, that I lost some of myself.

During the first year I went to boarding school, I was stage manager of our class play, *The Red House Mystery*. I had hoped to be an actress like Mummy, but my talent for organization outweighed my acting ability and I ended up behind rather than on the stage. Miss Sedgwick, the difficult head of the theater department whose twisted claw hand lay hidden most of the time under huge shawls, helped me understand that my job was important and that my new friends in the cast were counting on me.

The afternoon of opening night the phone in the dormitory hall rang and a friend yelled to me, "Call for you, a man. I don't know who it is."

I opened the door to the little wooden telephone closet that always smelled of tennis shoes and adolescent hormones, released in conversations with boyfriends and parents. I picked up the receiver and said hello.

A voice I didn't know replied, "This is your father. I am in town. I want to see you."

I stood transfixed, shocked, and awkward, reflecting back his awkwardness. "Collin, that's great. That's great, but I'm sorry, I can't see you," I stammered. I reached out my hand and braced myself against the wall. "I'm managing a play and we have our first performance tonight." And then, hoping he would be pleased with me, I added, "Would you like to come see it?"

"I am your father and I've come to see you. I want to take you out for dinner," he replied sternly.

"But I didn't know you were coming. I haven't seen you in so long." I could feel myself slipping down onto the hard bench in the phone room. "Why don't you come to the play and then we can go for dinner," I pleaded. But he insisted, he didn't want to come to my play, he just wanted to take me for dinner. He didn't have that much time and he wanted to see me. I didn't know what to do. Finally my anger and hurt, compressed over many years, exploded and I yelled, "I don't want to see you"—blurting— "ever again," and I hung up the phone as if I were in slow motion, prolonging my connection with him, knowing I would hardly ever speak to him again.

I tried to walk to my room without crying but I dropped to the floor, shuddering against the wall. The dorm mother, a severe Danish woman named Mrs. Fog, found me there shivering, my teeth chattering from too much adrenaline. She led me down to the apartment where the headmistress lived and gave me a pill, probably a tranquilizer. The headmistress came quickly to talk with me as I sat trembling on her couch, feeling embarrassed that I had been overwhelmed by my conversation with Collin, and had made a "scene." I don't remember what she said, I just remember feeling as if I were drowning, fighting to reach the surface again and find my composure, knowing I had pushed my father away and that I might never see him again.

Alex found out that his landlord was going to evict the tenant on the fifth floor, a single woman with three young children, and that we could have the apartment as soon as she was turned out. We felt like vultures hovering but we hadn't found anything else and it would be fun to be in the same building as Alex—besides the rent was seventy-three dollars a month. We waited until the sheriff's men hauled a torn avocado-green couch from the fifth-floor apartment, clunking it down the stairs, its broken springs bouncing at each step.

When the couch was on the street, the former tenant and two of her three children sat on it—waiting for someone or something. The mother was a slight Puerto Rican woman with stringy black hair pulled back tight in a bun. She was wearing a dress that hung slack from her body like an untied halyard slapping against a mast and it seemed as if all her ligaments and muscles had lost their strength. She stared out at the street, her eyes blank. One little girl was sitting against her and sucking her thumb, the other sat on the couch and bounced a ball against the pavement. I didn't see her little boy.

To try to erase this family from my mind, I turned my back on them and went to inspect what had just been their home and now was mine. There was a child's doll with nylon blond hair and a broken arm lying in the living room and a pair of a woman's pink underpants in the kitchen. The walls were painted surgical green and the floors were cracked black and white linoleum with speckles. The place was dirty but I knew with a lot of Pine Sol I could scrub it clean. This was a railroad flat: a large front room like Alex's with a kitchen big enough for a table, which also contained the bathtub, and a hall leading to the toilet. The toilet was a challenge—and eventually I gave up trying to get the smell of old urine out of the remnant of green linoleum on the floor in the tiny dark room. The bathtub had a wooden cover marred with scratches and gouges, stains and rings, which also served as a kitchen counter. We had to heave the cover up and balance it against the wall when we wanted to take a bath, hoping it would not fall on us.

We had a home now and we brought in our furniture from storage: my large bed went in the room off the kitchen along with the handsome old-fashioned cherry bureau I bought from friends. We put up pictures and curtains and settled the small love seat my grandmother bought me in the little hall outside the toilet. It was hard to see how we could invite anyone to this apartment who wasn't a very good friend, but then, we were in a neighborhood where we couldn't expect people to visit anyhow.

When we were married we were given beautiful Egyptian-cotton sheets with my new initials entwined in blue embroidery. When I made our bed the first time it looked beautiful and luxurious and the sheets were cool and smooth against my legs. At the end of the week Tom took the sheets and other laundry to the Laundromat, but when he brought them back they were wrinkled. I don't think I had ever seen wrinkled sheets before that. I tried to pull them taut on the bed but they puckered, as if in sour resentment.

"Tom," I said, when he got home from running, "next time you do the laundry, would you get the sheets ironed."

He looked at me with surprise. "Ironed, why ironed?"

"They look awful and they are sort of scratchy this way," I replied.

"We can't afford that," he told me, repeating, "we can't afford to get sheets ironed. That's a ridiculous waste of money."

I felt chastened but I couldn't argue with him—I didn't have a job yet. Somehow, the sheets stick in my mind as the first sign that I was stuck in a different life, a life I had not anticipated and for which I was not well prepared. I was beginning to feel as if I had traded one set of insecurities for another when I married and I wondered why Tom wasn't looking for a job, and how soon my efforts to find work would succeed.

The next evening Alex and his friend Polly knocked on the door, and when we let them in we saw they were each carrying a kitten. One, a tabby, looked like a man in a herringbone suit with a white tie, the other was black and wearing a tuxedo.

"Please take them just for the night," Alex said. "My cat doesn't like them and a friend found them abandoned. Tomorrow we'll find a home for them."

"Oh, sure," I said, knowing the home would be with us because I couldn't resist kittens.

I loved cats and so did Collin. He had let me play with his kittens when I was very little. His new living room was small but there was lots of light. I wore a yellow dress. He had two gray kittens with white paws. As I played with them they crawled over me and chewed on my fingers. One sat in my lap for a long time quietly, and when it left, there was a brown stain on my dress. Collin fussed over me, cleaning my dress, but I felt as if I had soiled it myself

After my parents divorced Collin lived in another apartment, where I visited him. Sitting in the dark little apartment in Harlem made me think about living in New York City with Collin and my mother and, after he moved out, with my mother and grandmother. How different it was. Their apartment had been much larger and in a safer neighborhood, near Sutton Place. Mummy and Grannie had someone to clean. Collin would pick me up from the huge brick Presbyterian Church on Fifth Avenue where I went to Sunday school. I was very tall for my age, and when Mummy went to register me the teacher said I should be in the first-grade class because I wouldn't fit behind the desk, which made me feel awkward and clumsy.

Collin was a pilot in World War I, ferrying bombers to England. I have photographs that show him standing, legs apart, bold and handsome in his uniform. He loved machines and delighted in explaining them to me. One Sunday, sitting in a square of sunshine on his blue rug with the white and yellow stripes, we took apart a camera, another time a large clock, carefully putting the eviscerated pieces on a dish towel in lines paralleling the rug. We cleaned and oiled each part before he showed me how they fit together. Maybe my belief that I can solve problems, understand how things work, comes from these afternoons.

I had tried to make myself call him after I got engaged, but I couldn't. I had a sent him an invitation to the wedding, but only *afterward*, and almost as a gesture of defiance. I thought being married might make calling him easier, but it didn't, it was still too depressing and frightening, though often I thought of him.

I always called my father Collin because I felt I had to, but I don't know why. In spring and summer when the weather was fair, we sailed boats in the little pond in Central Park. Charting a course across the pond, we wet our fingers and held them in the breeze, eyed the competition, set the rudder, and adjusted the sails. He held me by my waist as I stretched over the nubbled cement rim of the pond, holding the white hull like a dove waiting for wind to pull her from my hands. Then we ran laughing to the other side watching the boat voyage across the choppy waters, the sun catching her brass and the tricolor pennant on her masts.

I went to college in New York City because it was as close as I could get to Kevin, who was at Harvard, closer than Bryn Mawr, where everyone thought I should go, and close to Collin. I wrote to tell him I would be there, but though we talked on the phone several times, I saw him only once when Kevin and I went to dinner with him and his mistress, Millie. He seemed strangely diminished, but then I was taller. He was going bald, and getting fat. He drank too much, and I was embarrassed and sad. Sometimes I would call him, but there seemed little to say, and after a few moments he would ask if I needed anything. I could not tell him what I really needed, so when he asked if I needed money I said yes. A few times he sent me a check for a hundred dollars. But my mother told me he also stopped sending her the payment they had agreed upon for my expenses, a hundred dollars a month. When I was fifty-four, my aunt told me that when my parents wanted to make love they whispered the word "teedle" to each other and that when I was born they called me by the same word, "Teedle," soon shortened to Tee. It was the first time I thought that they might have once cared about each other. Now, as I started my marriage, my father was a ghost in my past, more awkward to me because he was alive, and there was always the promise and threat of a reconciliation.

Being called Mrs. Russell made me feel a man had valued me enough to marry me and give me his name, but I was also worried. Anne had told me that the first six months of married life were very tough, and I had read in brides' magazines that if you could get through the first six months, you could get through anything. I had expected to have to adjust to living with Tom as his wife and I wanted to be supportive—the term "a good wife" stuck in my mind—but we were living in a tiny space in a dangerous neighborhood. We had very few friends we could ask to come to our neighborhood and the few times we were asked to parties by old friends, I didn't feel comfortable. I couldn't reciprocate and people we met seemed distant and cold to me. Sometimes they passed joints at a party and we didn't want to smoke dope; it seemed to cast a pall over conversation and people sat around giggling, talking in occasional monosyllables. When we refused to smoke with them we felt like outcasts, and it was easier not to go to the parties.

I was changing in ways I didn't notice but which began to add up. When I was nineteen I had succumbed both to Kevin's suggestion that we make love and that I start smoking. I smoked from then until the day after I married. I would let the smoke trail out between my fingers as they arched around the cigarette; I pretended I was Bacall, and Bogie was just a few feet away. I tried a cigarette holder for a while, and then when I was broke I rolled my own—but they came out looking like Tampax. I tried Russian cigarettes with the long tube and mysterious black-coal dust scrunched at one end. Once I smoked a Player's Navy Cut from the packet with the picture of the aptly named and handsome Tar. But I settled into unfiltered Camels; it was satisfying to think I was smoking a man's cigarette—the cigarette smoker's cigarette.

The weeks before our wedding I smoked so much that my lungs ached and it was hard to draw breath. After a week of living in New York City I realized I hadn't smoked—the pain had simply been too much. As the price of cigarettes had gone up dramatically and Tom had never smoked, I stopped also. I have since learned that nicotine is a more powerful drug than heroin and I have watched friends trying to quit. I wonder now why I was able to stop so easily.

I also changed my eating patterns to suit Tom's, but somehow I didn't realize that I was entirely cutting out sugar and desserts, a palate inherited from my English mother. I was simply changing my patterns to match his and I didn't notice that I was actually eating much more healthily, but as I ate less and less fattening food over the next two years, I lost about twenty-five pounds. Tom's diet was different from mine, but there was nothing overtly strange then about it. He simply ate very little fat or sweet food, at least when we ate together; besides, we were living off money friends of our parents had given us for our wedding, so we had to be careful not to spend it on rich and expensive food. I learned to enjoy simpler dishes like pasta and vegetables, and cheap dishes our friends Polly and Alex knew how to make.

After a month of living in the apartment on East Ninety-ninth Street, the landlord told Tom and me the apartment just below ours was coming vacant; it was smaller and the rent was only forty-five dollars a month. Tom said he wanted it as an office in which to write and study while I was at work and working on my master's thesis, and it seemed too cheap to pass up.

On Halloween Night in 1969, Tom was writing in his study and I called him for dinner by pounding on the floor and yelling out the fire escape. After supper he went back downstairs, but soon I heard him yelling—and running back up the stairs.

"We've been robbed, we've been robbed. They took the wine we got for our wedding and some silver. Guess there wasn't much else to take. They must have known I was going upstairs."

"Did you lock the window when you left?"

"No, I was just going to be gone a short time."

"Damn it. Let's call the police."

We called, and after a long time a detective called back.

"Wine, huh, and silver? How much was it worth? Under three hundred? Well, drug addicts I guess. Window open—well, you're just inviting them in. Sure, I'll file a report, see if I can get to you this week." But he didn't.

A week after the first robbery the super still had not installed the new locks. I came home from work to find Tom standing in the bedroom, the bureau drawers pulled out, my underwear spewed over the floor, my jewelry box emptied, and the two kittens sitting on the bed. It made me nauseous to think of hands pawing through my underwear, of men throwing our things into a pillowcase, wrenching off the lock on the door, tearing open the window, frightening the kittens. I felt violated and afraid myself, and wondered what I was doing in such a dangerous place—worried that Tom was not taking responsibility for us.

When I placed second on the city civil service exam I was thrilled, thinking I would have a real advantage in finding a good job. I was told to appear on a certain date to talk about my choices with representatives of city agencies. On the specified day I showed up, as did at least six hundred others, in what turned out to be a huge room. The person who had scored first on the exam was called and instructed to walk through another door. One minute later my name was called and I was ushered through the same door, which opened into a gigantic hall with at least fifty long rectangular tables, each with several people sitting around it. There were large placards on the tables announcing the department of city government for which the recruiters were working. I stood there stunned, realizing that the people who had placed third and fourth and fifth would be coming into the room, and that my "advantage" in placing well would soon evaporate.

The first table I noticed was for the Housing Development Administration—I hadn't thought of working in housing before, but I was intrigued by the effect of physical structures on social problems and decided to risk spending a few minutes learning about HDA before I walked down to the table for the department of social services. At this table a young woman briefed me about HDA, read my résumé and placement, and said, "You are perfect for this wonderful job we have working for a special assistant to the commissioner." She made it sound like a really interesting job that fitted me. Now the hall was full of people scurrying from table to table and I signed up with HDA without going to any of the other interviewers.

Tom was studying for the comprehensive exams for his master's degree at the New School and working on his book. He had talked several times with an editor at Scribner's he had known when he worked there. "He says it's written like Joyce's *Portrait of the Artist as a Young Man*. He says it is poetic and evocative." We were excited and hopeful, and I enjoyed working to support our dream. But I worried when he told me that he hadn't had a "real" job since he had worked in the religion division of Scribner's, assigned to travel to schools of theology to sell texts and that he had gotten bored making these trips and started making up his reports. He seemed proud that Scribner's praised these "works of fiction," but it scared me to think he had been so deceitful.

Hoping that being married would deliver me from feeling lonely and vulnerable, I sometimes felt more like a child wanting a parent to protect me than a partner working to be a member of a team. I could accept where we lived as a temporary adventure, I could accept that I worked to support us so Tom could write his book, but I felt letdown, even betrayed, when Tom behaved in ways that hurt or shamed me. One night a friend of Tom's, a lonely and shy man, came over to see us. He was one of the few friends who dared visit and I thought it would be fun to have a guest. Our apartment was so small that we had to use the kitchen as a living room, and the bedroom was open to the kitchen. We were standing in the bedroom when, in his awkwardness, Tom's friend opened the top drawer of my bureau. I was shocked, and I felt violated. I was sure Tom was going to tell him to stop, but he didn't. The friend pulled open the second drawer and started to go through my underwear. Again I waited for Tom to say something but he didn't, and finally I blurted out, "Stop that, what are you, some kind of pervert?" I was trying to make it funny. But it wasn't. I felt so unprotected, just as I had when I was a child, fearing that I hurt him as I tried to defend myself. For years afterward Tom berated me for offending his friend, never seeming to understand how deeply hurt and frightened I had felt because Tom had done nothing to stop what was a gross invasion of my privacy; no matter how many times I told him, it didn't seem to matter.

Another time, right after we married, we were at dinner in Washington with Tom's father and stepmother. As we were sipping asparagus soup, Tom and his stepmother were talking. Suddenly I heard him say something about me having my period. His stepmother looked surprised and embarrassed, I froze as everyone looked at me, and then a flush of hot blood suffused my body and turned my face magenta. Today, such a comment might have little impact on a new bride. At the time it felt completely inappropriate, as if Tom were claiming power over me by revealing what should have been private. I felt shamed and helpless, more like a possession than a treasured companion.

I couldn't entirely ignore how and where we lived, and how different it was from what I had expected. Harlem was a strange place for us to start a marriage, a symptom of our defiance against our parents' way of life, perhaps. At night we could hear our elderly neighbors screaming at each other, clumping across their living room, rattling our tin ceiling, throwing pots that crashed and bounced, reverberating along the floor over our heads.

Sometimes, when I climbed the steps from the subway, I watched the people who lived in the elegant high-rise apartments below Ninety-sixth Street as they walked home before I turned up toward the brick-and-glass projects a block from where we lived, and again I wondered what I was doing there. But I was determined not to fail at my marriage, as my parents had failed at theirs. Instead I thought about what fun we had with Alex and Polly, that we all agreed about the war, about the foolish pretensions of Washington society, and that it was fun sitting on our big bed and on mismatched chairs watching the Knicks, eating popcorn.

Tom told me a lot about his family, and I read about them in his book. I had gotten to know his father, a tall man with twinkling blue eyes and a red face. I thought of him as dithering, bustling in nonproductive ways, always taking so much more time to do anything than was necessary, always using more motion than was needed. He was gracious and kind to me, but I felt sorry for him because he seemed so easily overwhelmed. I remember one time we were staying with him and his second wife, Danielle, at the big house they bought together on Q Street, and Tom went to put our laundry in his father's machines. While we were out, the clothes in the dryer started to burn because, I learned later, Tom had stuffed the machine too full. The smoke began to billow out of the machines and all his father could do was yell and yell and wring his hands. When we came back from doing errands we found him screaming that we were burning the house down . . . but the dryer was still churning around, the smoke still pouring out of the laundry room. He hadn't known how to stop it. How amazing, I thought, all he had to do was turn the machine off, open the door, or unplug it.

Once, when we were together in the old kitchen in the Adirondacks, Danielle held a small kitchen tool in her hand and asked, "What is this?"

Our friend Barry, who had himself been born into extraordinary luxury, looked at her and said, "It's an eggbeater." She had never seen one before because she had been raised by maids and married a senator who kept her as she had been accustomed to being kept as a child.

It was a different world, one we had left willingly. When the *Social Register* showed up in our mailbox in the apartment house in Harlem—perhaps the only one that ever made it north of Ninety-sixth Street—Tom exclaimed, "What in God's name is this awful book doing here?," holding it at arm's length as if it were infectious. "I bet my father put us in here." The next day he called the Social Register Association and told them they had no right to put us in the book without our permission.

Tom wrote about his family and I empathized; after all, I had had problems with my own family. His book validated my own experience, and I was incapable of looking at either of us objectively. Just as I didn't recognize the damage in myself, I didn't see the damage in Tom either. His family seemed sad and strange, but I was proud of Tom, just as I was proud of myself, for surviving. As we traded "war stories" about our parents, I appreciated his understanding and sympathy in listening to me.

By late winter Tom was ready to send in his manuscript. He carefully packed it and sent it by registered mail to his friend the editor. We were excited about learning the man's reaction to Tom's finished work because he had been so encouraging when they talked on the phone and because his opinion carried a lot of weight with the publisher. But then weeks went by and we didn't hear anything, and when finally Tom called him, the man didn't return his phone calls. The weeks dragged into months. One day Tom came home from running to find the carelessly wrapped manuscript sitting in the front hall of the building with a note from the editor saying he had quit to work for his lover, who was a hairdresser.

It was a terrible disappointment. Tom tried to find the editor but never succeeded. He started sending chapters of the book and new pieces, mostly poems, off to other publishers and magazines, but no one ever called, and each time he got another rejection slip it was another blow, eroding his confidence in himself and his dream of being a writer. I felt sad and helpless watching this happen, because my own dream—brilliant author and wife discovered in garret—was dying as well, and because Tom was torn apart and didn't seem to have anything else he wanted to do.

Confined to the small apartment, I noticed Tom's running more than I had when we lived together in the big house in the Adirondacks. He always wore layers of heavy clothes to induce a heavy sweat, which I was used to, but when he got home from running around the reservoir and stripped off the drenched pants and shirts, the smell of his sweat filled the kitchen. He hung his clothes out the fire escape to dry until the neighbors complained, and then put them in thick garbage bags until he could take them to the Laundromat. Strangest of all to me was the abuse he accepted to his feet; somehow I had not realized that his leather shoes chaffed his feet so much that they bled, staining his socks pink and leaving a trail on the floor. I first noticed crimson droplets of blood streaking across the kitchen floor, diminishing on the way to the bathroom. I thought I had cut myself, but when Tom came home the next time after running, I looked at his feet. "My God, your feet look awful! You're bleeding."

He looked down and shrugged. "The shoes are stiff—I can't cut them, and I just get blisters."

"Doesn't it hurt?" I asked.

"Yeah, I don't really feel it when I am running, though," he said.

"Shouldn't you let the blisters heal?" I asked. "You might get an infection."

"No, no," he replied. "I've got to run. It's the only way to deal with Reynaud's. It's okay, I'm used to it." Each night he swabbed and bandaged the blisters and I thought he was heroic for coping with the condition so bravely and it never occurred to me to question him or learn more about Reynaud's.

My job was dreadful; Tom was finished with his program at the New School, and when the phone rang one day and Tom's father offered us cheap rent in a beautiful little house he owned in Georgetown, we accepted immediately. We hired two men to help move things to the truck; the elder, a short black man with a halo of white hair, who didn't look particularly strong, moved the bureaus and the bed on his back in a slow beautiful flow of energy, rhythmic and controlled as a ballet dancer. We had a penny collection in a giant mayonnaise jar and in an impetuous gesture of neighborliness Tom gave it to a small slightly retarded black child who had been watching us move. Sometimes I have worried about that child and wondered if he got his treasure home or was mugged before he reached safety—and if he could even have explained how he had gotten the money. Then we drove away, the back of the truck clanking ominously whenever Tom switched gears, and I wondered if the back end would fall off and careen down Third Avenue at 125th Street, annihilating pedestrians and starting a race riot. But finally we were out of the city and our first real difficulty was crossing the small wooden bridge at the end of the driveway to Tom's father's summer house in the Adirondacks, where we would live until we moved to Washington in the fall.

I was hopeful about moving back to Washington. I looked forward to being near friends and my family, to unpacking the wedding presents we had stored in Mummy's basement, and beginning life as a young couple in our own little house in Georgetown. I thought about living closer to Mummy and hoped that physical proximity would lead to a closer emotional bond as well. Tom and I had spent two weeks with her in Ireland that summer, a trip, she said, that could substitute for the honeymoon we never had. Tom's younger brother Michael, who his father suggested would enjoy the trip, my mother, Tom, and I—an odd honeymoon party, but I was grateful Michael was with us because Tom and my mother never seemed to agree about anything: where to go, which way to turn, how much time to spend when we got there. Michael and I tried to be peacemakers, but Mummy and Tom each complained to me throughout the trip. I remember most clearly the moments I was by myself, walking from the car where Mummy sat parked next to a menhir and dolmen at the side of the road along the Dingle coast, the stones jutting from the emerald grass into the air like a steeple and no less sacred and later walking through a field with a sheepdog owned by Mummy's friend. Nettles stung my legs and suddenly the dog leaped into a hedge and tore out a nest of baby birds, crushing them in his mouth before I could stop him.

When I called Mummy from New York to tell her we were moving, she seemed pleased, though I thought I heard a note of reticence in her voice, as if she were slightly embarrassed by me, or perhaps just by the marriage that produced me. I worried that living in Washington might be complicated. The war was raging in Vietnam and in our living rooms. Day and night we endured Nixon, watching his surly face squinching into a sneer, feeling his fingers pointing right at us, as if he spoke for the generation of our parents in condemning us. It was a struggle to return to the fold like black sheep, but I did so, much as I had gone to college in New York City, hoping for some reconciliation or at least contact with my father, but in hopes this time of being with my widowed mother. Perhaps I was going back to Washington now to make my own place there as an adult, to try to help fill the void in my mother's life that Desie's death created. I don't know. I just know I went full of hope, thinking that I was coming home again.

5

Coming Home

September 1969

When Tom's father rented us a small house he owned in Washington for a hundred dollars a month, I couldn't believe our good fortune. Built as slaves' quarters in 1803, the little Federal house nestled at the foot of a hill in Georgetown. The brick had softened over the years, scoured by city wind and soot to a gentle, variegated red, and the front door and two dormers were painted a handsome dark green. The original house contained a small room, now the front hall, a good-size kitchen, with two bedrooms and a bath upstairs. More recently someone had added a large combination living room and dining room, which opened through French doors to a terrace and a huge, though untended, garden. When I walked out the doors I found a rotting tire filled with dirt and festering rainwater, brittle black plastic bags, broken bottles, and other debris, but I stuck a spoon in the dirt and turned over rich black loam.

It had been easy to leave New York. We had a few friends there, but not many, perhaps because we could not reciprocate invitations easily; my job was disappointing and I doubted I could make it any better, and Tom didn't have one. Washington was home, where we knew many more people and where Tom's family had lived for generations. His aunts and uncles, cousins, father and stepmother all lived there now, as did Mummy and Grannie. I was excited about coming home, but it wasn't easy. I worried that the conflicts I had felt as a child would not resolve themselves just because I was an adult, and that it was perhaps easier to be an adult if I was not living in the place where I had been a child.

On one side of our house there was a public school that served children bused in from Anacostia, because the students who lived in the neighborhood all went to private schools. The playground was twelve feet below the level of our garden. A brick wall topped by a tall chain-link fence and draped in wisteria separated us from the playground, which provided a ready supply of errant tennis balls and conversations with the aspiring tennis buffs who landed them in our garden. Tom had been a nationally ranked tennis player when he was in high school and played on Princeton's undefeated tennis team for four years. He enjoyed watching people play and giving them pointers while he was reading in the garden.

Later I would unearth colonial pipe stems, white as bird bones, and broken pottery, some marked "made in Nippon," and others that seemed much older. I once found a pockmarked revolver buried in the ground. I grew tomato vines that scrambled around the convenient trellis of the chain-link fence; hot red peppers, their hats a fiery torment; and other vegetables, including okra, which grew pods a foot long when we went away for a week and I didn't pick them. The rose of Sharon burst into pink trumpets and the wisteria unfurled its purple clouds along the fence, attracting bees and butterflies. The packs of seed I scattered over the rich earth burst into a cutting garden of orange, magenta, and pink zinnias, red lobelia, deep blue Chinese delphinium, and other bright flowers that spread their color throughout the house. I plucked and pruned, planned and planted and the garden seemed enchanted— responding with exuberance to unaccustomed care and compost.

Sometime during the year we drifted into being vegetarians, not so much as the result of a conscious decision, but because we had little money it was hard to afford meat. When, months after not eating meat, we bought a steak, the richness of the bloody red meat sickened us and we decided not to buy it anymore. Instead, we grew mung beans and other vegetables, and substituted cheese for meat as a cheap source of protein.

We settled easily into the little house. It was exciting to unpack barrels of wedding presents that my mother had stored for the year since we had been married. I had made a floor plan from memory on graph paper, the way my mother always did when planning a new house, but as we arranged our things according to my belabored plan, Tom said, "You know the rocking chair would be much better over there by the couch, and I think the three Giacometti lithographs would look better in a row, over behind the table." I had to agree. He seemed to have a much better sense of how to place things, a natural sense of aesthetics. He had traded in his Eurail pass to buy the three Giacomettis when he was working in Paris as a tutor and had seen them staring at him from the window of a small store. I thought they looked like Tom; two drawings of a man's skeletal figure and the third, a face with eyes that held you in their grip.

We moved in our furniture and I began to work on the interior. The floors were painted a dull brown, and one day I scraped a little of the old paint away to find richly grained wood, so I decided to refinish the floor. Each day I uncovered a bit, and by the end of the two years we lived there the floor shone in the light that flooded the room through the French doors.

We were so worried about being broken into, as we had been in New York, that we bought an expensive Schlage lock from Meenahan's hardware store on Wisconsin Avenue. Tom said we couldn't afford a locksmith, so he took the old lock apart and spent several hours installing the new one. I walked past where he was sitting cross-legged in front of the door and noticed that there were extra parts on the floor.

"Why did you leave those out?" I asked.

"Well," he answered, "I couldn't tell where they went, so I figured they were extra."

"I don't think it will work properly," I said, restraining myself because I worried that he was ruining the lock, but I didn't want him to feel badly about it.

We had to pay a locksmith to take the new lock out and reinstall the old one because Tom had thrown out the parts he thought unnecessary. It seemed such an odd thing to do—just throw out parts the manufacturer had designed to make the mechanism work. Was he thinking that as a man he ought to know how to install the lock, or was he just impatient and unwilling to figure out how to make it work properly? I wondered but I didn't know. It scared me to have been right in wanting to call a locksmith in the first place, as if then all I had were my own resources to rely on.

Tom got a job as a part-time football coach at the private school where I and my sister and brother, and Tom's sister and brothers, had all been students. Tom had gone to the more prestigious of the private elementary schools in the area, the "feeder" for the most demanding day school that prepared all its boys for college. I was looking for work in a government agency, but one day Tom told me there was an opening at the school that he thought would be ideal for me. He said it would be convenient for us to work in the same place since we would have the same long vacations and could spend the summers in the Adirondacks. I have since wondered if having me at the school made being there somehow easier and safer for him. I took the job, but reluctantly. I hadn't wanted to be a teacher, and I was going to teach things I knew nothing about, sports and English, not what I had worked so hard to learn, anthropology and sociology. I wondered if I would be taken seriously by teachers who had known me since I was in second grade. I felt as if I were giving in and giving up some of what I had wanted to do, but Tom kept telling me that my goal of helping people by working in government was foolish because I would be starting at the bottom, unlike my stepfather, who had started at the CIA so close to the top.

In the beginning we enjoyed being "home." We loved to go to the old movies playing at the cinema near our house, and to rallies against the Vietnam war. We met Jim, a fledgling doctor and tennis player who flailed away at balls and sent them flying into our garden. If we had wanted to, we could have relied on him for a steady supply. Tom often talked with him when he was home because Jim had irregular hours, too, and Tom was home most days until early afternoon. We invited Jim to dinner one night with Kendra, another friend, whom Jim didn't know. Later Jim told me that when he asked Tom about his prospective blind date, Tom had said, "Well, she isn't very attractive and she isn't too bright," but when they got married and Kendra asked him about this, Tom replied that he hadn't wanted to get Jim's hopes up.

I loved playing at being grown-up, now that I lived in a charming little house in Georgetown, a perfect place to have friends over, not in a tiny apartment in a dangerous neighborhood in Manhattan. Mocking myself a bit, I still knew how to provide a full table of food, compatible guests with just enough in common and just enough that separated them to provide a wonderful evening of talk. I thought it was expected that we would have friends for dinner, it was something our parents enjoyed and one of the requirements for a young couple just entering the adult social scene of Washington's upper crust.

Many of the many people our parents had invited to our wedding were friends of both families and gave us lavish presents. Mrs. Bray gave us an entire set of Orrefors crystal, slender wine and water goblets catching the light on candles, and champagne glasses, which sat on shelves in the kitchen. We had silver flatware, not good silver, but plated, which Mummy had given us, and many salvers, servers, bowls, and trays—one from my father's sister with the initials I had discarded, BLT, but hadn't been able to tell her. I had collected Herend plates, and the French service we had chosen at Martin's were a second complete set. We had an oval cherry dining table that, with the leaves in it, could seat ten comfortably.

But Tom started to pressure me about food when we began inviting people over. I tended to overdo it because I was afraid that what I offered guests would never be enough, he to be too restrained, and it made us both tense to discuss our differences. In New York we had never been able to invite friends for dinner, except Polly and Alex and sometimes Diana, a classmate of mine who had moved into the same brownstone. Because we all lived in the same circumstances, I never felt I had to offer a fancy meal. So it was not until we moved to Washington that we had an opportunity to invite more than two or three friends for dinner, and to disagree about how to treat them. Finally we were both working, though Tom's job was part-time and we had given up the much larger salary and benefits I would have earned doing almost anything other than teaching. I knew we didn't have much money, but in my mind I envisioned the lavish parties my mother and stepfather had given at which Lester passed silver trays and serving dishes piled with roast beef and Yorkshire pudding, broccoli with hollandaise, and an elegant raspberry sorbet rising in an eight-inch dome festooned with sugared flowers, twining leaves, and vines of icing. I struggled to plan ways to mimic the luxury of my upbringing without spending much money because what Tom said made sense to me. We didn't have as much money as our friends; we had to be careful.

I had to justify what I was planning to serve, to show him that I was making an effort to be economical. For one party I thought about a menu and then presented it to him. "If I buy whole shrimp that aren't cleaned or cooked, I can get them for several dollars less a pound. We won't have them by themselves. I'll make shrimp pilaf. What was that wine you and Jim found that was so cheap? Can't we just serve that and no other drinks? There's a lot of lettuce in the garden now, and I think the cherry tomatoes are ready. There's lots of okra—but I don't think anyone likes okra but me. And I won't have to buy flowers, there are tons out there."

"Yes, that sounds okay," he answered. "I'll get the wine and ice, but you don't need any other vegetables. Just the salad from the garden should be fine. And you don't need bread."

"Well, bread is cheap and it will fill people up. And I can make a carrot cake."

"There's no need for cake. You don't need more fattening foods—Jim is getting too fat anyhow."

At the time I didn't recognize any other agenda or concern except that we had to be careful about what we spent. I was still a new wife, trying to make a home for us and fit into Washington society.

Once, we sat ten friends around the table dinner—thick home-made mushroom soup and then a ham quiche and salad, French bread with herbs—not expensive food, but good. I had been taking weaving lessons, and had made ten place mats in colonial over-shot, red with white threads creating intricate patterns. The candles stood tall in their silver candlesticks, the bread in the silver wire basket lay within a white linen napkin, the casseroles rested in silver serving dishes, silver trays held cheese and silver pepper and salt shakers, the little silver mustard pot, all new and highly polished, seemed to preen in proud display.

I was sitting a few places away from Tom, not at the far end of the table, as I needed to be able to get up and go to the kitchen. Jim and Kendra were there, smiling and talking with their dinner partners. I loved watching as people dipped into the soup and seemed to enjoy it. "Barbara, this is delicious. Where did you buy it?" Sarah asked. "It's simple to make. I just cut up a lot of different kinds of mushrooms," I replied, not wanting to tell her how long it took, or how you had to squeeze the mushrooms in a towel to separate the juice for the stock. Jim and Tom had found a wine named Château Palmer, which they thought was a great bargain, and I laughed to myself, thinking, "That is going down well."

Nan, my dear friend from boarding school, who lived in New York, was sitting at the far end of the table. She asked for the butter, which was on a silver plate my godmother had given me, next to Tom. I wished I had put two plates of butter on the table, but Tom had told me that was excessive. It was such an ordinary request that I paid no attention until I saw Tom cut off a pat of butter and hand it on a knife to pass from hand to hand until it reached Nan at the other end of the long table. We all froze. Nan looked at me, sadness blowing over her face. I remember feeling as if the lights had dimmed on a stage, locking us in place at the end of a scene. Then they went up again and I don't remember what I said, but I know I made a foolish joke.

At the time I was too shocked to say anything to him, but I thought Tom had insulted Nan and that his behavior was odd and controlling. The moment is framed in my mind as the first time I felt embarrassed, scared, and vulnerable because of Tom's behavior about food. I worried that he appeared odd to the friends gathered around our table, and that perhaps they thought I had made a terrible mistake joining my life to his. And so I made a silly joke to cover my embarrassment and to deflect our guests from thinking about what Tom had done, a silly joke, the first of many, interjected over the years to soften an awkward moment, to shield us from our own reality. I was too scared to think of him as strange or odd because he was the only security I had.

But then, after a few months living in Washington, I felt nauseous in the morning, was always tired and my breasts ached. I described my symptoms to a friend—who responded that she had felt the same way when she was pregnant. "When you were what!" I exclaimed; this was not what I had expected. I had been taking birth-control pills, but the ones I had been prescibed were later taken off the market because they had failed so many times. Now I was pregnant, due in July, and Tom and I were excited. We told our parents. Tom's father and stepmother seemed very happy and proud to be prospective grandparents, my mother said she was pleased, and my grandmother was ecstatic.

My mother's mother was very tall and must have been beautiful when she was younger. She had a fine, even nose, handsome brown eyes, and a beautiful curving mouth. She married young because she was not allowed by her Victorian mother to talk to a man alone, even the village minister, but she discovered she had married a very proper man who bored her. Grannie remained in this marriage until her children were grown and married, then she left, coming to America to join Mummy, who was separated from Collin.

I was three when I first met Grannie. She and Mummy spent so much time talking to each other that I became jealous and picked up a pan of water I had been playing with and dumped it in Grannie's lap. Mummy was furious but Grannie understood that I was hurt and jealous at being left out; she made friends with me, and we had been friends ever since. When I was twenty I had been sick for several months, and when I felt better, Grannie told me it was time for me to get a new dress. She whisked me to the top floor, the sale department, of Garfinkel's in Washington. She swept along the rejected dresses, occasionally pulling one from the lineup. Suddenly she proclaimed, "This is the one," and pulled out a black satin sleeveless dress with a plunging V-neckline and fringe from below the bust to just below the knees, an impossible, outrageous dress.

I loved it. It made me feel sexy and funny and very glamorous, and every time I wore it I had a good time. Grannie had seemed to enjoy that I was a "budding" young woman, pleased that my boyfriend Kevin was so handsome. She once asked me if he had the "sex spot." I was stunned, and laughed, asking her what she meant. "On the back of his head, just above his neck. There will be a little bump. Look for it." I did. He had one. It was so hard to be feminine or womanly around Mummy, but Grannie made me feel as if she was launching me on a great adventure. When I called Grannie to tell her that finally she was going to be a great-grandmother, she was thrilled.

"Oh, but how marvelous. That is simply wonderful. When, when are you due?" she asked. "In early July, I think," I replied, "so school will be over and we will have some time." "That's good. You shouldn't work too long. Now, how are you feeling? Are you feeling sick? What about going on the school bus?" She made me feel loved and cared about.

Tom and I had fun being prospective parents. Our new status seemed to bring us more acceptance in the family, more congratulations from friends and relatives, but also a sense of responsibility, like a thin mantle settling over our shoulders. Tom's father talked with him about how Tom was going to support us, what kind of job he could get. He had always left open the door to a job in his real-estate office, and Tom could have worked there as an agent at any time. The office was small, only a few women worked there as agents, but they worked the most lucrative turf in Washington, Georgetown, and made sales without even advertising property. Tom didn't want any part of being a real-estate broker, a job his father had always talked about hating because it was boring and demanding, and, he thought, demeaning.

That fall Tom had started studying for the ministry again, though by spring he seemed to have lost interest in the classes, and thought he could get a job teaching tennis at the end of the school year. Now Tom's father offered to pay the medical expenses for the baby—a gift that allowed me to go to obstetricians associated with Georgetown University hospital and further delayed our confrontation with financial reality.

My doctor gave me lots of pamphlets to read, and I borrowed a medical text on pregnancy from Jim, though I tried not to look at all the pictures of what could go wrong. I learned that I should anticipate different symptoms in each trimester, and I was eager to get past feeling sick in the morning. The doctor told me that it was good I had stopped smoking and that I should expect to gain about twenty to twenty-five pounds, but that more might be bad for the baby.

Tom was also worried about my weight. "You've got to be careful," he said. "You see those women who gain lots of weight. They puff up like marshmallows and then they never lose it."

Always insecure about what I looked like, I worried that being pregnant would lead to arguments with Tom as I got fatter. I wondered what he would think as my body changed. "Lean horse for the long race," he said again, turning to me as we stood in the kitchen. I remembered my shock and repulsion on seeing my pregnant aunt's huge belly as she walked around her bedroom naked. My aunt was unselfconscious as she walked in to the bathroom to take a shower, but I looked in amazement at the red marks across her swollen belly like claw scratches from a huge cat. I had so rarely seen anyone naked. My mother sometimes walked into her bedroom when I was there with a towel around her waist, her nipples dark from childbearing.

Tom and I had always been shy around each other physically, never allowed ourselves to be naked in front of each other except when we were making love. We never took a shower together, we never walked around without being dressed or at least swaddled in a towel. If he ever complimented me about my body, I don't remember it. I had always felt too big, too tall, too heavy, and any kind remarks he may have said about my body I sloughed away in disbelief. I remember only knowing that he wanted me to be thinner, that he admired the thin, taut bodies of athletes.

At the same time being pregnant was a bit of a reprieve from the pressure I felt to get and to stay thin. When Tom told me not to eat ice cream, not to put cream in my tea, not to eat dessert, I could respond, "Look, I'm eating good food, broccoli and mung beans, and we aren't eating meat. I'm not eating junk food, McDonald's french fries, which I love. The doctor says I will gain some weight," I said, trying to lend what I was saying credibility. "It's important for the baby's health that I gain some weight," but I was scared to say how much. "Besides, I'm eating for two," I added.

Because I worked a full day at school while Tom took courses at a seminary in the morning and coached in the afternoon, I chaperoned the school bus to get to work. Each morning the bus picked me up at 7 A.M. and then for the next hour and a quarter we gathered the students on our route to the school in McLean, Virginia. I sat in the first seat on the opposite side of the driver, which meant that I had to turn around to talk to students. In one hand I clutched an ammonia capsule and in the other I held on to the cold clammy steel of the bar in front of me. I never actually threw up, but I certainly came close every morning.

Tom's sister Melinda also taught at the school. I knew Tom had always had a very difficult relationship with his sister, which hadn't improved since I had first met her when we had gone skiing together, but I couldn't blame him for this; she could be exasperating. I never understood what was wrong; Tom told me she had been born premature, that his mother had had such a tough time delivering him because he weighed over nine pounds at birth and she was a slight woman, that she was terrified of having another child. His sister seemed locked in permanent adolescence, absorbed by herself, and so insecure she had to get reinforcement constantly. She would take pictures of friends at parties, get thirty copies made of all the prints, bind them into expensive scrapbooks to give as surprise presents, but she charged everything at the pharmacy that had served her family for years, and she couldn't pay her bills. She seemed unable to control her spending, and Tom resented that his father always bailed her out. I knew so little about the effects of prematurity that I believed all her problems were due to her early birth. Later I realized that, like Tom, she had been raised by a mother who almost destroyed her, and to appreciate her struggle to grow up. She has since become a compassionate and well-grounded woman.

We started that fall to look for teaching jobs in other schools. After two semesters, Tom had decided not to pursue the degree in theology, though I'm not sure why, and he had given up writing his book. He liked teaching and wanted to teach English, while I wanted to teach anthropology, which limited the number of schools with possible jobs. I was teaching remedial English, coaching girls' teams—a joke really, as I had avoided sports as much as possible when I was in school and didn't know the rules of the games let alone ever having played them. I tried to get the girls to organize themselves and referee, but they often saw through this ploy and resented that I wasn't doing what a coach was supposed to do. Sometimes I forgot I was pregnant. One afternoon, when the hills around the school were covered with snow, we took trays and plastic disks and a few toboggans and raced down the slopes. At one point, caught up in the excitement, I grabbed a dish and plopped myself down, landing on my extended belly, suddenly feeling my baby inside me. Then I was offered the chance to teach a two-week course in urban anthropology to students from the inner-city school and our own ninth-graders in late May. I loved planning this course and spent an exciting week with my band of twelve students, six from Potomac, six from inner-city schools, going around to many interesting sites in the city—my belly preceding me.

The morning of May 25, 1970, I woke up bleeding a bit, my abdomen rippling with the Braxton Hicks contractions that had afflicted me whenever I exerted myself too much, and fluid tinged with blood leaking between my legs. But I refused to accept that anything was wrong, that I could be in labor. I was not due for another six to eight weeks, and I was not going to have a premature child.

I strapped two Kotex between my legs to stanch the flow, thinking that the pressure of the baby had just made me incontinent—denying that I could be in labor because it scared me to think I could have a child like Tom's sister. It astounds me now to realize how completely I fooled myself; I had, after all, prepared for this birth by reading a complex and detailed medical textbook. I went to school and taught classes all day long, though at one point I went to the nurse and asked what I should do. She told me I should go home and call my doctor. When Tom arrived at one-thirty to coach, I told him I was having a hard time but thought I could last until the day ended at three-thirty.

When we drove home, the contractions were stronger and I was becoming fearful, but I thought that if I rested I would be all right. A little later Mummy called, and as I sat on our bed clenching my teeth, I told her I was fine, that everything was fine, that I felt fine, and the baby was fine. When I hung up I lay back on the bed, the pains coming strong and regularly. Finally I called the doctor, and found he was not on duty, though his associate whom I had never met was there. Tom and I were supposed to start Lamaze classes that night, but the contractions became too painful to ignore. Tom called his brother because he had read that the most dangerous group of people on the road, those with the highest accident rate, were expectant fathers, so his brother came over to drive us the three blocks to the hospital.

When we got to the Georgetown University Hospital we met the doctor for the first time and Tom asked him if he could stay with me when the baby was delivered, as we had hoped to do if we took the childbirth class. The doctor replied, "I don't take attendance in the delivery room," but added that Tom might have to leave if he felt faint or there was a problem. When the doctor examined me he told me I was going to have the baby in half an hour, but that because other expectant mothers were there before me, he would give me medication to slow down the process. I lay on the gurney, waiting with the other women, like planes circling Dulles Airport, worrying about having a baby born too early.

I was too frightened to tell Tom how scared I was that I was going to let him and his family down. I felt like a complete failure and I was stunned. The doctor had once told me I was an obstetrician's dream—built for having babies—but here I was having a child a month and a half early, a child who might turn out like Melinda. As the nurse prepped me in the delivery room, I thought about how I had failed, failed to protect my baby, failed Tom and his family. We had made love the night before; was that the reason I went into labor? Had I pushed myself too hard working with my students? I knew I shouldn't have gone sledding. I knew I had done something wrong, but I didn't know what it was.

The doctor came into the small green room and said, "We're going to give you a saddle block to stop the pain because you haven't taken the classes." I couldn't protest because I didn't want to risk hurting the baby. Then the nurse added, "We're setting up a mirror so you can see the baby being born," and I was relieved, at least they trusted me to be able to watch. As I lay spread-eagled, my legs in the air imprisoned by the stirrup cups, exposed and vulnerable, Tom came in, took one look, and said, "Wow, I've never seen you like that before." His words made me feel awkward, self-conscious, and embarrassed, but I said nothing because I did not want to embarrass him or myself even more.

The doctor was standing in front of me, the nurse at my side, Tom nearby. "Push," they said, and I tried, but the baby didn't come. "Push again, now push." The heaviness of it felt dead and I was scared the child would be stillborn. I kept wanting to close my legs so the baby would have to stay in my womb until it was fully ready. But they told me to push, and the contractions, though I couldn't feel pain, were like heavy waves rolling over me. Finally we could see the child, just the top of a head covered with wet, black hair, and then, quickly, a gush of water and blood, and then they put this little red-blue wiggling mass covered in cottage-cheese-like mucus on my naked breast and I was horrified, but knew I was supposed to be ecstatic. This is all happening too fast, I thought, and I am not ready to have a baby.

"It's a boy," the doctor said.

"Balls as big as mine," Tom responded, which made me wince and wish again he were not in the room.

"Seven pounds, eleven ounces," the nurse announced.

"Is that premature?" I asked.

"Oh, heavens no!" she answered. "This is a big healthy baby. I wondered why he wasn't coming out faster—not premature this one," and I wanted to burst into tears. I didn't understand what was happening to me.

Then they all left and told me to fall asleep . . . and finally I did.

When I waited for my child to be brought to my room, I wondered if I would know him. If I walked into a room where he was sleeping with the other babies, would I know my own son? We did not have a name. We had no clothes, no bassinet; we had nothing because we had planned to shop for our baby after school ended in June. When the nurse brought him to me, he smelled like cinnamon and was so soft and sweet—but I was still in shock and I went through the motions of mother love but without the feeling. We decided to call our son Stephen, which was not a family name but one we both liked. The first time the nurse brought Stephen to me to breastfeed, Tom was sitting across from me in a chair. She tried to teach me to hold Stephen and encourage him to suckle, but I felt awkward and stupid, and I could feel Tom's eyes on me. Instead of feeling love and delight in sharing an extraordinary moment, I just felt embarrassment because I didn't feel I was learning how to be a mother very quickly, and I was scared I wouldn't know how to care for Stephen when we took him home from the hospital. Not until several days later when I saw him curled in his basket in the front hall of our house, his fingers and toes tucked beneath him, did I begin to love his vulnerability and want to protect him, not until then did I begin to feel like his mother.

I was lying in my hospital bed the night after his birth. My breasts ached from a horrible engorgement of milk that had made them stiff, tender, and swollen. I asked the nurse for aspirin—anything—but she said she couldn't give me a painkiller because the doctor hadn't ordered it. Today I would have asked her to get another doctor, but then I thought I had to just bear the pain and so I did, though it wore me out and I spent much of the night in tears. I didn't feel I had a right to disturb the doctor. After all, lots of women had babies without taking pain medication.

The doctor told me the baby was full term; we just hadn't known when the term started because I was taking birth-control pills. He told me that because I was built perfectly for childbirth, with capacious hips, I had carried the child easily, and that because I was strong and healthy, my baby was strong and healthy. I was so relieved that I didn't wonder until later how his partner had managed not to realize that I was six weeks further into my pregnancy than we thought. But now that really didn't matter. I felt as if I had been stunned, shocked to the point where I could hardly feel. Suddenly I was a mother when I thought I still had time to be a teacher. I couldn't make the transition easily, couldn't seem to let go of the hopes I had for my students, and I resented leaving them. I didn't know how to take care of a baby; I hadn't learned from my own mother; I had no one to help me, I had never liked baby-sitting, and I was scared.

After the delivery Tom called my mother to tell her the news. The next afternoon she came to visit me in the hospital room, sitting stiffly at attention, perched on the edge of a little straight-backed chair, and toying with the button on her dress. "How are you feeling?" she asked. "I'm okay. I feel a little uncomfort-able, I guess," I replied. "It was such a surprise, but they say he isn't premature and he is healthy. Have you seen him yet?" I asked her. "No, but I'll look at him on my way out. Is there anything you need for him?" she wondered. "I feel so stupid about all this," I replied. "I didn't expect him until mid-July. Here it is the end of May. The doctor missed it completely. We were going to buy the layette after school got out," I apolo-gized. "I can do that for you, I have a little time tomorrow morning," she offered. I was very grateful but I felt I had done a bad job in planning and I was imposing on her. "The flowers are certainly beautiful. Who sent you the iris and baby's breath?" she asked. "I think that's from Tom's friend Bob, who married us," I said. "And the roses?" she added. "Those are from his fa-ther and Danielle," I replied. I wanted to talk about how scared I was and about how I didn't know how to take care of a baby, but my mother seemed curiously listless and withdrawn, as if she were just there because she had to be. After a few minutes of more awkward small talk, she said, "Well, I don't want to tire you out. When are you going home?"

"Tomorrow, I think."

"I'll get the key from Tom's father and leave the clothes in your house," she said, adding, "I'll stop by and see you after you're settled in."

I cried after she left because I had hoped that my baby would create a connection between us, that we would talk about caring for a baby, that I would learn what to do and how to do it, that she would help me. Later she went to Garfinkel's to buy a layette and a bathinette to change him on, but she had no advice or words of encouragement, and I felt her relief when she got up to leave me in the hospital. I didn't see her for another week. I know she tried to seem interested in her grandson, but she just wasn't. I realized later that she probably didn't want to be a grandmother—that it just reminded her that she was getting older, that her exquisite beauty was dimming, and that she was lonely.

When we drove Stephen home from the hospital, Tom opened the door for me just as a large D.C. transit bus spewed black exhaust all over us. We tried to cover Stephen but the fumes spewed out and made us realize now we had someone to protect.

The first time I handed Stephen to Tom, when Tom was sitting on our bed, he took him and held him close, nestling him against his chest. Suddenly he thrust him away and exclaimed, "Do you think this means I'm a homosexual?" I could make no sense of this question, but it saddened me that he thought that just holding his son in a loving way meant he was gay.

Oh no, I thought. There are men who are married for years, and they don't really want to be, but they don't want to admit they're gay and so they marry and they have kids. Could he be like that? It was a brief thought, one that passed through my head and back out because I was too scared to confront it. "Oh, come on, don't be so silly," I said to him, "of course you aren't gay." I reached over and took my son from his father, frightened to think that holding his child made Tom so nervous, and feeling lonely because the responsibility for Stephen seemed now to fall on me.

The first time I put a diaper on Stephen I laid him on our bed and sat next to him, reading the directions the hospital had sent home with us. Insert A in B, pin D to E—I was so confused I finally abandoned the piece of paper lying on the bed and just did what seemed logical. The remnant of the umbilical cord was still attached to Stephen and each day I had to clean, disinfect, and rebandage the wound that marked the place where we had been connected. I had to learn to clean up the baby shit that seemed like an explosion all over the diaper and his legs. One day he peed a great arcing stream that landed on our cat Nathan, who bolted from the room. After that I turned him over when I changed his diaper. To make him stop crying, sometimes I sang to him after I fed him, but until I read about using a pacifier I didn't know how to calm him down after I had fed, changed, and held him.

I was physically exhausted, emotionally depleted, scared about how I was going to take care of the baby when I knew so little about what I was doing. I thought it was my responsibility as the mother to know how. But I didn't, and Tom knew even less than I did. He seemed to think that mothering was a genetic inheritance, that it came "naturally." I was scared to tell him I really had no idea about what I was doing and felt vaguely guilty for not being confident, in fact for feeling almost overwhelmed.

Tom helped with some of the work, but he was teaching tennis and would come home exhausted. I wondered sometimes why he was so tired when he was sleeping a full night, and I resented that he was still working only part-time while my job never seemed to stop, but I knew the heat of a Washington summer was debilitating and that he didn't enjoy teaching the wives of prominent men because they often seemed mindless and boring to him. During the day I washed Stephen's clothes in the bathtub because Tom's father didn't want to buy a washer or dryer and we didn't have the money to buy the machines ourselves. The process often took several hours; my back ached because the only place big enough to wash in was the bathtub, and my hands turned red. Sometimes Tom went to the Laundromat but he said it was so disgusting, full of people who drank and threw up or urinated there, that he didn't want me to go and hated to go there himself. I could hardly blame him.

The second day after we got back from the hospital the doorbell rang, and there stood a friend of my mother's wearing a little hat perched on her neatly coiffed hair, an elegant, starched dress, white gloves, and holding a beautifully wrapped present with a card. I stood there, my hair frizzing in the Washington heat, my T-shirt damp with drying breast milk, my blue jeans stained with baby crap, and my feet bare. The house was as much of a mess as I was. I was up for most of the nights and getting about four hours of sleep because it took me so long to feed and change Stephen. Stephen was a very good and easy baby to care for, I eventually realized, I just didn't know how to do it.

"Oh, please come in, Mrs. Brown," I mumbled, embarrassed at the chaos around me.

I could feel her eyes paring me down to a stub. We made polite talk and she admired the baby, who was, mercifully, asleep in his basket. Lucky she didn't ask to see him when he was sleeping in the bureau drawer we used because we didn't have a crib for him yet. I remember that she said, firmly but kindly, in a voice I knew intended to be helpful, "Remember, you must not spoil him. Just feed him on a schedule or you will never get any peace."

The next day another well-intentioned friend of my mother's appeared looking almost identical and saying almost exactly the same thing. After a few more days of this I began to think that it was rude of these women to show up unannounced, but then I realized they had never known a new mother without a baby nurse and an impeccably clean house. They gave nice presents and were trying to be kind and welcoming, but they seemed to think of babies as manipulative creatures. I felt intimidated by them until I saw the pattern in their behavior. I also decided Dr. Spock was right and that Stephen couldn't get up and go to the icebox when he was hungry or to the toilet when he wanted to relieve himself and so, for now, he was pretty dependent on me and that we might reach an accommodation if we were patient with each other.

When I had found out I was pregnant, I thought Mummy would be happy to have a grandchild. I see now how foolish this was, but at the beginning I thought a grandchild would be a wonderful present, a baby to play with, enjoy, and love, someone to fill part of the void in her life left when Desie died and her children grew up and moved away. Des had told me that many nights, when he was home from college, he listened to Mummy crying. She felt people asked her and Desie to dinner only because of Desie and his job, and there may have been some truth in that. Now I hoped we could give her an excuse to give parties, go with her to places she might not have gone to alone, but it never happened and I was never able to ask her why.

Instead, I grew resentful that we were never included in dinner parties, never invited to plays and ballets that she asked my sister to attend. I began to realize she didn't like being a grandmother. One day I wrote her a long, long letter, detailing my sadness and pain. I told her I hated it when she gave me presents I couldn't use, because it showed how little she understood my life. She had given Frankie, Joan, and me expensive fur "tippets" that Christmas, the kind in which the "sacrificial" fox clasps onto its tail as it circles your throat, wrapping them in colorful hat boxes and arranging for us to open them simultaneously. Mummy didn't seem aware that I never ate meat and I didn't have the money to go anywhere I could have worn or would have worn a piece of fur, or to understand that what I really wanted was a washing machine. I took the fur back to the store, but the saleswoman told me it was "millinery and couldn't be returned." Finally I sold it for fifty dollars at the yard sale we held just before we moved again, to a young Georgetown matron who was thrilled to find such a bargain. I wrote in the letter to Mummy that I didn't understand why she never asked me anywhere, or came to see us when we invited her. I told her it hurt me that she seemed so uneasy around us and with Stephen. Then I wrote her name and address on the letter, put a stamp on it, and tucked it under a mug on top of my bureau.

I told Tom I had written the letter, but I didn't know what to do with it. I added that I wasn't ready to send it—but a few days later Mummy called, screaming at me that she had shown the letter to her best friend who thought it was totally unfair. At first baffled, I then realized that Tom had mailed the letter. "I just saw it with the stamp on it and thought you wanted to send it," he explained. "But I told you I didn't want to mail it yet," I said. "I forgot," he replied. "It was just sitting there." I blamed myself for being careless, but again thought I shouldn't have trusted him. But at least now Mummy knew what I thought and would never have had the courage to tell her face-to-face. After that we still saw each other but not often and only when she invited Grannie with us to Sunday lunch.

One Sunday we sat around her dark mahogany dining table with the Georgian silver candlesticks and heavy silver flatware eating lunch. Stephen was waving and cooing in his basket on the table. Grannie, my sister and brother, Tom, and I all marveled at the little things he was doing. For about fifteen minutes we were absorbed in him. Finally Mummy could stand it no longer and reached over to pick him up out of his basket, holding him against her. Joan turned to her and said, "Mummy, it looks so funny to see you with a baby."

Mummy turned to her and, pointing to each of us, replied, "But I took care of you and you and you."

I remember being amazed that Grannie interjected, "No, you didn't, you had nannies."

I think Mummy was ashamed of Tom and me. At Grannie's insistence she did hire a photographer to take a picture of Grannie, Stephen, me, and herself—the four generations—but when I showed up in a cheap cotton dress she frowned and I knew I had embarrassed her. Tom also made her uncomfortable, sometimes because he stood up to her, sometimes, perhaps, because she worried that he wasn't really working, just coaching part-time. The separation between my mother and me, and between me and my younger sister and brother, made me increasingly isolated and vulnerable—cut off from a countervailing weight that might have helped me balance my life.

I remember asking my younger sister to dinner and splurging all our food money for the week so that we could give her a good dinner of things I thought she would enjoy. I cooked most of the day, simultaneously cleaning the house and cooking and caring for Stephen. By seven o'clock, when Joan was expected, the silver sparkled, the crystal glowed, the house was clean, the baby was clean, the laundry was washed and put away, even I looked relatively good. The casserole bubbled on the stove, the rice was fluffy, the wine was cold, and the hors d'oeuvres were lined up on a silver tray. By seven-thirty, Tom was needling me with questions about why Joan was always late when she didn't work and didn't have anything she had to do and how selfish she was and inconsiderate. By eight, the casserole had become filmed over like brown paint in a can, the rice was dried out, and we had eaten the hors d'oeuvres. Finally I gritted my teeth and called Joan's apartment, but was still surprised when she answered.

"Hello."

"Hi, it's Barb. I thought you were coming for dinner to-night."

"Oh. I forgot. Sorry—can we do it another time?"

"Sure," I replied, trying not to cry, knowing Tom was going to be mad, knowing dinner was ruined, and we would be eating mung beans for the rest of the week. "Sure, it's no problem," I said, feeling as if I was being pulled apart.

We had so little money, now that the school year was ending, and now that we had a child. My relationships with my siblings were strained because I was in such a different place in my life, married with a child when they were single and poor when they had inherited what seemed to me to be great fortunes. It was impossible then to sense the danger I was in when Tom attempted to support me—as I struggled for my own sense of place and identity within my family—by tearing the rest of my family down as he tried to build me up. He didn't like the way they treated me, which I appreciated, but I see now that he also pulled me even farther away from them.

But for perhaps the first time in my life I loved someone completely and felt completely loved in return. I remembered the very young mothers I had met when I was a welfare caseworker, children themselves for whom a baby offered the first loving and accepting relationship in their lives, so that by nurturing their babies they nurtured themselves. But I did not see myself in their vulnerability, I simply loved being with my son, watching him sleeping, and rocking him in my arms.

At night I nursed Stephen while sitting on a mattress on the floor of the living room, where Tom insisted we sleep. We had brought the mattress downstairs because, though Mummy had given us an air conditioner to deal with the heat and humidity of the Washington summer, Tom said we couldn't pay for the electricity to run it. As I sat there sweating and leaking milk, and as Stephen gradually filled his belly and slept, I felt trapped and helpless. More than anything in my life I loved this baby, but I didn't like the way I was living and I didn't know how to make our lives better.

"Look," I said to Tom, raising my head to look up at him from the mattress. "Mummy gave us that air conditioner because it is so damn hot here. Stephen gets fretful and I don't know what to do to quiet him down. Besides, he's got a heat rash all over his tummy," I added, pulling up Stephen's T-shirt to expose his belly covered in the bubbling rash.

Tom looked at Stephen's stomach but said gruffly, "It costs a lot of money to run an air conditioner. I'm working hard as I can. I don't like going out every day, beating my brains out on a tennis court with dumb blond wives of rich politicians, but that's what I have to do," he barked.

"I don't think it costs that much to run an air conditioner," I said meekly, but I was scared of his anger, not because he ever hurt me physically but because I didn't want to displease him. I didn't know why Tom begrudged us the comfort the air conditioner would have provided, but now I think it was a way he defied my mother, and controlled me, and I wonder how I could have put up with his behavior.

There were other things that worried me. One night Tom was late coming home and when he arrived he seemed shaken. "What's wrong?" I asked.

"Nothing; no, really nothing."

"But there *is* something, I can tell."

"I had an accident."

"In the car? Are you okay?"

"Yes, in the car. I couldn't see. It was very dark. I hit a dog."

"Hit a dog? Oh, my God, what did you do?"

Silence.

"What did you . . . ?" I said, puzzled, knowing what he'd had to do was obvious: stop, try to find the dog, try to read its tag in the headlights, or run to the nearest house and knock on the door, get help, get a flashlight.

"What happened?"

"Well, it was very dark and I couldn't see."

"Did you get out?"

"Well, no, but it was very dark."

"Did you leave the dog?"

"Well . . . yes."

"We must go back—go back and find it."

"I don't remember where I was."

I imagined the dog lying, dying against the cold curb of the street. In my mind I saw its blood running down its tongue. I saw a little girl, coming out of the house in the morning and finding the dog, or a father calling that night, stooping to pick up the dog and cradling it in his arms, walking to his house. How could Tom leave the dog to die alone without its owners, without the people who loved it, particularly when he had told me so many times about all the dogs in his childhood who died, run over near his house, because they were Chesapeake Bay retrievers, frenzied hunting dogs that wanted to roam free and escaped the prison of the house? Tom had left the scene of an accident, he was a hit-and-run driver. He had run away because he couldn't confront what he had done, and that scared me. It was a deep failing I saw in him and that I began to fear. I was almost positive I would not have run away from the dying dog, that I would have made myself talk to its owners and admit what I had done. I wondered why he was so scared and what else he would run away from.

Years afterward, when one night we were driving home in Maine, the door to a small pale green house opened right on the road and a dog ran directly in front of the car, a big black-and-brown dog. It crunched against the front left wheel, shrieked in a thin keening, and then yelped into the distance. An old man ran out yelling, "Oh, my gawd, oh, my gawd, it weren't your fault, it was mine. It's my daughter's dog—a champion, her prize dog, and it just ran from me. She told me not to open the door, not to let him out."

I told Tom to stop the car and he did. I felt as if I were expiating our sins, forcing us to deal with this accident the way I thought Tom should have handled the first one. We jumped out into the cold night, slipping on the freezing ground, stumbling down the center line of the road to find our way, chasing after the terrified dog, knowing it would run from us but not knowing what else to do. Finally, the owner and her husband appeared and told us it was not our fault, to go home, probably the dog would come to them if there was no one else around. The next day we went to see them and the dog, a huge Doberman pinscher, was home, sitting on a large red cushion, and seemed delighted with the rawhide bone we brought, the biggest one we could find.

Tom seemed more vulnerable than I was physically as well. Very early one morning he had found an angry red line running from a blister on his foot up to his groin. We were both scared, knowing that could mean an infection. When he got back from the hospital he said the doctors told him he could have died and that he must be more careful. The threat of a quickly moving blood infection that would disable or kill him always hovered in the back of my mind, and I thought he was like a fine racehorse that required unusual attention, whereas I was more like a sturdy, reliable Percheron.

That summer, when Stephen was three months old, Tom told me that he wanted to go to Greece, where he had once lived with a family while tutoring their young sons. He painted pictures of white sun-washed houses, sparkling teal-blue seas, and welcoming people. He told me about how cheaply we could live, about how much he loved running there because it was so warm he wouldn't have to wear all the layers of sweatclothes in order to purge himself of fluids. Even though I was scared to leave the country with a very young baby, I finally gave in. I knew exercising was critically important to Tom but was also a daily battle with the elements and his body, and one that took a toll. Winter is coming, I thought. It will be better for him in a warmer place.

I was worried that if I didn't agree to go with Tom to Greece, he would always hold it against me, always tell me that I had stopped him from doing something important to him. I worried about how we were going to earn a living, but Tom said we would hardly need any money, it was so cheap to live abroad. Our parents and friends tried to discourage us. As the time grew nearer I felt more and more apprehensive but tried to hide my fears from Tom and myself, my friends and family. I tried to think of the trip as an adventure, reminding myself that people in other countries had babies, too, and would help us. But there was no one I could speak honestly to about how worried I was. I had to be loyal to Tom, and loyalty required not telling anyone else how I really felt. I didn't want to betray my fear for fear of betraying my husband. Tom seemed to be thoroughly enjoying the idea of leaving Washington and taking an extended trip to a place he had loved when he was a bachelor. But now he wasn't a bachelor anymore; he had a wife and child.

At the last minute Tom decided it would be more fun to go to Amsterdam and then Paris. We left in early fall, flying into Schiphel airport, and found a room in a hotel in Amsterdam. We took Stephen everywhere we went, walking him in a little pram we bought, covered by a handsome acrylic blanket in dark red, blue, and green plaid, not realizing we were exposing him to new germs and a changeable, damp, and cold climate.

The Dutch people we met were kind and helpful, but one night in the little room we had found in a small inn, Stephen started crying, cries that soon turned to screaming. All I could do was walk him around and around the room as I looked at the brown-and-white wallpaper with scenes of men and women in clogs, standing next to windmills, holding Stephen, rocking him and shaking him in my increasing desperation. Tom walked him around the room, too, but seemed irritated that I could not calm Stephen and I felt guilty that I had no idea what to do. Finally the middle-aged woman who ran the hotel with her husband came to our room and told us that other guests were complaining. We had to do something and she suggested calling a doctor. This seemed so obvious, once she said it I wondered why it had not occurred to me in the first place. But Stephen had never been sick; he was, after all, only four months old. The doctor came and prescribed baby aspirin; and after swallowing the crushed aspirin, Stephen slept. A few days later Tom decided we would go to Paris, a city he loved, and in which some of his friends and his former employers lived. I thought we would be safer there with friends to turn to, and that caring for Stephen would be easier because I could at least speak some French.

We took the train to Paris, through the fields of tulip bulbs covered by mud and snow, and when we arrived we found a room in a small hotel—with no elevator that required that we carry the baby carriage up four stories. After several days Tom's friends found us an apartment that was temporarily vacant while its tenants were on a trip.

The apartment was elegant and beautiful, like a fading grande dame. It had high vaulted ceilings and moldings with complicated twining flowers and vines tracing their design around the room. But the flowers were dirty and so were the Aubusson carpets; the peach taffeta curtains were stained along the bottom edges with dirt and wine spills. We were told to feed the caged mouse in one of the bedrooms and not to make long-distance phone calls. Nothing seemed to work well. The toaster blew up, the faucets leaked, and when we once made a long-distance collect call to Tom's father, the phone went dead. The apartment was dirty and smelled like the mouse. The smell in the cage was suffocating and I had to grit my teeth and put a bandanna over my nose when I changed the newspaper under the cage or fed the mouse and added water to the grungy plastic dish.

We went to places like the Sainte-Chapelle and art galleries together, and in the evenings we went to bistros and once to the Trocadero. We enjoyed sitting in the restaurants, trying to read *Le Figaro*, drinking cheap red wine, but when I think back on this time, I realize how much of it Stephen and I spent by ourselves. Tom had started running twice a day, perhaps because he wasn't working. The weather was getting colder and he had to wear many layers of thick clothes in order to make his body sweat hard, in order to make him feel clean and to purge water out of his system. If he didn't, he feared he would bloat, but running dressed that way produced lots of laundry, as did a four-month-old baby. One day we needed to go to the American Express office and also do the laundry, so we hauled the large bag of laundry with us, perched on Stephen's stroller as we walked through the streets of Paris.

While Tom was running or doing errands I took Stephen for long walks in his carriage. I enjoyed trying to reactivate my high school French and the French were kinder to me when I was a young mother with a child than they had been when I was there as a shy sixteen-year-old. Perhaps they were just touched by our minor emergencies—"*Nous avons besoin de . . .* " and then I fumbled through the dictionary to find the word for diapers—enough to excuse my stumbling grammar and limited vocabulary. I enjoyed trying to talk with other young mothers about their children as we sat in the parks, watching the French children rolling hoops in the Bois.

I rewarded myself each day by stopping at patisseries for warm, fat brioches and flaking croissants. I knew Tom would never tolerate such indulgences and I treasured the time I had alone with Stephen so that I could eat what I wanted. I was scared sometimes that Tom would find us when I was eating something he wouldn't approve of, but also enjoyed the slight feeling of danger and my subterfuge. I would check out the street, looking up and down the Champs-Élysées to see if Tom was walking to meet us, and then turn the carriage quickly into the patisserie, delighting in looking at the lines of pastries and bread, making my choice, and then hovering at the door to check the sidewalk again before I left. Sometimes I risked standing in line at the kiosks on the street where they sold crepes because I loved the ones with sugar and Grand Marnier so much. I was worried I would gain weight, and Tom would be angry with me, but when finally we were home and I weighed myself, I found I had pushed the carriage so far that I had actually *lost* several pounds.

In the evenings Tom and I sat in cafés with Stephen and drank red wine. Tom seemed more at ease with food here; perhaps because he had enjoyed living in Paris before and loved the city. We sat at Café de la Paix and watched the funeral procession for Charles de Gaulle, one long black limousine after another, like a parade of black ants winding down the street in front of us. One night, while we were eating delicate Vietnamese spring rolls, Stephen swayed in his portable seat and fretted slightly. I put my finger in his mouth to give him something to suck on and he bit me. "Wow, a tooth."

We were so naïve. The money we had gotten for our wedding was almost gone, and we didn't have jobs. Tom had given up writing his book, and the Hemingway image was fading. I enjoyed Tom's friends, the writer and his wife who was an heiress to a large fortune. They entertained us graciously in their huge, elegant apartment, serving *langouste*, a delicate crayfish I hadn't encountered before and wine Tom said cost a ransom even in Paris. But they can afford to write mediocre books, spend their time between Paris and Spetzia, I thought. We can't.

One evening in the apartment I sat on the floor next to the bed and spread a towel down on the dirty carpet on which to change Stephen. When I took off his diaper I saw little red bites in his groin. First one pair, and then another. I sucked in my breath and separated his legs, finding two more bites. Six bites. "Oh, my God. Tom." I called to him in the living room. "Come here, look. Look at this. These are fleabites. I can't stand this," I cried. I could begin to feel the tears coming. "I just can't stand this anymore. This is no good, this is no way to care for a baby. I am going home. I want to go home."

The angry red marks against Stephen's soft, vulnerable skin forced me to realize that we were not taking good care of him. What Tom wanted and what Stephen needed were at odds, and I had to protect my child. The bites broke the spell for me, and when I told Tom how I felt, he agreed. We called the friend who had rented our house in Georgetown and she told us she had just decided she wanted to leave because she was growing afraid of living in the house as a single woman. And so we returned to Washington, back to the little house in Georgetown, as if we had not been away for two months.

The first winter we were in Washington we had marched in protests against the war, much to the dismay of our parents and other relatives. Now, as we returned, the streets of Georgetown were clogged with jeeps and tanks filled with troops. It was an unsettling sight, a bizarre intrusion into our lives. As the military vehicles churned through town, we ran down familiar streets made unfamiliar by tear gas and other young people, some in uniform some out. When I was pregnant with Stephen, Tom had said he didn't want me to march in the protests anymore. Early one morning, as I sat in our upper room looking out the window, I saw a young man with long hair wrestling with the white picket gate that closed our fence. When he saw me, he said, "Oh, I'm sorry." "No, no take it," I answered, knowing he intended to put it on a barricade. I felt rather self-righteous, but delighted in his flashing grin and our exchange of the peace sign. Later we took Stephen on a protest, jiggling in the pack on Tom's back, but when we realized we could not protect him from the blowing tear gas, we knew we were being irresponsible.

We didn't have the money to take Stephen to a doctor, so I took him to the clinic at Georgetown Hospital. Each time we visited, another intern saw him and seemed to identify another problem: "What do you mean you didn't have a PKU test? You were supposed to have that done before he left the hospital. Do you know he could have been allergic to milk and that would have destroyed his brain cells?"

"I never heard of that and no one said he needed the test. I'm sorry."

"I think I feel a hernia," another doctor said during our next visit.

The next time we went to the clinic I told another doctor, "They said last time that he has a hernia."

"Hmm, I don't feel a hernia. Well, let's check next time. No, no hernia now. Kidneys? Hmm, seem a little small and misplaced."

And when I told the next doctor that the other doctor had said there was something funny with Stephen's kidneys, he replied, "Does he pee? Good. Oh, guess they moved back."

A doctor detected a heart murmur one month, and it was still there the next month. "Well, there still is a heart murmur. We should do some tests."

By this time I was worried that we were jeopardizing Stephen's health by not having a regular pediatrician and my mother, who was on the board of the Children's Hospital, arranged to have him tested with a barium X-ray. When the doctors took him away from me, I buried my head in my arms, heartbroken. Tom was disappointed, even angry, because he thought Stephen was never going to play sports and I thought that I had failed them both. As I sat there, a nurse came out of the examination room and told me that Stephen had to pee on camera for the X-ray technician and wasn't doing it for them. They asked me to help calm him down and I went in to find him sobbing, sitting half-naked on a stool in front of a huge X-ray machine. The room was cold and the lights shone brightly on him. I went to him and held him in my arms for a long time, and then I tried to explain what we needed him to do. But he had just learned not to pee except in the toilet. It was confusing for him, and when he finally let loose a stream of urine, the technician cheered, which surprised Stephen so much that he stopped peeing. Finally, by putting Stephen's hand in warm water, and singing about rain, we got him to pee again, and the results of the test were all negative. He was fine, but then I worried that we had put him through the tests when there had been nothing wrong. After that, we were able to find the money to take him to a pediatrician because by then Tom was teaching tennis again and I had a part-time job setting up an after-school program in the elementary school next to our house.

Late that summer Tom's friend Charlie told us that there was a job opening for an English teacher at the school where he taught in Connecticut and suggested Tom apply. Tom told Charlie he wouldn't take the job unless I could teach anthropology part-time, and somehow, when he went to meet the headmaster, another Princetonian, he was able to convince him to hire us both. I was relieved that he had finally found a full-time job, proud that the headmaster had liked him enough to hire me as well, sight unseen.

We hadn't "made it" in Washington. My relationship with Mummy was fragile and tenuous; I hardly ever saw my sister or brother, and even my grandmother seemed only rarely interested in us or Stephen, having become preoccupied with her widowed daughter. We had a few friends, but we had not become a part of any social group, and in fact, we had been ostracized by people like Tom's cousins. We didn't have the money to go to parties or participate in benefits—and besides, I was always tired.

It was easy to move and we felt lucky and excited that we would be working in the same school, finally teaching what we knew something about. It was a chance for Tom to establish himself in a career and for me to teach a subject I loved. I would have time to care for Stephen and we would make new friends. Any problems there were between us, any doubts I had about Tom settling down and working, I could ascribe to misunderstandings between him and his family, and between me and mine. Our problems getting along with our own families held us together and deflected us from looking at our own relationship.

Getting ready to move, we had a yard sale, putting the things we didn't want out on the sidewalk against the white picket fence: Tom's tennis trophies, the fox-fur tippet from Mummy, and the gold-leafed shell bookends and hideous red tray with the large scratch that we had gotten as wedding presents. We packed and cleaned. The last night we were to spend at Tom's father's house so our belongings would get to Greenwich when we did. Tom offered to do the final cleaning and inspection. I did not know him so well then, or I would have known to refuse, but I was exhausted from caring for Stephen, running the after-school program, packing and cleaning, and I was grateful for his offer, so Stephen and I went to his father's house for the day. When Tom returned I asked him if he had brought my favorite hat, which I had left on a banister by mistake, and he said no, he had not seen it. I worried that perhaps he had missed other things as well, but he said everything was taken care of. After we had moved to Greenwich, his father wrote that he was very angry with us for leaving the house in such poor condition. I was ashamed, but there was nothing to do about it. We had moved again. But this time we were moving to two jobs, we had a child, the school had rented us an apartment that sounded wonderful, and we were starting a new life.

6

THE OUTLET IS GOING TO GET ME

August 1971

We drove into the school just off the main street in Green-wich, Connecticut. As we turned into the driveway I saw the low brick buildings, plain but solid, and read the school motto, which was sandblasted into the granite lintel above the main door: WITH ALL THY GETTING, GET UNDERSTANDING. Over the years I came to learn exactly how fitting this motto was for a school that served the sons of families in a community committed to getting.

How perfect it seemed. Neither of us knew anyone in Green-wich besides Tom's friend Charlie, who was now divorced from Bonnie, or much about the community, but we were eager to learn. I had spent the summer in the Adirondacks preparing my courses, designing lesson plans, rehearsing lectures, setting up interactive questions and answers, writing tests, and by the end of the summer I had a complete script for the next year but very little idea of what I was doing. I had, in effect, forgotten that the script would only be known to me and that I was leaving out the most important element—my students. Nevertheless, my notebook gave me some confidence.

The school secretary, an intense, petite woman who had been a nun, had found us an apartment near the school with a bedroom for ourselves, a small bedroom for Stephen, and a very large living room, with two walls painted avocado green and two a rusty orange. We joked about living inside a pumpkin, like Cinderella, before I painted the room white. Later I built a platform for Stephen so he could have as large a room as possible and attached a long string to the overhead light in his room so he could turn it on and off. To decorate the room I made a six-inch-high alphabet out of shiny red contact paper and put it on the wall over his crib. He would ask what the names of the shapes were and I told him "X, Y, Z." One day he found the letter X on a sign and I realized he was learning to read.

At first Tom seemed to thrive on his new teaching duties. His sometimes zany sense of humor, irreverence toward tradition, sincere interest in his students, identification with them against authority, his knowledge of literature, and the creative outlets he found for their energies all endeared him to his students. On Fridays he started giving a trivia test that seemed to amuse them and they vied with gusto for the coveted prize—a Lipton tea bag. He assigned readings in such publications as *The New Republic*, which sometimes shocked the students' assumptions, and he developed close relationships with several that continued in correspondence for years after they had graduated and we had left the school.

But we got the message from our parents, sometimes subtly, sometimes not, that being classroom teachers wasn't really important enough.

"Oh, Tommy," his father said when he called one night, "I just heard that the Madeira School is looking for a headmaster. Why don't you apply?"

And a few months later he added, "You know you might apply for the job as head of Potomac School, that would be a *real* job."

I was more sheltered from this pressure as I had Stephen to care for, and besides, women didn't really have to work. Men had to work to support their families, and all that expensive Princeton education and New School master's degree would be going to waste if Tom was going to be just a teacher. Tom got a lot of pressure from his father, and perhaps also from himself. In a society that doesn't pay teachers well, and measures worth in dollars, the message is strong: if you aren't paid well you aren't doing well, you aren't doing anything important. Teaching is for those who can't do anything else.

There were times when Tom's liberal views conflicted openly with those of the conservative school parents. In the early fall the faculty attended a "banquet" put on by the board of trustees; after his speech the head of the board said he would take some questions. There were a few polite questions about the sports program and then Tom rose from his seat and stood to face the long head table. In a strong voice he boldly asked: How, in a time of social change and turmoil, the school could refuse to consider the implications of its investments. There was stunned silence as the other board members and their wives stared at Tom. I knew many other teachers were concerned about the board's conservatism, and that even the headmaster thought that the board chairman was a blustering drunk; still, Tom's audacious question made me uneasy. Later in the year, at Parents' Night, the head of the board of trustees stormed into his classroom waving *The New Republic,* screaming "Don't let me ever catch you assigning this filthy Communist rag again." Tom replied that he thought the writing was good and that the boys should be exposed to different perspectives, but the red-faced man with the protruding belly that even his impeccable suit couldn't hide wasn't listening and stomped out of the classroom.

Meanwhile pressures were mounting within Tom, but I didn't see them. I was consumed by caring for Stephen, our apartment, and preparing for my anthropology and sociology classes. I was so happy that Tom was busy at school, working in a full-time job; perhaps my hopefulness that we would make this venture work blinded me again to the reality. After school Tom would go running and take a sauna at the Y in Greenwich. He liked the camaraderie of sitting in the sauna with the other men, and he liked telling me how much he was running around the track. I was glad that he was making new friends, or at least had people to talk to after work. He was enjoying running as his new running shoes were softer and didn't chaff his feet, unlike the tough leather ones he had worn in the past, and I didn't notice for a long time that he was running now at least two times a day, and sometimes three.

At the end of the spring semester, the school offered us a much larger apartment in a house they had bought opposite the school and were dividing for two faculty families. Tom's boss, the chairman of the English department, and his wife and son would have the grander half of the house, but our half would include three bedrooms, a good-sized living room, an eat-in kitchen, and most exciting, a dishwasher and a washer and dryer. It seemed a wonderful opportunity to have an affordable and larger apartment right across from the school and reassuring proof that we were appreciated, and after a long summer in the Adirondacks, we moved in.

The summer before we moved we lived in a little cabin owned by Tom's father on the same property as the main house. Tom was taking classes at the Breadloaf School of writing, about an hour away, and I was caring for Stephen in the cabin, whose usual occupants, field mice, were hardly disturbed by our presence. In the mornings and evenings I watched them as they ran along the beams and open studs of the dark and musty 1930s prefab Hodson House, which was pegged together with metal pins, worrying that they would bite Stephen like the rats mothers had told me about in Harlem.

Early in the summer I was often nauseous in the mornings and realized I was pregnant again. Tom was at school most of the week and his sister Melinda came over frequently to ask me to do things with her or go to parties she was giving. When Tom's father berated me for not accepting all these invitations, I was hurt and upset but swallowed my anger. But no one seemed to care that I was tired and felt sick, and I was eager to get back to school.

At the end of the summer we returned to move into our new apartment. On two floors, half a house, it offered much more space and comfort than we had had before. I bought blue-and-green-plaid silk very cheaply from the Thai Silk Company in Bangkok as well yards of aqua-blue thick cotton material for a dollar a yard. When I was a child we had visited the store owned by a friend of Desie's, and I loved the material. I made silk curtains for the large sliding glass doors that opened onto a deck and garden and a new couch cover, and was quite pleased with the results. Stephen had a large bedroom down the hall from us, I had a room, an enlargement of the upstairs hall for a desk and sewing, our bedroom was spacious, and there was another small bedroom for the baby. It seemed perfect.

The headmaster and I had agreed I would teach three instead of two courses that year, and fortunately, the baby was due during a two-week minicourse session in late January. With luck, I wouldn't miss any school at all. Unfortunately, we immediately realized, the poorly insulated wall separating the two apartments did not protect us from the screaming matches between the couple in the adjacent apartment: Tom's immediate boss, Ben, and his soon-to-be ex-wife. Nor did it shield us from the sobbing of their son John, or even from hearing him reciting his homework, walking in his room, or whistling, which he did incessantly.

We complained, but the head of the business office, who had

overseen the construction, was not sympathetic and thought we should be grateful to have an "affordable" place to live. We were grateful—but we were caught between exhaustion from lack of sleep, and embarrassment about having to tell the school the source of the problems—the domestic difficulties of our housemates. Some nights they would yell at each other as they fumbled for keys in front of their door right under our bedroom window. After partying, they were so drunk they would fall out of the car, try to balance themselves, laughing or yelling. They were not kind to each other nor was Ben kind to his son. Once I watched him watching his son, and as soon as John walked past him, Ben stuck out his foot and tripped him. John went stumbling across the room while his father laughed. "That's life, kid. You've got to be pre-pared for the falls."

January 25, 1973, the morning I was to give my students their exams, I woke up early because I was so big with child that it was hard to sleep; I kept bumping into my stomach. As I stretched and stood to get out of bed, suddenly there was a flood of water from between my legs.

"Tom," I called, "hey, guess what? This is it. The water broke. Wow, right on time."

"Oh, good. What good timing. Early in the morning. I think I'll go running; I probably won't have so much of a chance later. Is that okay?"

I wanted to say, "No, it's not okay, it's selfish and I'm scared. I don't know when this baby is going to show up. I know the second birth is usually faster. No, it is not okay, you make me feel as if the baby and I don't matter." But instead I said, "All right," be-cause I knew how important running was to him, because I knew he got agitated if he didn't run, because I didn't want to be a problem, because I was scared to say what I was thinking and feeling. I called Sharon, Stephen's baby-sitter, who was going to take him for the night. When she came to pick him up, she asked me if I was all right and I told her I was. She shook her head when I told her that Tom had gone running, but she swallowed what she wanted to say, just as I had. I told her he was coming right back because I didn't want her to know how scared I was or how I felt he had let me down. Then I sat alone for an hour in the kitchen of our apartment because the floor was linoleum and easy to clean and I thought about what I would do if my daughter arrived home before her father.

I remember feeling my baby being pulled out of my body, feeling my body deflate, and my simultaneous elation at seeing my obstetrician holding the cord that had joined us, and the placenta, thin as a bat's wing, that enfolded her. I lay on the gurney after Katherine was born, filled with love and joy and adrenaline. Why, I thought, do they have to leave me here? We should be having a party. When the orderly wheeled me back to my room, I lay quietly, waiting for the nurse to bring her to me. I knew Mummy was scheduled to have a minor operation sometime that week, but when the phone rang, I was not prepared for what I heard.

I heard Grannie saying, "The doctor found just a little bit of cancer. Mummy has just a little bit of cancer."

Later I found the surgeon had taken a tumor the size of a grapefruit from her womb at the same time Katherine was taken from mine.

When my obstetrician, Dr. Mantarino, stopped by the hospital room to see me, he said, "Good morning, Barbara, how are you feeling? The baby is beautiful. A girl, aren't you lucky? Now you have one of each."

"Yes, yes, I am, and thank you, but my mother, my mother has cancer. The surgeon operated on her today. I need your help. I am her oldest child, she is a widow, and my sister and brother are much younger than I am. I need to know as much as I can about what is going to happen. Will you help me?"

He paused. He was a short, round man with dark hair, deep

brown eyes, glasses, and a cherubic smile, a friendly, kind man who seemed to love bringing life and joy into the world. He had been a help to me throughout my pregnancy—enjoying that I brought Stephen to the examinations and seeing Stephen's delight in listening to the heartbeat of the baby inside me, counseling me to take it easy while I was working, though he knew I could not, helping me interpret the Braxton-Hicks tremors that constantly reminded me I was taking on more than I could handle easily, and preparing me to be less cavalier about this pregnancy than I had been about the first. I enjoyed my conversations with him, and he always answered my questions thoroughly. Once he said to me, "You know you could have been a doctor." And I thought, Yes, you're right, but I never thought I could be much of anything.

When I was in college, Mummy encouraged me to be a secretary and told me to go to the Washington School for Secretaries one summer to learn typing and shorthand. I did learn to type, though the school rules, "Wear a hat, stockings, and gloves to school, brush over the carriage, and keep your feet on the floor at all times," seemed archaic and matronizing. I skirted them by taking the elevator to the floor above the school, pretending I had used the ladies' room, and been at school for a while so I didn't need my hat and gloves, and by playing hooky to go to the National Gallery, which was two blocks away. Desie caught me when he was home sick one day and the school called to ask where I was, but he understood why I hated the school and rather liked that I preferred the gallery instead. Now I realize that Mummy saw being a secretary as a way her "penniless" daughter could always earn a living, and was probably parroting advice from one of her friends—but I was insulted at the time, and fearful at the thought that she might be right.

Now, as Dr. Mantarino looked at me, I saw the worry in his eyes, and he said, "I'm so sorry. Of course I'll help. What kind of cancer does she have?"

"I'm not sure. It's either in her uterus or her ovaries. I know she had a hysterectomy when she was much younger, but maybe . . . I think it was partial."

Dr. Mantarino said, "Well, it's important to know which kind of cancer it is. I'll be frank with you because that's what you have asked me to be. If she has uterine cancer, the chance of recovery is good. If it's ovarian cancer, then it metastases easily and things are not so good."

"All right," I answered, "I'll find out."

And he added, "She may not want to know everything you want to know—so be careful."

When I talked with Mummy after the surgery, she sounded well. But then, she was an actress, and British. And when I asked what kind of cancer she had, she said, "I think it is uterine," and I sighed, not audibly, I hoped, and thought, It's going to be all right. But several days later, when I talked to her again, she said, "Oh, the doctor tells me it is ovarian cancer. But you know, I'm so relieved, I don't have to have radiation therapy."

Shortly after, Dr. Mantarino gave me a paper written by two doctors. Reading the paper was like reading an ancient language with some similarity to my own but different rhythms, and I lost whole sentences and even paragraphs. I read and reread the paper until I understood that Mummy had no chance of surviving ovarian cancer. Radiation was the preferred treatment, but she could not have radiation therapy because she had developed colitis when she was married to my father, perhaps because living with him made her so nervous that she got sick. The cure rate with surgery and chemotherapy was zero percent for women with stage-three ovarian cancer, and Dr. Mantarino thought, from my descriptions, that Mummy was in stage three. There it was, written in black-and-white, a death sentence. I read that section of the report again and again until I could find no way to deny the statistic, could find no circumstances to mitigate this brutal number. Then I called Dr.

Mantarino and asked him how long she could be expected to live, because I thought someone had to know. "There's no way to be sure. The only good thing about ovarian is that it is quick. It's a very aggressive cancer. She has perhaps six to eight months," he replied.

Tom tried to help me to understand what was likely to happen. During most of his own mother's illness he had stayed in Paris because he was tutoring and living there, but he knew from his brothers, sister, and father about the ordeal his mother had suffered. He told me the doctors would probably be deceptive about Mummy's prognosis and might subject her to tests that would benefit future patients, but cause her great pain. I valued Tom's insight and thought his experience with his mother would help me cope with what seemed my own mother's inevitable and imminent death.

Mummy had arranged sometime before my delivery for a baby nurse to stay with us for two weeks to help me cope with having only two weeks between giving birth and teaching again full-time. I was going back to work so quickly because I thought we couldn't afford to live on Tom's salary alone, that I needed my professional life to keep sane, but I see now that I also needed to be "indispensable" and I wonder if I was already worried that Tom's hold on his job was precarious.

I was concerned about having someone else living with us, worried that Tom would be irritable and make comments about her, that she would not like what we ate, and that it would be hard to share our small apartment with a stranger. When the nurse arrived, I was relieved to see that at least she was not dressed like the formidable German nanny who had come to the farm in Maryland to care for Des when he was born, uniformed in starched white from cap to stockings. When this nurse, a slight, mousy woman of about forty-five named Miss Martin, arrived, she seemed innocuous, and it was a relief, with so many things going on, to have someone to help care for Katherine, particularly at night, so that I could sleep.

The first afternoon she asked me, "What time does the family have dinner?"

I hesitated because I had hoped she would go out for dinner, or perhaps eat in the room she shared with Katherine, though I knew that was unlikely. I was sure she was used to caring for babies born to mothers who didn't work and had far grander houses than we did, but I answered, "Well, usually around seven, but we just eat in the kitchen or on the couch in the living room."

"Oh, that would be jolly," she replied, and I appreciated the effort she was making to be accommodating. We ate that night in the living room. Tom and I sat on the couch, and Miss Martin decided to sit on the rug next to the coffee table. I began to notice the ugliness of the cheap paneling, the tacky butterscotch rug, the roughness of the cotton I had bought from Thailand. I saw us through her eyes and thought of all the other places where she had worked.

Tom liked to cook, but he wasn't very good at it and I worried that Miss Martin wouldn't like what we were eating. We usually ate at a small table in the kitchen, but it wasn't large enough for us now with Miss Martin. Tom made his favorite dish, "hot slaw," and some salad. I remember watching Miss Martin as she picked her way over the cabbage with a layer of cheese, and I watched Tom under lowered lids as he swirled ketchup over his meal, and ate with a spoon out of the bowl. I was grateful that she never complained.

As the week went by, Tom seemed to recede into the furniture. He was so quiet I knew he was making an effort to make Miss Martin feel welcome, but as the days wore on, she seemed more intrusive and he seemed more withdrawn. I was pulled between the children, Tom, Miss Martin, preparations to go back to work the next week, and my mother's illness. Everyone seemed to need something from me, and I was exhausted. I would be on the phone with Grannie, letting her talk about how well Mummy was doing in the hospital, how all the nurses loved her and said she was the most beautiful and brave patient they had ever had, how Grannie knew Mummy was getting the best care because her wealthy friends had managed to get the most eminent surgeon at New York Hospital. Stephen would want me to read to him or play a game, but the house was filthy and I hadn't done our laundry in days. I was worried about the new course I was teaching in ten days, and Miss Martin kept telling me how difficult Katherine was: "The most difficult baby I have ever cared for. You are going to have a real problem with this one."

"I don't know what I am going to do," I answered. "I'm really going to miss you."

"I wouldn't ever leave those cats alone with the baby, you know cats smother babies," she added.

When Tom came home from teaching and coaching, he immediately went running. He grumbled about how the house was dirty and I was spending too much time on the phone with Grannie and with the children. Finally I said, "I don't know what to do, but you seem upset. What is it?" And he replied, "I want to get rid of that woman. I wish she would stay in her room and let us eat by ourselves." I knew what he meant, she did seem always to be around. Tom added, "This is all so different, I feel pushed out of my house." With the new baby, my mother's illness, a live-in nurse, and my work for school, I realized I couldn't pay as much attention to Tom, but I had hoped he would understand. And then he said, "And the changes upset my rituals." Rituals? It seemed an odd word. He said it so lovingly, it made his routines seem inviolate, sacrosanct, and I began to feel that they were, at least to him, and that he needed them more than I could understand.

I thought about how having children, a wife, friends, and a job all seemed secondary to him. Most important were the patterns he had created that anchored him but that made no sense to me: running in the morning, taking a cold bath, leaving work as soon as he could to run again and take a sauna at the Y. Anything that pressured him to change his pattern was irritating and inconvenient, an unfair imposition on his time and space.

At first, when Miss Martin told me Katherine was a difficult baby, I was sure she was right. Though I hadn't noticed anything "difficult," I wasn't able to spend as much time with Katherine as I had with Stephen and I thought, "Miss Martin must be sparing me the difficult times; she's the expert." But I began to see her as the source of Tom's irritation and think she was projecting her loneliness onto us, and to wonder if she did that to all the families she worked for. I began to resent her intrusion into our lives and her saying Katherine was difficult when I had begun to realize she wasn't. I saw it as a ploy, though perhaps not one of which Miss Martin was aware, to extend her time with us, and to make her feel indispensable. Grateful that I had already had the experience of caring for a baby, I began to see Miss Martin as an insidious wedge between new parents and their child—particularly dangerous if it were their first child. Tom and I decided to ask her to leave after a week. I was worried that I would not be strong enough to do everything I had to do, but it seemed easier than dealing with Tom and Miss Martin.

I spent the seven months between Mummy's diagnosis and her death feeling like Cassandra. I knew how Mummy's illness would end, but I did not know how to tell Joan, Des, Frankie, and Grannie. Grannie's only other child, her son, was dying in a nursing home in England of the wounds he suffered on the beach of Dunkirk, and the tuberculosis he contracted during his recovery. His life had always seemed so sad to me, because his beautiful young strawberry-blond wife became manic-depressive and bloated to three times the size she was when they married, and became alcoholic, "a weight around his neck," Grannie always said. And I always thought how very odd it was that he married someone with the same name as his mother, particularly as the name they shared was Muriel. Watching Grannie struggle against the inevitability of the premature deaths of her only children was terrible, in part because she was relentlessly brave and hopeful, and in part because it terrified me to think about the horrifying prospect of outliving my own children. I did not know how to tell anyone in my family what I knew, that Mummy was going to die soon, within the next six or eight months, because I knew they did not want to know. I tried hinting to them, but it made them angry. Besides, Mummy looked fine: she didn't lose her hair, she didn't look different, and she didn't talk about the other side effects from chemotherapy. Everyone was protecting everyone else from the truth.

While Mummy was recovering from the surgery, we had a meeting with her doctor at the hospital in New York. Des was twenty-one, Joan twenty-three, and they had lost their father seven years before. Frankie was there, and Grannie. Tom and I sat next to each other in the antiseptic gray room and listened while the doctor talked. He told us that Mummy would have the best treatment and that a cure was possible. He said, "She's a wonderful, brave woman. I hadn't wanted to care for her because the only reason she got in here was all the calls from her fancy friends with connections." I knew he was right, that this prestigious hospital was one of the best in the world for the treatment of ovarian cancer. The surgeon added that he had been struck by her courage and beauty, by her grace with other people, and by her ability to reach out to them and make them feel as if they mattered.

I thought about the many times I had heard people say this, each time wondering why it was so hard for her to reach out to her own children. Months later, as she was dying, she arranged for one of the nurses to get medicine for her son, because the child was severely stunted in his physical development, a growth hormone that had been impossible for the family to obtain. But she once told me she wished she had never had children and that she thought she was a bad mother. I hadn't known what to say to her at the time, but I remember thinking how sad that was for her and for us and that she must think we were turning out badly.

When the surgeon reached the end of his presentation, I was baffled. He had not mentioned any of the difficulties of dealing with ovarian cancer that I had read about. He had not talked about how quickly it metastasizes. He had said Mummy was in stage three, but he had not defined the term or told us that this meant the cancer was probably already reaching far into her body. He had not told us the truth.

I hesitated, because Joan, Des, Frankie, and my grandmother were there. I wished I could meet with the doctor alone; I wished I could be frank, but I didn't think I would get another chance to talk with him, so finally I asked quietly, pitching my voice low in the vain hope that Grannie wouldn't hear my question and the doctor would not be affronted, if he was familiar with the paper Dr. Mantarino had loaned me. I read the long title, but now I cannot remember it. He beamed. "Oh, yes," he answered, "I helped write it."

So cautiously I asked, "Do the statistics I read in that paper apply to my mother?"

He looked at me and the blood drained from his face. He looked at me for a very long time, his blue eyes hardening, and then he said, "I have to believe that each of my patients will beat the odds. The statistics may say less than one percent survival, but I have to believe that those will be my patients. I have to think they will all survive or I could not go on in this line of work."

There was an ugly silence in the room. I could feel the man's hostility toward me. Then Tom said, "But you wrote the paper. You said women in stage three don't have much chance." Tom pushed, adding that he had had experience with his own mother's death and that he wondered if the experimental and aggressive treatment the doctors planned was going to do any good or if it wouldn't just prolong my mother's agony. I knew he had resented all the tests his mother suffered through, though he had been in Paris for much of the time she was ill. We had talked many times about the arrogance of doctors, about their insistence on experimental treatments that would add to their knowledge at the expense of their current patients, and I knew he was still angry.

So there it was, out in the open, but everyone was staring down at the floor. Frankie, Joan, and Des were sitting silently, Grannie looked at me like a wounded old dog and said, "But the doctor knows best. He knows what he is doing, and he is going to cure her." And the doctor, relieved to be offered an escape hatch, slipped through it by saying, "That's it. We have to do the best we can and be positive about this."

Everyone seemed to resent Tom's intrusion, and I wondered if they thought he shouldn't be there, as he wasn't one of Mummy's children. Many weeks later, when I was at the hospital alone, the doctor asked me, "Who was that obnoxious young man with you, who was so strange?" I realized he meant Tom and I answered, "My husband."

"Oh, I'm so sorry. I'm so sorry for you," he replied, but I didn't have the courage to ask him what he really meant. I never understood why Tom's question or manner had made the doctor react so strongly, and I wondered what he had seen that I had not.

But as it turned out, Tom was right, the treatments were terrible. Grannie told me one time she stayed with Mummy while the doctor cut into her flesh without anesthetic because the test required that she be fully awake. She bore the pain without flinching, but Grannie told me that one of the nurses fainted during the procedure. I wish I had been able to spare my mother that pain, when there was no chance of a cure. And yet, to give up was precisely that, and I did not think she or her other children or Grannie could bear it. Even when her body began to break down and in the mornings she was puzzled by spontaneous bruising she found in deep purple blotches on her legs, she could not ask what was going to happen.

And I would answer, "Yes," because I didn't know what else to say.

That spring Tom told me he wanted to go to the Breadloaf School of writing again that next summer to study and write as he had the summer before. We were standing in the kitchen of the apartment in Greenwich when he said, "I've decided to study for a degree at Breadloaf. It will be for the whole summer so we need to find a cabin to rent up there."

"But Mummy is really sick," I said anxiously. "How can we go up to Vermont?"

"I've got to go for school," he insisted. "It's really important to my work at school."

"But I don't want to go," I pleaded. "I don't know anyone there. I don't know what I'm going to have to do to help take care of Mummy. I want time to be with her and Grannie, and Joan and Des." But he was implacable. Finally I gave up arguing with him, fearing if I didn't agree he would always say I held him back when he wanted to work on his writing; still, I hoped I could balance his needs with those of the rest of my family.

Memorial Day weekend we went to the Adirondacks to look for a house to rent, near Breadloaf, and when we returned I went to school to pick up some papers from my mailbox. When I opened the kitchen door of our apartment, Tom said, a little laugh catching in his throat, "This is sort of odd, given the situation. There was a message on the machine from your aunt Dolly. Your father just died of a heart attack. I wouldn't have told you so quickly, but I know you didn't really care about him."

I laughed, too. What else was there to do? It seemed so odd. But it was not that I didn't care about my father and losing him and the chance to know him, just that I had always been expected to feel he was unimportant. To lose him then, like a footnote to the rest of my life, at the time when every bit of my energy was going to my mother, sister and brother, my grandmother, Tom, the children, and my students, when there was nothing left over and I was running on empty, seemed so sad. There wasn't even time to mourn. And so we went to his funeral in a tiny white chapel at the graveyard. There was no one there but his mother, my grandmother, my aunt and her husband, and Millie, my father's companion. No one else to mourn. I wore a white dress I bought at our school thrift shop and thought how pathetic this was, and about the contrast between his funeral and Desie's, at which the Washington Cathedral was full to capacity, and a line of limousines disgorged eminent people.

It would not be for many years that I was able to mourn my father's death and the end of a chance for us to know each other, and not for many years after that that I began to understand the damage inadvertently done to a child who never had a father, and almost never had a man to love. I didn't tell my mother, or Grannie, or anyone else that my father had died. There didn't seem to be any reason to tell Mummy when she was so sick, Grannie had never liked him, and my sisters and brother had never met him, but I thought sometimes about the fact that I was about to be an orphan now, too.

While Mummy was ill, Joan and Grannie were living in Washington, and Des was a student at Harvard. When Mummy was in the hospital in New York, I was the nearest person in the family to her. Each week I went to the hospital; I could not afford fancy flowers and so I bought her a large paper bee to hang above the vases of flowers sent by her many friends and admirers—so many the nurses had to take them out of her room at night. I made her a balsam pillow, gathering the needles from the Adirondacks over Memorial Day, sewing a silk liner, and then crocheting a cover for it in the softest wool I could find, in the blues of the sky and ocean. When I brought it to her she looked at me and thanked me, saying she would put it under her arm when the nurses drew blood, and I watched the veins on her thin hand as they pulsated grayish green against her white porcelain skin. I wondered how long the nurses would be able to find a place to put the needle, and one of them told me soon they would use her thighs.

When I went to the hospital I left Greenwich on the morning train, and from Grand Central I took the bus, walking the last few blocks, and then went to her room. Most often she was asleep, but one of us—Grannie, Joan, or I—was always there. Des had to be in classes, but he came when he could. "How terrifying this must be for them," I thought. I was not sure how to be with a dying woman, but I had at least nursed children. "What do I do?" Joan asked.

I pretended that I knew how to comfort Mummy so Joan would think she, too, would know what to do, and I said, "Well, I think we should talk about things we loved doing in the past so she knows how much they matter to us. And I think we should always try to sit below her so she doesn't feel dominated. And she will just want to sleep a lot and have us here when she wakes up."

When it was my turn to be there, I read my books for school and waited for her to wake up. Sometimes she was awake for only ten or fifteen minutes during the hours I was there and once she said, "Oh, you're here. I know it's just for a few minutes, so it isn't out of your way." At first it seemed she thought my effort to see her was inconsequential and I felt hurt. But then I realized she didn't want to be a burden to me, and I didn't want her to know that it took me eight hours to make the round-trip and that I got home to a dirty household, with crying children and an irritated husband.

Increasingly Tom seemed to feel her illness intruded on our lives. He did less and less to help in the house, leaving dishes in the sink, dropping clothes, never emptying the garbage, or doing other household jobs. He said he had too much to do with his work at school, that the children were upset that I had to be away, that my work at school would suffer. I was exhausted. There were too many nights when I slept only a few hours—hours sometimes punctuated by our neighbors' fighting—because I had to correct papers, clean the house, calm the children, talk with my family. I was vulnerable to Tom's criticisms; I worried that he was right. I felt pulled again, taut with the pressure, but there was nothing I could think of to do except to keep doing what I was doing. However, toward the end of that spring, I did talk to the business manager of the school again, begging him to help us by rebuilding the wall between the two apartments so we would not be awakened by our neighbors' altercations. He was sympathetic, and perhaps because he was the first person I had confided in, even in a very limited way, I started crying. I realized then how tightly I was wound, and wondered how I was going to deal with the next several months.

Bob, the minister who had married us, now lived in New York and came often to visit Mummy. I asked him one day why she didn't ask more about her illness. I told him I didn't think she had any idea that she was dying or that there were no weapons to fight ovarian cancer. She had said to me several times, "Well, they just have to start doing something to cure me," but I knew there was nothing to do. Toward the end, her favorite nurse told me that they could no longer find a vein from which to draw blood, even in her thighs.

Bob said, "She doesn't want to know the answer, so she won't ask the question." But one day, as I left her room, she turned to me and winked and in that wink I learned that she knew what was happening, but that she was playing out the final scene with as much elegance, dignity, and courage as possible.

But then she lay dying, and there were many times before that when it seemed she might endure—that she would get out of the hospital, be in remission, as beautiful and funny as ever. She had moved to the Watergate Hotel just before she learned she was sick, and that strange place made all our lives much easier because it was convenient for her. She traveled between the Watergate and the hospital in New York, between staying with friends and taking short vacations with the men in her life. She brought one of them to visit us in Greenwich one time, when Katherine was only a few months old. The friend took some photographs, the only ones ever taken of them together, but he put the roll of film in his glove compartment and the film dissolved in the heat while the car was parked.

Tom still insisted we go to the Breadloaf School in Vermont so he could study for the summer. It made no sense to me. I wondered how I would go to see Mummy in the hospital in New York City, how I would help my grandmother who lived in Washington, D.C., my sister and brother, and also take care of my children. But Tom said he needed to write and he needed to do it at Breadloaf in Vermont. Just as I had felt I had to go to Paris, I felt I had to go to Breadloaf. I didn't want to be in Tom's way, I didn't want him to resent me, or the children, or my family for holding him back from doing something that was important to him.

We rented a little log cabin near the school and hired Anna, a large placid fifteen-year-old, the daughter of another teacher at our school, to help us. The house was big enough to require some tending—a room for Anna, a room for us, a room for the children, a living room and dining room, and a kitchen. I hardly remember it; we were there such a short time. I was not taking courses, and had only the children to care for—and Anna. Anna was a gentle sweet person, but not a friend, and there were few places we could get to easily without the car, which Tom drove to school. I had no reason to be there and many reasons not to be.

Very soon things seemed to go wrong. Tom was worried about his work at school and seemed to be retreating from us. He was gone a lot, and when he came home he was miserable. "I'm not sure I can do this. Everyone is much younger than I am. They are sort of shallow. I don't really like any of them. There is so much to do and I don't have time," he said quickly, the words a blur. "There just isn't time."

"What do you mean?" I answered, wondering why he had no time when he had all day for himself. "This is what you said you wanted to do." I felt torn between thinking, We're only here because you insisted and wanting him to enjoy his work and succeed in the writing that I knew meant so much to him. I could feel anger well up inside me, but I was also starting to get scared. He looked thin and drawn, and the skin around his eyes was strangely pulled back.

Tom began to be even more abrupt with us and with Anna, gruff, tense, and demanding. As I heard his car in the driveway, I could feel my shoulders tighten and my stomach begin to ache. Anna asked me why he got upset, why he was always running, and why he wore so many sweatclothes. She asked me why he rarely sat with us to eat and why he didn't seem to eat anything except bowls of cheese and mung beans covered with ketchup. "Oh," I said, trying to smile, "I think he's just worried about being in school with lots of people who are younger and don't have families." She looked at me, mystified, so I added, "I know he exercises a lot but he has this circulatory problem he inherited from his mother. She died of it, so he's got to be really careful. One time last year he didn't exercise and he bloated up like a watermelon." Listening to my own words, I almost believed myself. Anna's father was a huge, burly man with a ready, confident smile, a teacher all the students loved and trusted. I thought she must think us a strange family, and as Tom's behavior became increasingly odd, I worried that I was exposing her to something she couldn't understand.

Tom said he had been exercising even harder than usual because it was the only thing that made him feel better, helped him feel anchored. I worried that he was pushing himself too hard, playing tennis relentlessly against a backboard, running for hours in layers of clothes to purge the water from his body. "I've got to run it out or I bloat," he said, and I remembered the awful red puffiness that swelled around his eyes the one day he was too tired to run, and that he had told me he gained fifteen pounds of water. I worried he wouldn't have time to write for the classes if he was exercising so much, so I tried to be sure he had no other responsibilities at home. But what worried me most was that he didn't seem to enjoy the work, didn't seem to like being at Breadloaf, didn't even seem to like the people in his classes.

By the second week Tom was skipping some of the classes and had gotten behind in his academic work. He seemed incredibly tense, taut, like a rope holding a mountaineer from falling off a cliff. He was curt and abrasive to us and I watched helplessly, not knowing what to do, as he spent less and less time with us. I found later that he had withdrawn from his work at school as he was withdrawing from us, feeling safe only in his daily rituals that revolved around exercise.

Our bedroom had two single beds with old-fashioned white metal frames. Usually Tom got up before I did, but one morning when I opened my eyes, I saw him curled up in the bed, hugging his knees, and he would not unwind. He held his body in a fetal position and rocked back and forth saying, "The outlet is going to get me, the outlet is going to get me."

I looked over at the outlet on the floor, not understanding what he meant. "What do you mean, the outlet is going to get you?"

"The outlet is going to get me. It is going to shock me. The outlet is going to get me."

"But you have to get up and go to class."

"I can't, I can't get up. The outlet is going to get me. I don't understand it, but I know it."

I stumbled out of bed and stood next to him. He was lying

under the thin white coverlet, and he looked like a skinny child, but his face was haggard, like that of an old man, his eyes tightly closed. Oh, my God, what is happening? I thought. I don't understand what is happening.

When I am in an emergency, I get peculiarly calm, as if the hurricane whirling around me has driven me into myself and I am the eye of the storm, still and focused. I called Tom's father, who was staying in his house in the Adirondacks. "Mr. Russell," I said, "I'm really sorry to bother you, but Tom has gotten sick and we need your help."

"What's wrong?" he asked.

"I don't know. I don't know, but he won't get out of bed," I answered. "He's just lying there and he won't come out. I think going back to school has been hard for him, but I don't know what's wrong."

"All right," he replied quickly. "We'll be there as soon as we can. I understand," but I didn't see how he could understand when I didn't. Next I called the medical center at the college. The school nurse told me to take Tom to the clinic and that the doctor would see him there. When I told Tom what I had done, he seemed grateful and passive.

"I'm better now," he said. "I'll just stay here in bed until Dad gets here." I shut the door of the room and looked back at him, feeling more like a mother than a wife, perhaps even more like a nurse taking care of her patient.

When Tom's father and his wife arrived, he went into the bedroom to talk to Tom, and when he came out he said we would all take Tom to the clinic. We drove to the town, found the clinic, a formidable gray granite building attached to the hospital. The doctor was dressed informally in a plaid shirt and I was comforted by the fact that he looked so ordinary. He took Tom into his office and I waited outside with my father-in-law and his wife. There was nothing and everything to talk about. I felt profoundly embarrassed, as if I was somehow to blame, though I didn't know how I could be. Tom had told me my mother's illness was a real problem for him, that I wasn't getting everything done to care for the children and the house, and I thought I had not done a good enough job. When the doctor came out of the office, he looked at us and said gently that Tom was very sick and needed to be hospitalized. He told us that Tom was severely depleted physically and emotionally and needed to stay at the clinic for his own protection until we could arrange to get him home and into a hospital.

Where is home? I wondered. Greenwich? Washington? I felt as if I were on a movie set, playing a role for which I had no script. If we went to Greenwich, then everyone at work would know what had happened. It didn't make any sense to stay at Breadloaf, where I knew no one, if Tom wasn't going back to class.

"How long will it be before he gets better?" I asked. "Do you think he will be going back to the program at Breadloaf?"

The doctor looked at me and I could see the stupidity of my own naïveté and hopefulness mirrored in his eyes.

"No, he needs a lot of rest. He won't be going back to the school this summer."

"What's wrong with him?" I asked.

"It's really too early to say. He is exhausted and it's going to take a long time and lots of rest to help him feel better." It wasn't a satisfying answer, but perhaps the doctor knew it was all I could hear just then.

I thought about being in Washington. The doctor told us there was a good hospital in Washington that he thought would take Tom. Tom's father and his wife said the children and I could live at their house in Georgetown, and I thought, Well, that makes sense. I will be near Mummy. I could stay at their house or go to my mother's apartment at the Watergate when she was not there, as I thought she would think it was too small for all of us together—me, the children, and herself.

When we left Tom at the clinic, we all felt relieved. He had become so withdrawn I knew I couldn't care for him and the children as well. I told Anna he had gotten very sick from exercising too much and that she should call her father. As I listened to her talking, I could imagine the man on the other end of the line. I wished I had a big, gentle, calm father to talk to so I could sob quietly and he would comfort me. When he drove over the next day to pick her up, he held me, too, for a minute, and said, "I'm so sorry, Barbara, so sorry," and I wished he would stay with us.

I closed the cabin, arranged for partial payment of the summer rent. Then Tom's father drove over again from his summer house with Tom's youngest brother, Michael. We went to pick Tom up at the hospital and drove to catch the plane home to Washington. I was scared to have Tom with the kids and me on the plane. Scared that Tom was dangerous to himself or to us, but the doctor had said we would be all right and I tried to believe him. Tom seemed dazed, very quiet and passive, and I wondered how much of that was from the drugs he was taking. Michael went with us to help, caring for the children while I checked Tom into the hospital, but he returned to the Adirondacks shortly afterward.

Now I think it was odd that Tom's father didn't go with us to Washington, that he left me to cope alone with the two very young children, my mother's illness, and Tom's hospitalization. But Tom had told me years before that his father, at about the same age as Tom was at this time, had had a nervous breakdown. Tom seemed ashamed of his father for not being able to cope, and we rarely talked about it. When Tom had wanted to leave the marine corps, his father's doctor told him it would kill his father if he went AWOL, and because both his grandfather and great-grandfather had been admirals, someone arranged an honorable discharge, but one that pained Tom deeply. I didn't dare to push Tom's father now, and so I gratefully accepted the help he was able to give. When his father had been hospitalized, his wife had taken over running his business. Later Tom would tell me that his father never coped with anything, he just turned away, and I began to think we were following the same pattern.

Several days after Tom checked into the hospital, his new doctor asked me to come to talk with him. I remember sitting with the psychiatrist in the hospital in a small windowless white room with a white table between us. We sat facing each other. He seemed younger than I was, though perhaps he was my age. There was no need for small talk. "Your husband is very ill," he said. "He has become completely exhausted and it's going to take a while for him to recover."

"But he *will* recover," I said, with more assurance than I felt. Sitting in this horrible little room, an antiseptic box, was like being inside a Band-Aid can. "What am I doing here?" I asked myself. "What has brought me to this point in my life?"

"Well, yes, he will get better. But it will be slow and he'll need a great deal of support and care."

I looked at the doctor's handsome face, a neat beard outlining a strong jaw, deep brown eyes flecked with hazel and light and struggled to accept what he was saying, to understand what it meant for our lives. "How long will he be here?" I asked.

"Probably about three weeks," the doctor said.

"I don't understand about the outlet," I forced myself to say. "He said the electric outlet was going to get him."

"He had worn himself out completely, driven himself so hard that his electrolytes were depleted," the doctor replied.

He didn't say "nervous breakdown," and I didn't ask. I just sat there staring at him, trying to smile and be natural, but I didn't know what natural was in such an alien place.

I could distance it all by playing the role of brave, young wife, but there was a seed inside me of resentment. "I do not need to be here," I said to myself. I could hear the psychiatrist talking: "He will tell you he doesn't need to be here, that he is fine. As he starts to get better he'll say he wants to go home, but he won't really. You'll have to be patient."

I was thinking while he was talking, I *have been* patient, and Tom's timing is just a bit inconvenient, and it all started to seem ridiculously ironic to me.

"Why are you laughing?" the doctor asked suddenly, and then it all blurted out of me and I realized that I had been laughing because there seemed nothing else to do.

"I'm laughing because six months ago I had a baby, and I have a three-year-old son. I have a full-time job. We live next to my husband's boss and his wife, who are drunks and getting divorced. The apartment walls are like paper—we can hear them fighting, hear their son sneeze. My father died a few weeks ago and my mother is dying now. I am laughing because I am her oldest child, because my grandmother is a widow and her son is in a hospital in England, dying from wounds he suffered thirty years ago at Dunkirk, because my half sister and brother lost their father when they were fourteen and sixteen and now they are losing their mother. So it seems funny to me that my husband is the one to break down." But then I looked at him and realized he was watching me intently, so I stopped talking, because I was afraid he would think I couldn't handle it all and I knew I had to.

When Tom shuffled down the hall to see me, his eyes were wild, the pupils strangely dilated yet flat, the whites of his eyes a complete circle around the irises. He looked rumpled and he moved slowly and with hesitation. I looked at him and wondered, Who is this man? Is this is my husband? He seemed dazed but almost at home.

"I'm allowed to go to the dayroom," he said, with a pride that saddened me. "We can sit there for a while." We walked slowly down the long gray corridor to a room with open French doors, two televisions, a couple of sofas, and lots of straight-backed chairs.

Tom chose a chair that faced the television and I pulled a chair next to him.

"Everyone in this place is nuts," he said. "I really don't need to be here. They tell me I just got too tired."

"Um," I replied, not knowing what else to say.

"See that guy over there? He's a paranoid schizophrenic. Just stares at the floor and dribbles all day. Hasn't said a word the whole time I've been here. And that man over there, he is really nuts. He just babbles and screams. I really need to get out of here."

"Yes, of course, I understand," I said, thinking Tom wasn't nearly *that* sick. How could it be good for him to be in a place with people like *that*?

I saw a scene in my mind from a movie. The hero is trapped in Bedlam by mistake, and the heroine must get him out. I wanted this all to be a bad mistake. I started to say to Tom that I would get him out and then I remembered what the doctor had said. I wanted to believe Tom, I wanted so much to believe him, but when I looked at him sitting in the dayroom watching the television, I saw the same wild, dazed, unnerving look that I saw in the eyes of the other men. And I realized Tom seemed more comfortable with them than he was when he talked with me.

I thought how odd it was that he shuffled mechanically, like a doll, and that his facial expressions seemed either curiously wooden or theatrical. There was no middle ground: either he was wildly animated, his face contorted with expression, or quiet and passive. Sometimes he talked about how much fun it was to play basketball, that he could really move the ball around the court because he was in great shape. He said the doctors were telling him he just had a potassium deficiency—that he didn't have enough electrolytes, that he hadn't had a nervous breakdown. Cure by Gatorade! I thought. Wouldn't that be wonderful? But he rarely asked about the children or my mother, just talked about basketball and the meals at the hospital, and whenever I went to see him, I left feeling empty and humiliated, scared that he would not get better, and that I would, from now on, have to be the "head" of this family.

Tom was hospitalized for about three weeks, as the doctor had predicted. I told Stephen that his daddy had gotten sick and would be coming home soon. We stayed at Tom's father's big house, but it was so large that I couldn't hear the children easily at night because they were in separate rooms with separate air conditioners, and besides, it was Tom's family's house, not mine. So when Mummy had to go back to the hospital in New York, I moved into her apartment at the Watergate. She and the rest of my family had been kind, which to me meant not asking much about what had happened, not making me feel guilty or ashamed, leaving me alone.

When my mother moved into the Watergate, she had crammed her life into this elegant little space, with all the best furniture, best silver, best porcelain and paintings from her larger houses. The rooms seemed crowded and somehow a bit frantic. I was uncomfortable there, too, though it was fun to walk with the children along the promenade by the expensive boutiques and pretend I could afford to do anything more than look. Looking at the beautiful people doing beautiful things in this beautiful place, I thought about how I had given it up because I wanted to, but that there really were some advantages to such a life. I took the children to splash in the pool, lying beside them on a towel, watching the men watching me, wondering what it would be like to have a different life.

One night before I went to bed I checked on Stephen and Katherine. Katherine was sleeping peacefully, just like a baby, but Stephen was fitful and in the dim light he looked strangely puffy. As I flicked on the light, a wave of shock went through me—he looked like a miniature Lyndon Johnson, his ears sticking straight out like an elephant's, his eyes squinting, and his lips purple red and swollen. Frantic, I called friends, my sister-in-law, Mummy's friends, trying to find the name of a doctor, but no one was home.

I had to act quickly, so I wrapped Stephen in the yellow silk quilt from Mummy's bed and rushed to the front desk, leaving Katherine sleeping in the crib. I ran down the deeply carpeted hall to the front lobby, holding Stephen tightly. The night clerk was leaning against a tall stool behind the dark wood desk, reading a magazine. "Please help me. My son is very sick. I have to go to the hospital. I've left my baby in the apartment. Please check on her. I need a cab. Please."

"Yes, of course, miss, right away," he answered, turning to call the cab.

We drove fast through Washington, and when we got to the hospital, I ran from the cab to the emergency-room door. I felt a hundred eyes on me all waiting their turn in the harsh yellow light, but when the doctor saw Stephen, she grabbed him, pushed everyone out of the way, and charged into a shining white examination room. I only remember that she gave him a shot of antihistamine and said that his system had begun shutting down.

We waited in the corridor. I was rocking and rocking, rocking him and rocking myself, swaying back and forth, back and forth, trying so hard to calm us both, worrying about Kathcrinc, waiting and waiting for the medicine to take effect. Finally the doctor called us back in. Stephen looked like himself now, and though he was very quiet, I could see he would be all right. A second doctor, a young man with glasses and thin blond hair, entered the room and the two doctors stood together looking at Stephen stretched out over the table. "See, here," the older doctor said, "feel with your hand, his liver is distended and it's not in the right position. Now, to the left, what do you feel? A little off, isn't it? Now, what about his groin? Do you feel a hernia?"

I could feel myself getting dizzy.

"Is there anything wrong?" I asked.

"Oh, no," she responded, "I'm just showing Dr. Jones; he's new."

"May we go now?" I asked.

"Are you all right?" she replied, looking at me for the first time.

"Yes," I answered, "but I've left my baby alone in an apartment, my mother is dying, my father just died, and my husband is in a mental hospital."

She looked at me again, her eyes wide. "Do you want Valium?"

"No," I replied, "I just want to go home."

I spent that summer between my father-in-law's house and my mother's apartment in Washington, the hospital in New York and the hospital in Washington. After Tom was released from the hospital, we went to live in his father's house in Georgetown. Living with him felt one-dimensional, unconnected. I wanted so much for him to be well, well enough to go back to work, that I never questioned what had happened to him. When he told me the doctors said his breakdown was just from depletion of electrolytes, that he hadn't had a nervous breakdown, I wanted to believe him, and so I did. There were times when I wondered if it was safe to be there with him. There were moments when I worried that Tom was going to hurt himself, or us; though I had nothing concrete to base that fear on. I worried about what we were going to do, and whether or not Tom could go back to teach. I began to feel as if his illness was like an eggshell, thin and fragile, yet still a barrier I dared not penetrate.

In retrospect, I think that if I had been really brave, I would have left Tom then.

At this time Mummy was still traveling between the hospital in New York and her apartment for treatment, and then she went to Newport, where she had rented two houses from a friend so she could be nearer the hospital and get out of the heat of Washington. She asked me to accompany her, telling me I needed a break and that she had rented one of the houses, which was a converted windmill, so the children and I could stay there while she was in the larger house with Grannie and other friends. Tom didn't want us to go, but I told him my mother needed me and that I was going. All during that summer I felt that wherever I was, I should have been in another place.

One night when I sat near Mummy in the beautiful living room in Newport, one that *Architectural Digest* would have ached to photograph, I saw a yellow cast to her face. At first I thought it was from the yellow of the walls reflecting onto her skin, or the yellow in the flowered chintz on the couch, but finally I admitted that the color of her skin had changed in the few days we had been together. That night I called our friend Jim, the doctor, and he told me the color meant the cancer had reached her liver. Jim said I must call her doctor, and when I did, he told me that she had to return to the hospital in New York City. She was lying on the couch and I went and sat next to her and took her hand. It, too, was yellowish, the skin mottled and yellow as a chicken wing.

"Mummy," I said, looking at her and trying to keep my voice even and stop the trembling I felt. "I noticed yesterday that your face was pale, and a little yellow, like jaundice. I called Jim, and he said I should call your doctor." I saw her teeth clench as she tried not to show her fear. "The doctor said you probably should go and be checked." Then she tightened her hand in mine and was silent for a minute. When she could talk she looked at me and said, "I think I took that rather well."

Together we decided that she would go by private plane with Grannie to the hospital, and that I would take the children home the next day and then join her in New York.

I remember looking at the water as the gray navy ships sailed through the fog, standing with Katherine in a carriage and Stephen beside me, watching the fog and blowing soap bubbles into the air. The air was so wet that the bubbles didn't burst, just remained floating in the air, hundreds and hundreds then thousands, floating over the water and around us, blowing slowly, suspended, the light catching them like snowflakes, softly and gently. I can still see

Stephen running up and down on the sage-green grass, catching the bubbles in his hands, smiling as they gathered on his sleeves, jumping and laughing in a moment without time. It is a magic memory that shields me from the pain of the rest of the summer.

I knew I was not included in Mummy's will. For many years she had told me that because I was not Desie's child, I was not entitled to Williamson money and that my father would "take care of me," a fantasy she wove to make her feel better, I thought. I hadn't told her Collin had died during the Memorial Day weekend of a heart attack, sprawling on the floor of his house in Connecticut to be found by his friend Millie. But one day, in midsummer, when I went to visit her in the hospital, she told me that Aunt Eleanor, Desie's sister, had told her.

"Tee," she said, "why didn't you tell me?"

"Well," I replied, "I guess there was just so much else going on, and I didn't see the point. I didn't want to bother you with it." And I dismissed my father and the difficulty of talking about him with her by adding, "It's okay, I hadn't seen him in years."

She looked at me and then at the balsam pillow I had made for her and said, "Did he leave you anything?"

"No," I answered, "but he really didn't have anything to leave. He left the house and furniture to Millie. Aunt Dolly told me he ran through fifty thousand dollars his mother gave him, and he was in debt. She told me they found bills stuffed in the sofa and under chairs and that the whole place was a mess. He was drinking a lot. But don't worry about it. It's over."

Several weeks later, after our stay in Newport together, and when she was in the hospital in Manhattan for what I knew would be the last time, she said she wanted to have a serious talk. I sat next to her bed, looking up at her, and she seemed to be trying very hard to focus and stay awake.

"Tee," she said, "Bruce tells me I should leave you some money in my will. I guess he's right. So, when I get better I will change it so that you and Des get half each. Joan and Frankie have enough, from their grandfather, but Des wasn't born when he died. I was pregnant with him, and I know his grandfather was going to set up a trust fund for him, but he died before he could. Aunt Eleanor put up a fuss and Desie didn't want to argue with her."

She was struggling with the words. I didn't know what to say or do. I had only a glimmer of an idea of what it would mean to have some money. I didn't feel worthy of it, not being worthy had been so drummed into me that I felt guilty at the thought that she would include me. But I was scared, too. I was scared by Tom's illness, by the responsibilities of raising two children.

She rested against the pillow and then said, "This will make things more even. For now, I think I will give you and Des each a larger share and then explain things to Joan and Frankie when I am better."

When I am better. The phrase hung in the air, floating over the hospital bed. I knew it wasn't going to happen. I felt so conflicted I could hardly figure out what I felt. Finally I said, "Thank you. Do you want me to call Uncle Charlie or get Mac"—her lawyer—"to come in and talk with you about this?"

"Oh. Yes," she answered. "Call Charlie and we'll talk when he has time."

I knew he had more time than she did, so I called Charlie and said she wanted to talk about her will. "Uncle Charlie," I said, "I think she wants to include me. I feel really torn up about this—but it would make a huge difference to my life, and with Tom sick . . ."

"I understand," he answered. "It would be a wonderful thing for her to do. I'll go see her immediately and take Mac with me." I had known Charlie since I was a child, and he had been very kind to me. I had gone to his office in New York one afternoon and told him I knew the odds were very poor for Mummy, and that I wanted to be with her as much as I could, but that I didn't have enough money to pay for flying back and forth to New York from Washington while Tom was sick. Charlie told me he thought it was essential that I be with her as much as I could be and that he would reimburse me for the trips. Now he, more than I, knew how important being included in her will was to me. And so he and Mac went to see her in the hospital days before she died, and Mummy changed her will. I wish I had been able to thank her properly.

My mother died in mid-August. When I left her for what I knew was the last time, because I had to go back to Washington to be with Tom and my children, and to arrange her funeral, I reached down to her on the bed. She was lying there, drowning in her own body's wastes, wastes it could no longer process. I leaned over and whispered in her ear, "I'll see you in a couple of days when I come back." I knew it was the last lie I would ever tell her. She smiled, just a trace of a smile, and tried to murmur something, but I couldn't understand what she was saying.

I went out into the hall and leaned against the wall, pushing my hands against the rough wallpaper to steady myself. Her doctor came out with Uncle Charlie, and Charlie said, "Tee, I'm sorry, the doctor has to ask you one more thing."

"All right," I answered.

"Will you give me permission to do an autopsy?" the doctor asked. "It is necessary, to learn from—"

I shuddered inside, but I managed to ask, "Will you cut her face?" because I wanted her to have one piece of herself intact.

"No," he promised, "we will not cut her face."

"All right," I said, and turned away quickly so they could not look at me.

I walked to the elevator, turning my crying inside. I didn't cry then, or when I had to identify her body as it lay in the funeral home in Washington, lying in a dark brown coffin, in a darkened room with one light over the casket, still as a marble Galatea, though her lime-green chiffon dress moved softly in the breeze of the air conditioner in a taunting suggestion of life. I didn't cry when I said, "Yes, that is my mother," though I could hardly recognize her with the rouge and the painted eyebrows disguising her yellowed skin.

Nor did I cry when Grannie collapsed against me the night before the funeral, though the pain of thinking how she must feel and the fear of losing my own children before me was almost suffocating. Mummy's surgeon had pulled me aside one day at the hospital and said, "You must expect that your grandmother will die in about two years." I thought this was an incredibly cruel thing to say and looked up at him, startled. "I know that is a harsh thing to say," he added, "but you have to expect it. You have to know that the death of her daughter—and you say her son is dying, too . . . well. How old is she?"

"Eighty-two, I think," I answered.

"She just won't be able to take it," he replied. Now, as I held her as she lay on the celadon-green-covered chaise longue in Mummy's bedroom, her body heaving, her bathrobe open, exposing the mottled, pale flesh, I knew he was right.

I didn't cry at my mother's funeral, though I almost broke down when her lover, Bruce, put his arm around me and tried to hold me. "You are so strong," he said, "so strong, how can you be so strong?" I knew that if I had trusted him more, I might have laid my head against the comfort of his broad chest and cried forever. But I didn't, and I didn't cry about any of the deaths, even the death of my marriage.

But the day I lost Nathan, my cat, to a coyote the following summer, I walked through the woods around Tom's father's house in the Adirondacks, calling and calling his name, hoping that a rustle in the fallen leaves meant he was playing hide-and-seek with me again, fearing I would find a bit of fur or bloody skin, crying and crying as I called because by then he had become my best friend.

7

BACK IN SCHOOL

September 1973

At the end of that summer we went back to Greenwich, back to the apartment where our neighbors were fighting, back to school. I worried about the number of other teachers who knew about Tom's hospitalization during the summer. Perhaps, I hoped, only the kind woman in the business office I had talked with about our health insurance was aware of what had happened. I admitted to myself that she had probably told everyone else, and Anna's father certainly knew, but no one ever said anything until years later, when we were leaving. Tom and I had both talked with the headmaster, Sherman, who accepted that Tom was capable of returning to work, that he had just broken down from exhaustion. Tom was worried, but found comfort in affirming that he had simply become run-down and had depleted his electrolytes and potassium.

The connection between electrolytes and the electric outlet stuck me as strange, but it was easier for me to explain Tom's illness as a result of physical exhaustion than to admit the possibility that he had had a nervous breakdown. Run down from running, I thought, and this even made me laugh.

When I walked in the front door of the school, Mr. Crosby, a middle-school history teacher, coach, and former army sergeant, the only black man in that bastion of whiteness, told me he had read about my mother's death in *The New York Times*.

"Barbara, I mean, I didn't know, didn't know she was famous. I guess that means you are famous," he said.

"No, Bob. She wasn't famous. She had been an actress, but that was a long time ago. I am just me." But other teachers and parents mentioned the obituary, and suddenly there seemed to be a little aura around Tom and me, one that intensified when Frankie won a Pulitzer for her first book. Perhaps other teachers were too kind or too polite to mention Tom's illness, perhaps the office manager and Anna's father never did tell anyone else, or perhaps Tom seemed so brittle that people left him alone. Whatever the reasons, no one talked with us about Tom's hospitalization, and I was grateful for this.

Mummy's death changed our lives in many ways. We had always been outsiders in Greenwich, and after she died, we seemed to move farther away. We were never accepted as friends or even social equals by the school parents, though now when some of them mentioned my mother or stepsister, or Tom's uncle, who had an important position in the administration, they seemed surprised by our connections.

One Parents' Night Tom and I stood outside our respective classrooms, which were next door to each other. I wore the pink wool suit I had bought for "going away" after we were married and Tom had on one of the suits his father had bought for him. Two parents we didn't know walked down the hall and began to talk with us. After several enjoyable minutes of small talk we turned to go into our classrooms and the woman said, with surprise in her voice, "Oh, but I thought you were parents."

"We are," I replied.

Still shocked that we were really teachers, she added, "Oh, but you know what I mean, you look so nice."

When we returned to Greenwich the fall after Tom's hospitalization, he started seeing a psychiatrist. I met the man only once when he asked to see me at his office and I remember him as strangely cranelike in appearance, with a crest of wispy wild gray hair. The doctor explained to me that some people were "wired" differently and that Tom simply was more fragile than I was. When I heard this, I looked at him and wondered what that meant. Did it mean that Tom would be all right if I didn't push him? That he couldn't handle pressure, so I must?

One evening after seeing the doctor Tom told me he had asked him if he was anorexic. Tom had seen an article in a magazine about the disease and wondered if he, too, fit the description. I was surprised by his question because I had so completely believed his problems stemmed from his inherited circulatory condition that I had not thought about other causes, but I admired Tom for asking. Perhaps, if the doctor had answered yes, our lives would have been different. But the doctor replied, "No, only women are anorexics. That's not what's wrong with you." I have since learned that even now, over twenty-five years later, too many doctors as well as the lay public think that anorexia is a woman's disease. I don't know what we would have done differently if we had known the name of Tom's affliction earlier, but I have to think it would have helped.

Instead, the doctor said Tom was processing his guilt and ambivalence about his own mother, an inner turmoil prompted by my mother's death. I wanted to believe this diagnosis, but it never really seemed to fit, and over the years I came to believe that Tom's breakdown had more to do with the fact that I could not give him as much attention that summer as I had before we had two children and my parents died. From that time, until I left him over twenty years later, Tom's behavior became more bizarre and erratic, more overtly controlling and inappropriate than it had been, as if a storm were building and each successive wave striking the beach would recede, only to wash against the sand with greater strength.

Several months later Tom said he no longer needed to see the doctor because he felt much better and he didn't really respect or like the man. "He's a little weird," Tom said, and I agreed. Because I had fooled myself into thinking Tom had just gotten exhausted from running, because I was ashamed to have a husband who needed a psychiatrist, and because I had my own pressures to bear, I was relieved by Tom's decision, when, in truth, I should have been even more worried than before.

Living across the street from the school was convenient, but our neighbors continued to drink and fight and disrupt our lives. By spring Mummy's estate was beginning to be settled and I asked Mac if I should buy a house. He told me it would be the best investment of the money I could make and urged me to start looking. I looked at houses near the school with a broker I found in the Yellow Pages, a much older pudgy man who didn't seem to have any more idea of what we wanted than I did. We looked at a number of houses that were like cardboard boxes, and then I saw a little ad for a house next to an Audubon preserve where we could "hear the pheasants, see the deer."

"Oh, that's what I want," I told him.

"But it's so far away from the school," he said, adding, "And it is such a little house, you won't like it at all."

I insisted that he take me there, and when I saw the land and the little red house set against a wooded hill, I said, "If it has a stream, I'll buy it," because I knew Tom wanted to be near a stream.

"It's over there," the broker said grudgingly, "not much of a stream, though."

I called Tom and said, "I think I've found it. But it just came on the market. There are lots of people coming to look later today.

Can you come look right away?'' It was pouring rain, but when Tom saw the house, he liked it, and he loved being next to the stream, and three hundred acres with trails for running. With Mummy's money, I bought the house in North Greenwich, set against Audubon's Fairchild Wild Flower Garden. It was a simple house, but there were pheasant, deer, and fox in the woods and we were right next to the trails through the garden. I doubt anyone else on the faculty could have afforded it, and owning the house set us even farther apart from the other teachers.

After we moved in I made the mistake of inviting members of my department and of the history department at the girls' school with which our school was loosely affiliated to our house for a meeting. I felt the tension as soon as my guests assembled. At one point a young women who taught at the girls' school asked, ''Is this a family home?'' and I had to say no, that we had just purchased it. The teachers seemed awed by our little house, and I could hardly add that the whole place would have fit into our parents' living rooms.

Yet we weren't to the Greenwich Manor born either. One spring one of my students from the girls' school, a beautiful senior with blond hair, blue eyes, and a shining smile, asked if she could baby-sit for us when we went to the Adirondacks. I told her I would love to have her helping with the children but that I couldn't pay her much. She said that was fine, but two weeks later she came back, blushing and looking down at the floor. She said, ''I am so sorry. My parents say it is not fitting for someone in my social position to work for teachers.''

One of my favorite students was a young man who was an albino with tunnel vision. He told me once that he could only see the denominator or the numerator in a fraction and that he was never sure when he crossed a street if he was going to make it to the other side. He had compensated for his handicap by developing an acute sense of smell, sensitive enough to detect the scent of

pollen on bees or the kind of hand his opponents held in poker—
but he could read only slowly and could not complete assignments.
He had been passed along since he was in kindergarten because his
father was chairman of the board of a major corporation. I was
able to help him get assistance from the Lighthouse because I
forced his parents to confront the reality that their son was almost
blind. One day, when he was visiting the school after graduating,
he came to see me. He said he had heard we bought a house.

"Is it very small?" he asked.

"Well, yes, Peter, it's pretty small."

"Is it in a bad neighborhood?"

"No, Peter, it's just off Reservoir Road."

He looked puzzled. "Is it very run-down?"

"You know, Peter, you should come see it for yourself."

Though his questions sounded rude, I knew he did not intend
them to be—he just couldn't conceive of teachers being able to
afford to buy a house in North Greenwich. Tom and I were caught
in a trap we had in some ways created for ourselves.

I was losing contact with my own family, too. The first Christmas after Mummy died we had gallantly assembled in Washington.
Frankie gave up her usual trip to Barbados with her mother and
stepfather, and Tom and I and the two children flew down from
Greenwich to stay in a house we had rented from our former
neighbors in Washington. Grannie was living in her apartment
near the cathedral and Joan and Des shared a carriage house they
rented from a good friend of Mummy's.

Tom and I were exhausted from a semester of teaching after his
illness, and I dreaded the logistical hassles of moving Katherine,
then almost one, and Stephen, three and a half, to an unfamiliar
house for a week and shuttling between our two families. The first
Christmas we were married we had gone to Washington to be
with our parents, but no matter how we tried to juggle our time
in order to placate them we ended up offending everyone.

Mummy was mad we had missed the "Traditional Christmas Morning Stocking Opening"; Tom's father was irritated we didn't spend the entire evening at the "Traditional Family Night Before Christmas Party." Somehow everything had instantly become a ceremony, rooted in a long family history, and we felt like taffy being pulled by jealous children.

That Christmas after Mummy died was very difficult. All fall I worried about Joan and Des and my grandmother. I spent as much time on the phone with them all as I could, but sometimes I got very little sleep. I was carrying a full workload at the school, though I spent only half a day there teaching four classes in a row. We were tired, and the rented house smelled of old clothes and dirt. We learned that our friends were getting a divorce and house-keeping, never their forte, seemed to have become a field of battle.

I think my sisters and brother resented having to spend Christmas there, but it was difficult for us to be mobile and Grannie couldn't cope with having us at her little place. The second night, Christmas Eve, both children contracted strep throat and had very high fevers. Joan, Des, and Frankie couldn't seem to understand that the kids needed to be kept quiet and Tom was furious. On Christmas, we opened our presents and tried to be cheerful, but we felt Mummy's absence intensely. After dinner Grannie went home and Tom kept hinting that my sisters and brother should leave, and they, irritated with his hinting, stayed because it was their Christmas together. Tom had stomped off to bed and occasionally came to the head of the stairs and grumbled about rude, inconsiderate people waking up his sick children. The kids couldn't sleep because they felt so sick. I spent the evening running up and down stairs until finally I went to bed while my sisters and brother continued to party downstairs.

The next Christmas, after Grannie had moved back to England, my siblings told me they were celebrating in their house in Maine and wanted us to join them. "The house is unheated and there's no running water," Joan said when she called me with the news, "so it's going to be an adventure." I could feel my heart and voice sinking. I wanted to spend Christmas in Maine with my sisters and brother but I knew I couldn't take two children in diapers to an unheated house with no water and a two-mile unplowed driveway. My sisters and brother had no children and couldn't understand the impossible position they were putting me in; instead, Joan told me that I obviously didn't care much about being part of the family. There was nothing I could do; it was how she felt.

I loved our land in Maine more than any place in the world. After Mummy had died, my sisters and brother built a house there, and though I didn't have enough money to contribute to this, I did own a share of the land. Tom and I and our children had been able to stay at "The Point" for the first two weeks of the summer before the others wanted to be there. It was a confusing arrangement, laced with more peril and pain than I could foresee.

I had missed going to Maine for the years after I graduated from college and before Mummy died, years when I couldn't afford the trip. The new house gave me a chance to watch my children play in the same tide pools where my stepsister and I had collected seed pearls from mussel shells. When I was a child, just as we passed the center of the bridge that connects the island to the mainland, we would yell, "Yahooooo!" a long deep exultation of larks migrating home for the summer. Each time I came back I felt that finally I was home. Since 1948, when Desie first brought Mummy and me here, this had been the place where I had felt most deeply rooted. For years, in the winters, in my mind I would follow the threaded roots weaving over footpaths through the high bush blueberry from the "green place" where the boats had docked to load rough-cut granite, quarried from this place, then to the pink feldspar granite of the shore, which held me like a grandmother as I read in the sun, folding me into her soft skirt. It was a place I loved so deeply it seemed every root, every rock held a memory.

"Yahoo," Tom and the children yelled as we crossed the bridge.

When we reached the Green Place again, the children could run, under our watchful eyes, and climb the wind-gnarled tree that had grown as they had in the year past. Our children learned to row at the Yacht Club, where I rowed my boat into the dock, swirling in circles like a one-legged water boatman. We played tennis on the exquisitely groomed courts of the club, the best Tom said approvingly that he had ever played on and that my parents had loved.

Tom was beautiful on a tennis court, so good that people came to watch us as we blasted forehands at each other. I had gotten much better under his tutelage and he was patient, confident, and sure in his coaching. I saw myself as my mother in my mind's eye, scurrying after a ball, never giving up, running until she was sweating—not something a lady did. Now I enjoyed that I could sweat and run and run. I loved hearing the cheers of Mr. Lister and Mr. Wayland, two ancient gentlemen who liked watching almost as much as they had enjoyed playing years ago. Playing tennis with Tom was still fun at this time. I did not yet feel like a yo-yo, thrown across the court, then back to the other side by his relentless forehands and powerful backhands, running after the endless supply of tennis balls he kept in an old red-and-white L.L. Bean bag, "so we wouldn't waste time," he said, until I was worn out. "Just want to give you a good workout," he explained. And for a while I accepted and enjoyed the challenge.

We went for picnics on Cadillac Mountain, seeking a sheltered spot on the rocks just off the crest so the tourists wouldn't find us, just at dusk when the sun was setting over the mountain, a cloak of orange and red, cerise and purple, gentling down over us. The seagulls always found us and we tossed crusts of bread or cheese at them and watched them catch dinner in midair. We picked blueberries and sat together in the sun, or went to the beach and let the children dig for the astoundingly blue sea worms that shocked me with their size and intense color the first time we found them.

It was hard to be part of a family splintered by geography, circumstance, and time. Grannie in Washington, Joan and Frankie in New York, Des in Cambridge, married and unmarried, wealthy and not so wealthy, products of three different marriages; we still tried hard. Once, in all the seven months of her illness, Mummy and I talked about what might happen to Grannie and my brother and sister if she died. We were in Newport, driving to do some errands, and I turned to her in the dark car and said, " I want to tell you something. I don't want you to worry about Grannie and Joan and Des. If something happens to you, I want her to live with us. Maybe they'll want to as well."

"Thank you," she replied. But that was all; she didn't want to talk about it, but I hoped my words made a difference to her.

After Mummy died, I asked Grannie to come to live with us. I was afraid that Tom would be angry and miserable if she accepted my offer and so I was relieved but sad when she told me her place was back in England with my uncle Kent, her son. She said she would try to get into the same nursing home he was in because they had "bedsitters" for older people, apartments you could rent and health care available if you needed it.

She moved to Bath, where her mother had lived, to number eleven The Circus, which seemed an improbably cheerful address. Tom and I flew to England to see her during our spring vacation the year after she moved. We found her ensconced in her little apartment, well settled into a routine that included meals with other people in the apartments, visits from her niece by marriage, Boff, and daily visits to her son, my uncle Kent.

I watched her moving slowly around the "bedsitter" and then sinking into the large Queen Anne chair with its bright chintz upholstery that she had brought from Washington. I looked around the bright room, lit by large windows facing a garden. There were many framed pictures of Mummy and Uncle Kent, of her three grandchildren, of herself when she was younger: Mummy as an ingenue with Grannie just behind her, a fox stole circling her shoulders, nipping its tail; Grannie in an outrageous tall hat with feathers judging the hat competition on the *Caronia* on one of her trips across the Atlantic, Grannie and her second husband on their honeymoon in London. Her green silver-and-enamel brush set graced her bureau, the couch was comfortable, she had a little kitchenette. She is well cared for here, I thought. But I wondered if she was ever lonely.

We couldn't stay with her long because she got tired and short of breath. The second afternoon we walked down the hall and then down the stairs in a slow progression, Grannie stopping to talk to other residents or the matron sisters who bustled about in their starched blue uniforms and white-winged wimples. When we reached Uncle Kent's room, the soft sweet smell of putrefaction shocked me even though it was masked by disinfectants. Grannie had told me, "He has a hole the size of a tennis ball in his chest and a drain. But he is very well cared for and they all say how much they like him." Uncle Kent tried to sit up on his elbows but had to lean his head back on the bed.

"Tee, dear, and Tommy. It is so good of you to visit me. Such a tiresome place to come to. I'm sorry," he said.

Grannie walked over to the only chair in the room, put her hands on the back rail, and sank slowly down until she could sit. She was solicitous and very cheerful, telling Kent what a lovely day it was and asking about his breakfast. "Now, Kent. Did you eat your breakfast? What did you have? Did you have some porridge?" she asked.

"No, I just didn't feel like it. I drank some juice," he answered, turning his pale face toward her like the sick child he was. Tom and I stood in the doorway, as there wasn't much space in the tiny room, and I tried not to get nauseous from the smell and thinking how sad it all was. Another day when we visited, Uncle Kent's wife was there looking as fat as a bloated tick, her oily skin glistening in the fluorescent overhead light and her short greasy hair pasted against her face.

Later Tom said, "No wonder the man is dying, look at how awful his wife is."

We could see Grannie only briefly before she tired and needed to rest, and so we had the only trip we ever took by ourselves. I had dreaded the trip, thinking we would have to stay in Bath seeing Grannie and Uncle Kent, and that Tom would be irritable and difficult, but instead it turned out to be fun. We went somewhere each day—Cornwall, Dorset, the Roman baths—and spent several nights away, but always saw Grannie once a day, either in the early morning before we left or the next night when we came back. I remember it as a wonderful trip, with very little tension between Tom and me. Tom would run each day, hanging his sweatclothes out of the hotel windows or on the little red car we had rented. I would explore the villages while he ran in the afternoons and then we'd go to dinner. One time we walked along a beach and I looked down to find fossilized ichthyosaurs and other creatures caught in a Devonian mudflow now exposed by tides. We were able to spend time with each other with no distractions, no responsibilities except to see Grannie, and we had a good time with each other.

When I saw her just before we left, Grannie told me she was leaving me her jewelry box and told me the history of some of the things in it, including the two gold-and-diamond rings I am wearing now from my great-grandmother and great-great-grandfather. I wished I had written down what she said, but I didn't want either of us to think we wouldn't see each other again. I called her from London the next day, just before we were flying out of Heathrow, and she sounded weak. "Grannie," I asked, "are you all right? You sound a little different."

"Oh, of course dear," she answered. "I'm fine."

"I'll come back if you want me to," I offered.

"No, no, you have to go home. I am fine, I am very well taken care of, and it's nothing, just a little upset stomach." She died two days later and her doctor told me she had had a stroke hours after I left her.

She left me twenty thousand dollars, all the money she had amassed in her lifetime, as well as the contents of her jewelry box and her mink coat. I wore the mink coat a few times to parent-faculty dinners, feeling self-conscious, and finally used it as a comforter on my side of the bed. There were several rings, one I wore often. One day I cleaned a ring with large crystal stones that was particularly dirty. I had been wearing it to school, but when I cleaned it, the glass shone like diamonds, which is what the stones turned out to be. I sold the ring, because I thought it was too expensive for me, something I couldn't afford to keep, which I now regret.

With Grannie's money we bought a sauna and a new car. We ordered a maroon BMW, but when I saw an orange car with a thin black stripe outlining its shape, shining in the showroom, I knew we were going to take the one in Princeton's colors. I wonder now why I used my inheritance to buy two things Tom wanted, and I realize I hoped that if he had the sauna at home, he wouldn't have to spend so much time at the Y and would stay longer each day at school. We needed a new car, as our Toyota station wagon was rusting, but a BMW? Now that we had some money, something was changing about the way Tom viewed the world and himself in it.

For years Tom had increasingly done the driving. First we had such unpredictable cars that I didn't want to drive them and he convinced me that they were hard to handle. When we moved to Greenwich, Tom went to get his new license, but didn't take me, though I had told him I wanted to go with him because the department of motor vehicles was located in another town, so it was hard for me to get there on my own. I think Tom would have taken me on a separate trip—but he said that it would be inconvenient. Again my fears played into his and it was easier for me not to insist.

Besides, I enjoyed having Tom drive. He had an unerring sense of direction while I have none, perhaps because my father used to leave me on street corners when I was a toddler. I doubt this happened more than a few times, but I have never forgotten what it felt like to be so small, and have the world swirling uncontrollably around me, a world of gray flannel legs and shoes, indifferent and unapproachable. Tom always seemed to know where he was and not to be scared if he didn't. He drove deftly and with confidence, the way he played tennis, dealing with the crazy circles and drivers in Washington, which seemed increasingly intimidating the less I drove.

During our first two years in Greenwich we had an ancient, embarrassingly ugly, tan-and-brown Chevy we bought from a friend's mother for a hundred dollars, paid for over ten months. You could look between your feet and see the road going by through the car floor, and after a rain the interior of the car had its very own wave, a moving puddle of dirty water that amused our students when they had to pick up their feet to avoid getting wet. After Mummy died we bought a blue Toyota station wagon that was reliable, but I was always the one who held our children and tended to them while Tom drove with assurance and delight in doing something well. I knew it seemed odd to people that I didn't drive when they saw me as assertive, confident, and competent, the only woman academic teacher in the upper school and soon to be head of the history department and dean of guidance.

When my D.C. license expired and I still had no Connecticut license, I couldn't drive. But when I bought the BMW and we moved outside of the town, I knew I had to have a license and I wanted to be able to drive the car I had just bought. Tom still tried to discourage me, but it was too inconvenient to have me immobilized and living four miles from school. I studied for the written test and was relieved when I drove the inspector around during the test and my foot didn't shake on the accelerator as it had when I first tried to get my license in Washington.

When I drove the solid, smooth BMW, I felt secure and deft

and I found that I enjoyed driving again, though Tom still always drove whenever we were together. But during the six years we lived in that house, we never had two cars, so I had to hire students to drive me home from school. It never occurred to me to insist that I use the car I had bought or that Tom should be the one to wait for a ride, even when I had more responsibilities at the school and was earning more than he did.

Now that we had our own house, a few miles away from school, it was harder to spend as much time at school as we had when we lived across the street. The headmaster, Sherman, complained that Tom didn't stay at school late, held short practices, that we didn't go to games, and left school events early. Instead of having more time, we seemed to have less. Tom started taking more saunas, a sauna in the morning before going to work, then another in the late afternoon when he came home, and sometimes even a third in the evening just before he went to bed. Getting ready to exercise, exercising, and then taking a cold bath and getting dressed were taking up more and more of his waking hours, and he was regularly going to bed early, shortly after eating his supper and exercising again.

Dinner was movable if not a feast. Sometimes we ate at the table, often on the couch in front of the television. When the children got older they complained about the food Tom cooked and begged me to do the cooking. Once, at the end of a long climb in the Adirondacks with friends, they opened the lunch he had made them to find grape-jelly-and-mayonnaise sandwiches, and the meals he cooked regularly for them were equally unappetizing. We sat on the red couch I had inherited from Mummy in the extension we had built to the house, a combination dining room and playroom—what the contractor called a "family room." "What would you like to eat?" I asked Katherine. "I like what we have at school. I like what you cook. Dad cooks all the time, and you should have a turn." Ah, another diplomat, I thought. "It's a little hard, Kit," I replied. "He really loves to cook and I just don't have much time. But maybe we can split it and you guys can help." I decided to make a quiche Lorraine, because it was easy, and I thought of other dinners we could cook together, but I worried about telling Tom.

When he came home that afternoon, I was standing in the kitchen, looking in the cupboards for ingredients. I turned to him and said, "Tom, Katherine and Stephen think it would be fun to help with the cooking. I miss cooking. Why don't we just split it?" I looked at him to gauge how he was reacting and saw his jaw tighten. I pushed on. "It will be easier for you. I'll just cook some supper and we can eat together when you get back from running."

He dropped his books on the table and said, "So, what were you thinking of cooking?" he asked.

"Well, I was thinking a quiche would be nice. We haven't had one in a long time and they're easy to make. I can cut down on the eggs and—"

"That's a terrible idea," he interrupted. "It's all eggs and cream; it's just heart-attack material."

"Well, what about something lighter? Maybe a carrot soup and then . . ." My voice trailed off. Katherine and Stephen were looking up at me, Tom was glowering. "We need to share this, Tom. The kids are growing up thinking school food is gourmet dining." And so we would try to share the cooking chores for a little while, but he was relentless. He complained every time I cooked, wouldn't eat what I prepared, and was grumpy and irritable—so always, we settled back into having him do more and more of the cooking because it was easier to eat bad food than to stand up to him.

That year a teacher and friend from school, Rob, who was only slightly older than we were had a serious heart attack and almost died. Thinking about him, and about my father and stepfather, forced me to reflect on my own mortality. "Your parents ate themselves to death. They ate so much bad fatty food and they didn't do any exercise. And Rob didn't do any either. Lean horse for the long race, you know," Tom admonished me again.

I had always resisted Tom's efforts to get me to exercise—it seemed the one area of my life I could still keep him out of. But I began to worry that I should try to exercise, that if I didn't, I might die early, too, as my parents had. Tom suggested I try the sauna I had bought, and when I did, my body exuded a bright blue sweat. I wondered what chemicals were polluting my body, and I thought the sauna would be healthy for me. I started taking a sauna a few times a week. Mostly I enjoyed the quiet, being by myself, and the smell of cedar. It seemed a sanctuary because it was the only thing I did during a day that Tom thought important enough that I should not be bothered. Protected space, almost sacred—that's the way he thought of saunas and exercising.

"You should run, you know. Rob's heart attack is just a warning." Many times Tom had told me to exercise but I had resisted, not thinking of myself as an athlete and feeling uncomfortable when he pressured me. But I thought about Rob's heart attack; I thought about the fact that he was only a few years older than I was, and I thought about my own parents' premature deaths. One day I decided to run through the Audubon garden. Trails through high grass and meadows led me to streams and ponds with frogs squatting on lily pads, turtles sunning themselves on logs. Running along the trails, stopping to pick up and examine scat or look at tracks, gave me a feeling of peace I felt nowhere else. Sometimes a fox crossed the path in front of me. Often I startled deer, their white tails flashing as the gland in their hooves emitted musk to mark a place of danger. And almost every night I heard the rusty-tin-can rattle of pheasant calling to each other, the promise that had brought me to this place originally. I enjoyed the peace of being in the garden, seeing the wild Turk's-head lilies standing above the tall grasses, their elegant orange caps like Persian soldiers at attention, or tiny deep blue iris tucked into clefts of rock in the brooks. Sometimes I found porcupines lumbering along the paths, and one night, as I paused next to a pond, I felt a soundless shadow pass over my head and looked up to see a great horned owl sitting on the branch of a tree. I soon realized that my time in the sauna and running were the only moments in the day when I could be by myself, and that by offering to care for the children, Tom was erecting a guardrail around this island of time for me, the only approved space I had. "Isn't it time for you to go running? You've got to get better shoes. How far are you going now?" The weight of his controlling questions was offset by the relief I felt having time away from him, the children, work, the telephone. But then he pressured me to get even more exercise. I would go running a couple of times a week, but then it had to be every day. I would take a sauna a couple of times a week, but it became easier to do it every day so I wouldn't have to explain why I didn't want to. But then running for a short time wasn't enough, taking a short sauna wasn't enough.

Tom's behavior at school also became increasingly inappropriate. He had never cared much about what he wore, but the clothes he now chose and the way he wore them began to look more and more strange, like the red-and-white-striped pants he bought at the school's secondhand shop. The stripes were wide, like those you see on an awning, and people said to me, "He looks like a clown, how can you let him wear those pants?"

He favored garish plaids and madras pants—often they had shrunk and were too short for his lanky frame. He liked orange, a color that rarely blended, and he usually wore thick red wool socks, the kind most people wear under ski boots, because they cushioned his feet. The pockets of his pants were stained with pools of blue ink, successive waves floating out from leaking pens. I hoped people thought of this as an endearing eccentricity, revealing a lack of self-consciousness, a disinterest in possessions. But much later, when I spent time with homeless people in Boston, I looked at their bizarre dress and realized the most seriously ill chose articles from the heaps of donated clothing not just for warmth but as strange costumes. It seemed they wore their pain on the outside as well as within, and I thought perhaps Tom had been doing the same thing.

Well-intentioned teachers, parents, and students commented at different times, "He's so skinny," and then, inevitably it seemed, "Gosh, don't you like to cook?" or, "You must not be much of a cook." How could I answer that I loved to cook and I used to be very good at it, but Tom just wasn't much of an eater? Several students said to me, in some awe, that Tom's table manners were worse than theirs. I rarely ate with him at school, but at home I knew he used a spoon or his fingers, and slopped ketchup over anything he ate. He seemed not to notice that there was often ketchup on his hands and that as a result he marked anything he touched—cabinet knobs in the kitchen, doorjambs, walls. At first I thought he had hurt himself, and was leaving a trail of blood.

With well-designed running shoes, his feet were no longer bloody and blistered, but the relentless running made them callused and a bruised deep red. One day he came in from running and said, "Shit, I think I've broken my toe."

"Oh, no," I replied. "Are you sure? What are you going to do?" I asked.

"I'm going to pack it in ice and see if it gets better," he answered. But it didn't. His second toe, longer than the big toe, was blackened and red with acute bruising. Tom limped from pain, but still went running.

Several times I said, "I really think you should see a doctor," but each time he answered with the same words: "I'm not going to a doctor, he's just going to tell me not to run on it, and I have to run."

"But if it's broken, it may not heal right and it might mean you won't be able to run properly at all. It might become a real problem for you," I suggested hesitantly. Years later a therapist told me that his refusal to take care of his foot, his insistence that he couldn't stop running to give it time to heal, were just symptoms of his anorexia.

He was coaching the running team because he had to coach something, but he insisted on having time for his own running before it got dark and his practices were very short in comparison to the hours the other coaches put in. He grumbled about meetings, relied on me to stay later than he did, got physically agitated if he had to stay past three-thirty or four o'clock because it would interfere with his exercise. His physical agitation was often embarrassing. He would begin to fidget if a meeting lasted later than three o'clock and look at the wall clock, grimacing and sighing. He would move around in the seat, holding his hands in front of him stretched out toward the floor, looking down and around, everywhere but at the other people at the meeting. Finally he would get up and say he had to leave, that the light was fading fast and he had to go running. It was always a relief when he left and we could concentrate again, but I worried about what the other teachers and Sherman were thinking.

Tom became even more insistent that he cook for us. When the former head of the English department decided to relinquish his position, Tom had taken the job. His father was delighted, but the pressure of running the department made Tom more uncomfortable, and later, when we were leaving the school, he said he wished he had remained being a teacher. When I was made head of the history department and then dean of guidance after the children were both in school, I was so busy that I welcomed his help. Tom had never cleaned in a way that I found acceptable; he would simply not see the dirt. It was easier to have him cook because then he didn't complain. But his behavior with food became sickening, so strange it was hard to admit what he was doing.

One morning when he was making porridge I saw him spit into the bowl he was about to serve. It scared me so much that I froze, unable to say anything. Other times I saw him rub his hand over his crotch and then on the long-handled spoons he was using to stir whatever he was cooking on the stove. I was horrified, but I didn't know what to do.

One time one of the children asked, "Why does Daddy wipe his bottom with his hand and then put it in the food?" "Oh, he couldn't be doing that!" I exclaimed. "You must be mistaken, he probably was just scratching." But in my heart I knew the children were right. I just couldn't bear the consequences—separation, divorce?—and I didn't know what to do to change Tom's behavior. I was too ashamed to tell him what the children saw, and relieved when he told me that these things were impossible.

"That's gross, why would I do that?" he asked, sounding puzzled.

"I don't know. I don't know, but they say that's what they saw," I answered.

"Well, they're wrong," he replied emphatically. But even I couldn't deny that the food was awful—desiccated, overcooked, or burned, served in smaller and smaller portions on smaller and smaller plates. I talked to Tom many, many times, trying to encourage him to talk with his doctor, trying to make him see that his behavior was inappropriate and offensive, trying to understand and forgive it as part of an illness. I was always too hopeful that if he just understood how I felt and just talked with the doctor somehow everything would be all right. I was always eager to deny, as he did, the seriousness and even the reality of the symptoms I, and our children, observed.

I found myself burrowing into my work and life with the children and students, hoping Tom could function, not talking about his problems, but thinking how much I would like to leave him. I wanted to leave, but I didn't want my children to have divorced parents, as I'd had. The curse of divorce had been so shameful in my own life that I couldn't see that it had lost some of its power in our culture over the years. I was prepared to do almost anything to keep my children from that pain. I thought having their father was better than a stepfather or no father at all, and I knew Tom loved them very much.

Teaching allowed me to be free afternoons and evenings, as well as vacations with my children. I was usually working while I was with them but we devised games that allowed me to both work and play with them. I would sit on the red couch in the playroom we had added to the house, while Stephen looked at a book, sitting cross-legged on the floor. Whenever he got restless and jumped up to sit on my lap while I was grading papers, I had learned to distract him.

"Stephen, can you dance like a bear? Run like a tiger? How would a butterfly move?" And I watched with most of my mind as the little boy lumbered across the rug in a heavy dumpy dance, or prowled between the furniture, and then fluttered gracefully over the sofa. One afternoon, a bit tired, I asked, "And what would a carrot do?" And he paused only slightly and then stood still on one foot, the other carefully tucked behind his knee and raised his hands in the air, waving his fingers to mimic the way he had seen the carrots growing in our vegetable garden.

In the summers we went to Maine for two weeks, and then to the Adirondacks for the rest of the vacation. I loved having time with my children, and Tom's father and stepmother had built a separate house for themselves, so we lived in the main house. Much later Danielle told me that they had done this only to get away from Tom, who was so controlling and judgmental they could no longer share a house with him even for a couple of months.

"Grand-man," Tom's father, and stepmother were our children's only grandparents, and they seemed to enjoy the role. Some mornings they would invite the children to breakfast, making a fancy menu advertising the special of the day—Pancakes à la Flume, Bear's Delight blueberry syrup—and setting the table with Ausable Forks and Sawtooth Knives, named after places they loved. Sometimes Grand-Man, as his grandchildren called him, dressed up with the realistic rubber masks he brought from Washington for the purpose—a fierce gorilla, Little Red Riding Hood's wolf, a fanged tiger. He prowled behind the outcrop of rock that separated the two houses and then roared or growled, daring the children to find him. Slowly they peeked around the rock, creeping carefully, Stephen holding Katherine's hand, until suddenly their grandfather leaped out roaring and flailing his arms and they jumped in the air and shrieked. Once Katherine seemed scared, but most of the time they knew he was playing and they tried to scare him back, their piping voices mimicking a growl but emitting a high-pitched meow instead. I was grateful to Grand-Man and his second wife even though we saw them for only a short time each year. I regretted that I could not give my children grandparents because I loved my own and the time I spent with them. And then one afternoon when we were at home in Greenwich the phone rang and when I answered it there was Danielle sobbing and saying, "He died right on the tennis court, right when he was going to hit a serve. I know you will think that it is my fault, I know you will."

"No, no, Danielle, we would never think that. I must get Tom," and I handed over the telephone and went into where Katherine was sitting on the floor, sinking to my knees to hold her in my arms. Three days after his father died Tom received a postcard his father had mailed that morning: a photograph of the tennis court at the exquisite club where he was to die that afternoon. Though it seemed a cruel irony, it was also comforting to know he had been thinking of us.

Tom genuinely missed his father, and talked often about what a gentle, good, and honest man he was. Grand-Man had been a kind person, a well-intentioned man, but he had had a nervous breakdown when he was Tom's age, a man overpressured by the ordinary demands of life. When he was married to his first wife, Tom's mother, he was careful about what he drank, perhaps because she was an alcoholic. But when he remarried three years after her death, he began to do things he had deferred throughout their marriage—going to parties, going on vacations, drinking more, and spending more money. He deserved to enjoy himself and his life, but he began to drink so much that he worried us. His behavior was erratic and Tom tried not to call him in the evening. One night we were at his house for dinner and we saw how seriously alcohol was affecting his behavior.

Dinner was very pleasant, cooked and served by their cook, Maria—lamb chops, asparagus with hollandaise, and new potatoes. But we had not eaten meat in so long it was hard to swallow the rich chops. We knew enough to avoid certain topics, but Danielle was much more liberal than Grand-Man and her outlook made our politics seem safer. Tom ventured a comment about President Nixon and Watergate.

"Dad, it seems the guy really is as much of a creep as I've thought all along. How could a president order thugs to break into—"

His father, who had been staring at his glass, looked up at us, his eyes bulging from a face as red as the wine, veins throbbing in his throat. "How dare you, how dare you criticize your president?" Somehow the argument degenerated until he picked up the brass poker by the fireplace and ran after Tom, chasing him around the dining-room table. If it hadn't seemed dangerous, I would have laughed. I wondered what my father-in-law would do if he caught up with Tom, but it seemed best not to find out, and we left, backing out the front door. But now that he was gone, another anchor had been cut from our boat.

Tom and I became increasingly uncomfortable at the school. Stephen and Katherine seemed to love being there and were enjoying friends, Stephen playing the trumpet, Katherine going to Brownies. But we had no friends except Charlie, whom we saw only at school. Tom identified more and more with his students and against the parents, and ridiculed parents and administration alike. "A pretty mundane crew, not an original thought among them. A bunch of petty burghers, really." He thought the parents were just interested in earning and spending money, and decried the way the school kowtowed to "important" parents. There was a lot of drinking, particularly among the bored wives of successful executives, and our students told us about the wild parties their parents went to. Too many Monday mornings I would go to the faculty room to hear the male teachers joking about how they "really tied one on," and then criticize their students for getting so drunk over the weekend that they couldn't think on Monday. Tom said he thought the school was mediocre and wanted to move on up to a better school, but though we had applied to a few such schools, we were never hired.

There were also many times that I felt embarrassed and "set up" by Tom. He would get upset about things that happened at school, things that seemed to him unfair, put-downs, slights, things that the headmaster had done or said. He made me feel as if I had to come to his defense, as my beagle Gwen had done with her first litter of puppies, becoming a real bitch, chasing deliverymen and Mary, our large, part-time laundress. Now, as I listened to Tom, he said, "It's so unfair. I have to coach the cross-country team, and now they want me to go to a squash meet in Darien. Maybe Charlie can go alone. I mean he's great at squash and he doesn't really need me." Or other times, "I can get Carter to cover for me. He loves to do extra stuff."

When I was chairwoman of the history department and had created a secure place for myself in the school, I often jeopardized my credibility by defending Tom. One fall a parent gave

the school a significant sum of money to start an assembly program that would bring nationally recognized speakers to the
school. The headmaster was thrilled and announced the first of a
series of six lectures. The speakers would talk about economics
and business, and about the state of the state and of the nation—
but in the evening. All students from the sixth through twelfth
grades would be required to attend, as would all teachers. The
faculty response was predictable.

"Goddamn dumbest idea they've had yet."

"Yes, and there have been some pretty bad ones. I mean, I work
here all day, I have to grade papers, and prepare for class. You
think I want to be here all night?"

"It's just an ego trip for some rich father."

"The kids are going to hate it. I bet no one comes."

"So who's going to tell Sherman?" I asked.

"Oh. Well . . . I mean . . ."

"I mean, there's not much to say," I added.

"If you feel so strongly, why don't you do it?" one of the men
asked.

I was the only woman there. First I was the only woman teaching in the upper school, then the only woman chairing a department, so telling Sherman was a bit of a dare.

"Will you back me up?" I asked.

"Of course," they all said, nodding in unison.

Tom and I talked about the next department-heads' meeting,
the one in which I would raise the issue of the evening programs
and register my concerns. He and the other men would chime in,
he said, and we would have an open discussion. When we sat
around the oval table in the conference room I said, "Sherman,
I'm worried that scheduling the program in the evening and re-
quiring attendance will undercut its chances of success, because
students and teachers will see it as punitive rather than as an opportunity. Could it be in the afternoon, or perhaps an all-day event
so the speaker can spend some time in classes?"

I waited for the other department heads to join me, but these erstwhile handwringers were silent and there was no chiming chorus. Instead, Sherman leveled his blue eyes at me and then asked if anyone else felt the same way, turning his head to survey the men sitting around the table. The room was silent. I could hear the seconds ticking by on the large wall clock with the red hand. Finally, triumphant, Sherman said, "Well, Barbara, looks as if you're out on a limb on this one. I certainly hope you realize how important it is to be enthusiastic about this; it's a great opportunity."

The first speaker turned out to be the senior senator from Connecticut, a parent at the school. His talk was interesting, but the students and faculty were tired, and their response was listless. At the second program, the auditorium was emptier than before, teachers had brought papers to grade and the boys were fidgeting and playing handheld games, or surreptitiously throwing spitballs. The third program was a disaster—the auditorium was half-empty, and the speaker cut short his presentation as students were talking and paying almost no attention. The last meetings were canceled.

Living in North Greenwich meant we were even more isolated; the drive was just long enough to deter us from staying late, or going in early to the school. We had one car. We had children. But Tom, fairly or unfairly, was perceived as not caring about his job, as not putting in the long hours expected. Sherman always seemed to need someone to pick on. He had nattered at other teachers until they left the school, and now Tom was easy prey. One day the headmaster read the student journals that Tom had locked away—journals he had promised his students were their refuge, in which they could write whatever they needed to write without fear of reprisals. Sherman read the journals looking for evidence of drugs and alcohol use, which he found. Tom felt betrayed, and knew he had unintentionally set up his students. Tom's criticisms of Sherman as a pedestrian thinker, a mediocre educator, soon reached him through his "ears"—another teacher we called the Mole. During the spring of 1979 some teachers began to confide in me.

"You know, Barbara, he's going to be fired."

"He can't last long here—Sherman doesn't like him anymore. The kids like him. Yes, they do. They feel like he's one of them. Well, that's not exactly a compliment, is it?"

"He's acting pretty erratic. I'm not sure what you are going to do."

I wasn't either. I had had to fire two of the men in my department—a very painful task, which I bore more easily because I was convinced having them leave was better for our students and for the teachers themselves, who did not love teaching. But I could hardly bear the shame of having Tom fired. I was earning more than he was, had more responsibility and status in the school, and also too much to do. I couldn't teach as well as I had when administrative duties didn't weigh me down. I would get to class without having read over an assignment, without having thought about how to present the material to that particular group of students, on that particular day, just winging it on past experience. Maybe no one else knew, but I knew; I wasn't doing the job the way I wanted to.

In the summer of 1979 we drove to Mount Desert Island to spend our two weeks in the house I shared with my sisters and brother at The Point, to the refuge of Maine, for that is what it was that summer. As we sat on the deck overlooking the sound and the distant mountains, smelling the rich smell of balsam and pines, listening to the thrushes singing in the evening, we began to talk about leaving our teaching jobs. I had told Tom what the other teachers said—that he would be fired soon. He disliked Sherman now, and it seemed unlikely they would heal their differences.

"We could live in the Adirondacks," he said. "You know,

there's a good school there. I bet we could get jobs. We could buy a house. Sell the one in Greenwich." And later he added, "You know, it's really cold in the winter. That isn't great for Reynaud's. I think it would be too cold. And there are not many people there in the winter."

"What about Maine?"

Yes, what about Maine? we both thought. "The temperature here isn't nearly as cold as on the coast, because the ocean around the island mitigates the temperature," Tom said, adding, "There are lots more people and things to do here in the winter." "I think the school is pretty good," I said, pleased that he wanted to move to *my* summer place. "Or maybe we could start a school," he suggested.

"Wow, that would be great. Maybe we could start a school— use the island as a base for an Outward Bound–type school," I added in excitement, beginning to spin ideas about a school I would like to create.

The more we thought, the better the idea seemed. We decided to leave at the end of the upcoming school year. We had contracts for the fall, and we knew we couldn't leave earlier. But then we thought about a colleague who had decided to leave and had been a "lame duck" for a year. It was awkward for everyone and so we began to wonder if we could leave in the middle of the year. We called Sherman, and asked if we could leave in January or June. Sherman replied that we could leave in June, but not January, and then added, "It would be much easier if you left in the beginning of the year or the end, but not the middle."

"The beginning? Not go back? At all?" We surprised ourselves with the idea, but the more we thought about it, the better we liked it.

We were sitting in the dining room of the Happy Crab, a small restaurant on the road to Southwest Harbor. "Happy Crap we call it here," said Pat, the brusque realtor from the oldest real-estate firm on the island, the one my parents used when they rented a house summer after summer because they never built on the land Desie owned. We were eating lunch, enjoying a rest stop between looking for properties. The restaurant was a one-story frame building with a high peaked roof, lots of flowers in whiskey barrels graced the entrance, and there were red-and-white-checked tablecloths and waitresses with blue aprons. The wooden walls boasted photographs of the owners and guests, none I recognized, old lobster buoys in red and green stripes, a lobster trap, a huge lobster claw, orange red against the wood, a collection of odd bottles and paintings by a local artist of boats and harbors waiting hopefully to be bought. "Here, let's go sit in a corner so we can talk without people listening," Pat said. "You know everyone knows everyone else's business, or thinks they do, and when you're with me, they know why. It will be all over the island soon." I hoped she was joking, but I was relieved when we sat at a table in a corner.

Tom's table manners had gotten even worse in recent years, until he made me think of the hogs I had slopped at a child, snorting and grunting their way through a full trough. It embarrassed me to eat with him. He ate with his hands or a spoon, seeming to forget that there were other utensils. I thought his fingers were losing the ability to "sense," because so often they would be covered in mayonnaise, mustard, or ketchup. He chewed loudly, often with his mouth open, smacking his lips in a way I found repulsive. If he didn't use his hands to pick at his food, he used a spoon to eat things for which he should have used a fork. Sometimes it made sense: "How can I get the gravy, the sauce, if I don't use a spoon?" But I was worn-out by nagging at him and grateful I rarely ate with him at school, and that even more rarely we were asked out or had to attend a dinner at the school.

I looked around the crowded restaurant, seeing men in rubber boots, the tops folded down over their knees, their hands holding gigantic sandwiches. There were mothers with small children, and several older couples, but no one seemed to be noticing us, and there was no one there I knew. I felt much less pressure being in that room than I had for a long time and I thought, "It will be all right here, people won't mind Tom's table manners so much. We will be accepted more easily. We will be all right." By then Tom had inherited some money from his father, and I knew we could buy some time.

It was the Fourth of July weekend. The summer people were showing up and I rather enjoyed shocking them with our plans. Within a week we sold the house in Greenwich for a profit that gave us more money than we both made working six years as teachers. We were incredulous. Through Pat we bought a large house on the ocean in Seawall, a modern house with a huge living room that had been damaged in a storm so violent that we were told it wouldn't happen again in a hundred years. It had a little guest house we could rent. We told Sherman we wouldn't be returning to the school, and he didn't sound quite as unhappy as I had expected he would—but I didn't care.

We told the children what we were doing. They seemed excited, but of course they understood even less than we did about what it would mean to leave Greenwich and move to Maine. We went to meet the principal at the school they would attend. He seemed nice, a man our age who was comfortable with our children, and pleased to have them in his school. He said they should each skip a grade—even though they were already young for their classes—because of their high scores on tests. Within two weeks we had completely rearranged our lives. We had made changes so enormous, changes we should have considered and planned, and perhaps reconsidered. I do not know Tom's motives nor even fully my own, but I know I was mostly acting out of fear and exhaustion, looking for a safe place in which to hide.

We went to the Adirondacks for the rest of the summer. And we did something for which I can never forgive myself. We went to Greenwich to arrange the move, pick up things at school, say a few good-byes. I tried to call my advisees, students I had counseled for three years, and tell them I had to leave. But we didn't take our own children. They never had a chance to say good-bye to their friends, their school, their rooms, their house. And I can only apologize to them now, because at the time I didn't know what else to do. I thought it would be better for them to keep our family intact, to move together instead of staying in Greenwich and having them bear the shame of having a father who was fired from his job. But acting out of fear and shame is never a good motivation, and I wish we had not moved so quickly and that at least we had given the children a chance to say good-bye to things and places and people they loved.

I was like an animal, seeking a dark place in the cave, crawling farther and farther away, cutting loose the obligations and responsibilities, crawling in, deeper and deeper. I wish I had known who to talk to. I wish there had been someone older whom I trusted and to whom I could have gone for help. But there wasn't.

8

NOT THE WAY LIFE WAS
SUPPOSED TO BE

September 1979

When we pulled into the driveway of our new house in Maine, I looked over the seawall to the ocean, and saw the coast guard cutter slicing through the waves with a cargo of buoys and channel markers draped with seaweed and dangling mussels that it was bringing in for winter. I walked around the house admiring the huge living room with its cavernous cathedral ceiling, the rich Portuguese blue-and-white tile around the fireplace, the blue-gray slate floors. I walked into our bedroom and opened all the closet doors in my dressing room. Dressing room, I had never had a dressing room. I felt as if I were playing house, mimicking my mother.

Now I, too, owned a real house. I walked into our children's wing, two adjoining rooms with a connecting bath. The contractor would put a skylight in the large attic and a ladder to turn this space into a room for Stephen, and the children could share a playroom. The back rooms were dark and I started ripping down the chocolate-brown wallpaper, shredding it, though Tom reminded me that we hadn't even closed on the house and I didn't yet own it. We joked about having to glue the strips of torn paper back on the walls.

We chose the house for its site—three acres, with three hundred feet of shorefront, bordered by an extraordinary seawall of pink granite popplestones ground by eons of waves into soft shapes that belied their strength. I can still hear the *click, click, clicking* as waves jostled the rocks, a dancer with a million castanets. We could see Gott's Island and Little Cranberry, and, over the Western Way, boats passing to and from the inner harbors. The pictures outside our windows changed with the seasons and weather to include schooners like the three-masted *Victory Chimes* or the *Mary Day*, her red-orange sails burning sunset against the water. I saw many more coast guard cutters, their bows painted with crimson sashes like ushers at debutante parties, lobster boats with men in yellow so'westers, and yachts festooned with flying flags. Once I saw three houses moving across my horizon, binoculars revealed the sight really *was* three houses. Later I learned a summer acquaintance had bought antique Capes to string together as a shorefront perch on Somes Sound. Another time I watched as a lobster boat backed up toward the house. I couldn't understand why it was coming so close until I realized the fisherman couldn't control the boat and it was crashing against the rocks. I ran down to the water as he jumped off the boat and held it with his hands as it beat itself against the rocks and his right leg in its thick rubber boot, braced to buffer his boat. I called the coast guard, but they didn't come, and finally a friend of the fisherman's hovered his boat near the shore, threw a line, and towed him off. When I checked a few days later, I learned that the fisherman's leg had been broken in three places.

There was a lot for us to learn about living in this place and only our two Maine coon cats, Christofur, who was a gift from my brother, and Katadhin, whom we found in the local SPCA, could claim to be natives. They soon discovered that with teamwork they could fetch large dead fish from the pebbled shore, tugging on either end until they worked the fish over the seawall and deposited it on the cocoa mat outside the kitchen door. One day the children found a metal sphere beached on the rocks by the incoming tide. The more we looked, the more it seemed malevolent, like an old war bomb. I felt foolish but finally called the police, who told me it was just a Japanese fishing bobber. "Don't worry, ma'am," the young man said, and I wondered if they joked about me afterward to each other.

The first storm hit in November. I was standing in the kitchen washing the breakfast dishes when suddenly a wall of water rose over the seawall and crashed down on the rocks, lashing against the plate-glass windows that lined the front of the house. As I watched the black green water curling into white, my stomach rose and fell with it. I sucked in air, shocked by the power of what I had seen. For years later I would have nightmares about the house—that the foundation that supported it had washed away and the house teetered on sand, as the tide slipped in and out beneath it.

Again at first I thought we would be all right. We had inherited money from our parents. I had made money selling the house in Greenwich and now had a little rental income from the guest house on our new property, and I had even inherited a small income from my father's side of the family. His aunt had died, and because he, too, was dead, the money came to me. I thought we had enough so that we could work at jobs we enjoyed, jobs that would not put much pressure on Tom.

Tom loved running along the road that followed the ocean, although he missed the hills of Greenwich. We had a sauna installed in the garage and Tom used it and ran whenever he wanted to because neither of us had a job. I spent my time first building a small garbage house to deter the raccoons that assembled on the back porch for an unintended handout, then creating a garden in the sand next to the seawall by lugging eighty laundry baskets of seaweed to the site and mixing it with truckloads of leaves and dirt brought by a contractor. I added packets of poppy seeds, and one morning in spring I awoke to find a wave of orange poppies blooming in the sunshine like the fields in Oz, my very own intoxicant.

We decided to teach as substitutes in the local schools in hopes of learning about the high school and finding more permanent jobs. Tom quickly got a long-term job substituting for an English teacher who was on leave for several months. I got calls from several schools, always before six in the morning. It was the hardest teaching I had ever done. I had no idea about the rules and regulations of which there seemed to be many, didn't know the names of my students or colleagues, but slowly I began to get a feeling for the different schools. The high school students enjoyed trying to befuddle me. When I called roll the first day, saying, "Arthur Jacobs?," a large-boned boy with improbably wild curling hair like a copper scouring pad responded, "Heah."

"No, that's my name," the attentive, proper dark-haired boy sitting near him interjected.

"Oh, I see," I said, smiling at them. "Arthur Jacobs is such a great guy everyone wants to be Arthur Jacobs. Is that what I should call each of you? Do you all want his grades, too?" The students smiled back, nodding enthusiastically, all except the "real" Arthur Jacobs.

A few days later, at the end of homeroom period with another section of students, a boy with thick glasses and a round owl-like face sidled up and said in a slow monotone, "Now, don't you just love the go-karts? I just love the go-karts in Ellsworth. I just love going 'round and 'round." I looked at him, about to answer with a quip, until I saw a glaze cross his eyes that warned me something was wrong. So I said simply that I hadn't been there yet, but that I had seen the go-kart concession and I watched him as he continued talking. Then I noticed the other students slowly putting their books and belongings together, watching me and waiting to hear what I would say.

Finally, after he moved out the door, two of the boys came up to me saying, "That's Marky. He's a little 'teched,' you know. He loves those carts, but he doesn't mean no harm." And I thought how gentle they were with him and each other. When I walked into the large classroom for senior English, I was, however, appalled that the teacher had left mimeographed exercise sheets for the students about the placement of apostrophes, something Stephen had conquered in third grade in Greenwich. I distributed the papers and then walked up and down the rows, asking students if they needed help.

"I don't get this. I don't know what he means here," a girl said to me. She looked anxious and she was tapping her foot nervously against the desk leg. "I'm from Bass Harbor and I don't get this stuff," she added.

I hunched down so I could be at her eye level and said, "Well, let's just go through it and you tell me what you don't understand. You use apostrophes all the time when you speak, so you already 'get it,' you just have to put what you know on paper." It was so easy to work with these kids, but for months afterward a few of them called me to ask for help and Tom and I worried that the high school would not be very challenging for our own children.

There were so many things to learn that I didn't stop to ask how we were, how Tom was. Not having to earn a living, leaving a school where he was no longer welcome, not having his father wanting him to take on a more important job, all released the pressure on Tom, much like letting steam off a pressure cooker about to boil over. And it was easier for me to focus on Tom and the children because my mother and grandmother had died, my sister and brother were older, and I was no longer working full-time. Even nature was gentle with us; there was very little snow that first winter, and being in a new home and a new community filled me with hope.

As winter crawled to spring, Tom seemed less and less happy at the high school. He was impatient with students who paid little attention to anything in class but their girlfriends and boyfriends, discouraged by their ignorance and disinterest in ideas and literature. He was disappointed by the assignments the teacher had left, which lacked imagination or intellectual challenge, even for the advanced-placement students.

We had always taught in private schools and had never been certified to teach in a public school. We soon discovered that certain courses were mandatory for certification and we went to the University of Maine at Orono to speak to the dean of education. The dean was not welcoming. I told Tom he reminded me of Cerberus at the Gates of Hell, and he seemed to gloat when he told us that even with many years of experience, with master's degrees and former positions as department heads, Tom would need sixteen credits to teach English because his undergraduate degree was in philosophy, and I would need at least eight. Perhaps we would have tried to earn certification if the dean had made us feel like anything better than debris washed up on his shore—but he upset us so much we gave up and just continued substitute teaching, though we spent some time thinking about starting a school.

As we moved into this community, we were labeled differently than we had been before, and it was through our children that we communicated with our neighbors. After a few days at her new school Katherine said a girl named Amy had asked her over and that Amy and her mother and brother lived in a trailer in the nearby town. There was something in Katherine's voice, a little hesitation, that made me ask if she really wanted to go. "Yes," she said, but there was still something that made me say, "Fine, but I'll stay home all afternoon, so if you want me to come pick you up early, just call me. Do you know our number?"

When I went to fetch her, she said she had fun, but that Amy's mother yelled at them all the time and called them "fucking bitches." I was shocked until I remembered the parents in Greenwich who were drunk when they came to pick up their children. I could see the little freckle-faced boy at Stephen's party in the school gym who played with such abandon, and then, when his mother teetered in to get him, the smell of liquor a cloud billowing before her, how his face drooped like a flag at half-mast.

In my naïveté I decided to give a big birthday party for Katherine and another later for Stephen. When we lived in Connecticut, and I worried my children would be left out of parties, I spent a great deal of effort on their birthdays—splurging after my mother died and I could afford to. One year I created a fair, complete with ponies and clowns, the Good Humor man in his truck, fishing and wishing wells, games and prizes. I loved giving parties and did it so rarely that my parties for my children were a substitute for those I would have liked to give for myself. The first spring in Maine I told Stephen he could ask his class, about twenty-four fourth-graders, to his birthday. I sewed calico bags for the children to take home favors, appliquéing their initials, I bought and made little gifts, and planned an elaborate scavenger hunt and other games.

Stephen's classmates seemed a bit awed. I remember the little boy with eyes so wide the white encircled the irises like fried eggs. "Is this a mansion?" he asked. "Yes, this is a mansion," he answered himself, proud to have been to one.

Oh, no, I thought, I know mansions and this isn't one of them.

At one point during the party Tom suggested we take all the spare change in the house and scatter it around for the children to find, which seemed inappropriate to me. I realized then that in moving to Maine, we had been transformed from "poor teachers" to "rich summer people from away." The metamorphosis was so quick, without planning or thought on our part, that I hardly realized what had happened.

The contrasts between the life our children had known in Greenwich and in the summers in Maine were sometimes stark and painful. In Greenwich all of my children's friends seemed to live in larger houses than we did; now Stephen and Katherine saw real poverty for the first time. Stephen had told me before that Rosie, a classmate of his, sometimes smelled and always wore the same acid aqua dress with yellowing ruffles. One day he told me he had just learned that she lived with her father, her mother, her sister, and her brother in their rusting station wagon in a parking lot in town.

Slowly we settled in. The spring of our first year I got a job running a small museum; the pay was insulting and the work part-time, but it was interesting. In the early May morning, after our first winter, pale light brushed unfurling birch leaves and fern fronds on either side of the long bark-covered path from the parking lot. I walked from my truck to the museum, its distinctive yellow stone walls and red tile roof catching the sun. The quiet of morning was punctuated by chickadees, and a partridge thrummed like a lawn mower starting up. Set in the woods away from Bar Harbor, the museum was a tranquil island on an island, but in summer, when the buses disgorged their passengers, there was a constant stream of visitors flowing dutifully around the exhibits.

The museum was dark and cool, a hexagon lined with old-fashioned glass-covered wooden display cases and bisected by another set of cases. Four dioramas showed how Indians, not "Native Americans," had lived in Maine. There was a long dark hall leading to my office, where, ensconced with boxes of artifacts and records, I oversaw this legacy of a rich man's hobby, a whimsical collection of split ash baskets, porcupine quill work, and stone and bone artifacts from nearby sites.

I had been hired because I had worked at the Smithsonian and

Peabody museums, though only as a summer intern, and because I had a graduate degree, though it was in sociology. I didn't know a lot, and the head of the board of trustees, a formidable woman, thought I would be malleable and attentive. The longer I was there, the more I found I needed to attend to, and I began to see this museum as an artifact in itself of what was at best benign neglect and at worst malignant, an example of how small museums are run as fiefdoms.

One morning in midsummer I turned on the lights and pulled up the dark shades. As light filtered past the high windows, it gleamed on the cases, fading the objects within. When I opened the storage drawers under the display cases, the artifacts jiggled together, abrading as they had for years, so that their dust lined the drawers. I sat in my inner sanctum thinking of ways to acquire some money for this little treasure of a place so the artifacts could be properly cared for, or ways to bring the exhibits to schools and nursing homes. I was sitting at my desk when I got a phone call from Winfield Anderson, a summer resident of Northeast Harbor, a man of such meticulous pretension that he always made me feel as if my slip or a slipped pedigree were showing. "Barbara," he intoned. "I have something urgent I must talk with you about immediately. May I come to see you at your office?"

"Oh, of course, Winfield, I'm here. Should I come to you?"

"No, no, Barbara, this will be fine. I will be there in twenty-five minutes." Twenty-five minutes later Mary ushered him into my office. As he walked around admiring the books, which included a complete set of Jesuit papers from the 1500s, I tried to put him and myself at ease with small talk, saying, "You know, Win, I read that the Jesuits hated Indian cooking, they were scathing about it, but they liked finding lobsters walking the shores, though some were six feet long. Can you imagine finding such a monster?"

Finally he settled in a chair and looked straight at me, his bright blue eyes boring into me. "We have a problem. I am embarrassed to bring this up to you, but I don't know what else to do. It's Tom."

"Oh, no," I said too quickly. "I'm sorry." I had been waiting for this. I could see Tom as he tromped into the changing room at the pool, his sweatclothes leaving a trail of droplets, the layers upon layers of faded sweatpants and hooded sweatshirts, gathered like a hump over his back, his face red and contorted, snorting snot. I had been waiting for someone to complain. I had begged Tom not to go to the swim club after exercising because I was sure other members would be irritated. I had felt ashamed, but he had paid no attention.

"You see, Barbara, we think he has been stealing towels."

"Stealing towels?" I replied, startled. "Why would he do that? We have lots of towels at home."

"Well, we heard he was starting a boys' school or club," Win answered. "Then I thought maybe his background, maybe he had been poor all his life and thought he needed the towels."

"Oh, Winfield. I am so embarrassed, I feel awful. No, I haven't seen towels at home except the ones I bought. We were thinking of starting a school, but certainly hadn't gotten to the point of thinking about towels." My mind was racing. "Towels. Why would he steal towels? This makes no sense at all."

Win looked even more serious and then he delivered the *coup de grâce*. "I'm afraid we can't have him use the club for the rest of the season."

"Win, will you talk to him, please?" I replied. "I get put in the middle and it's really hard for me. He would listen more to you. I've talked with him about how he dresses and using the club showers after running. I just feel awful about this. I've been going to the club since I was a child and I don't ever want anyone in my family to do something that makes other people there uncomfortable. But I can't believe he would steal towels. It just makes no sense to me."

Then Win added, "I was married before. I know sometimes we marry someone, and we find we have made a mistake. With Trudy I have found someone with whom I can share so much, be really intimate. I hope that will be possible for you."

And I thought, This is too strange. I hardly know Win. He is so pompous, sometimes he looks like a cormorant swimming around with its beak in the air, but he has articulated what I have been thinking. "Thank you Win," I answered, my stomach tight, my hands holding on to the desk for balance. "Thank you for coming to tell me this. I don't know exactly what I can do, but I'll try to deal with Tom."

Later Tom and Win talked and Tom said he might have taken a towel or two inadvertently, but that he once flunked the club manager's daughter in English because she combed her boyfriend's hair throughout class rather than paying attention. Now he thought she and her father were trying to get him in trouble. A vendetta perhaps? I was eager to believe him.

Perhaps as a result of this incident, sometime afterward Tom started seeing another therapist. Again, the man seemed kind but ineffectual. I had so little understanding of therapy then that I was relieved Tom wasn't seeing a shrink—just a therapist. When I accompanied him one time to see the therapist, I remember feeling embarrassed to be there, and again this somehow reinforced my own feeling that I must be healthy if I didn't need such help. Although Tom saw this man for a long time, he didn't talk about the therapy except to say that the therapist thought he was right to leave the school in Connecticut, that the head of the school had made working there impossible, had set unfair expectations, and picked on him and that he was dealing with his mother's death. And again I wanted to hear anything that made me think Tom was all right.

I spent part of most days at the museum. Tom picked the children up after rowing class, but I was not sure what else he did during the day. I knew he spent time with our neighbors, Brian and Francine, who had just started a real-estate brokerage business. One night he mentioned that Brian had suggested that we buy a building in Southwest Harbor and turn it into a restaurant. Brian had just listed an older house with a view of the harbor that was zoned commercial and wanted us to see it. It was pale green with white trim, hardwood floors, nice moldings. In hindsight I realize it also had small, rather cramped rooms, poor plumbing, and lacked the electrical power to run a commercial kitchen. At the time I thought about what fun it would be to have our own business, that having company every night in the restaurant would force Tom to be sociable, to find something to do now that he had given up teaching in the local school and we had abandoned the idea of starting our own a school.

We called SCORE, part of the Small Business Administration designed to help budding entrepreneurs, and were assigned to a man who had been in the restaurant business for over sixty years. Guido had grown up in his family's restaurant in Greece, busing tables, taking reservations, waiting tables, cooking, ordering the food; he knew everything about the restaurant business. He made an appointment to see us, but a few days before he was due to visit our prospective restaurant his wife called to say he had to have some medical tests and would get back to us. A few weeks later SCORE called to say that Guido was not well and they would assign someone else. As more time went by, we got more and more involved: thinking about work to be done, learning how to buy linens and flatware, what kind of tables to order, thinking about flowers and linen napkins. I could see us in the restaurant, Stephen and Katherine busing tables, then waiting on customers. Tom as maître d' . . .

One day the phone rang and it was Guido; it turned out the

doctors had mixed his X rays with those of another patient and he didn't have cancer. How bizarre this reprieve must have been for him, but how much worse for the other patient. Guido said he would be down to see us in the next few days. By this time I felt so confident that I wondered why we needed him and I thought it would be fun to show him all the things we were planning to do and have him nod his approval.

Guido arrived in a large Cadillac. He was a very short round man with big glasses and a large nose who exuded an aura of garlic and confidence. We soon realized he was a man of few words. He got out of the car, shook hands, and said, "Now I look." We walked him around the property. He tucked his hand in front, like Napoleon, and walked, firmly and slowly around the building, nodding, admiring the view, his face blank. We went inside and he walked through the rooms, upstairs, downstairs, the attic, the basement; he saw it all. He poked like a detective into every space, examining each room carefully.

Finally, when he was satisfied, he turned to us, sighed, and said, "Is beautiful. Is beautiful place. I love it. It could be a great restaurant."

I beamed, feeling proud that this old pro approved our choice and that we had "done well."

But then he added, "You spend a hundred thousand dollars, you make it beautiful, you break your heart. Whatcha gonna do when the chef hands you the apron?"

I felt my heart sinking like a bad meal through my throat into my stomach, where it clotted in a lump. I could feel it breaking right then because I knew he was right. I knew we didn't know what we were doing and that Tom would never be a maître d' and I would never manage a restaurant. "Whatcha gonna do?" Guido repeated. "You nice kids, you do somethin' else, okay? This business, it break your heart even if you know what you doing," and then he turned, opened the door of his solid, black car, shut it with a deep thunk, and drove away.

A bit later Tom told me that Brian had been talking with him about getting a real-estate license and about joining the brokerage. It began to seem like a good idea to both of them, as Tom could work when he wanted to, had grown up with the business, and knew a lot of people. Brian was brilliant and mercurial, his highs too high and his lows reducing him to hiding at home while his wife ran the business, but we didn't know that then. He had grown up on Swan's Island, one of twelve children, who were sewn into their long johns in November and cut loose in April. When he was in the army in Paris he met Francine, wooed and won her, and brought her back to the island, introducing her to a life of hardship and poverty. The real-estate business was a new venture, newer than we realized, but an opportunity for all of us. Tom convinced me to get a license as well so I could use it to supplement teaching and running the museum, and so we studied at night for our licenses and joined the agency in late spring of our second year in Maine.

We were struggling to find our place in this new world, but it was hard. We decided to rent the house and live in the guest house for six weeks because the rental income was very good, and we went to live in the house we shared with my siblings for the last two weeks of June before moving into our guest house for July. But there were repercussions I could not have anticipated. That fall my younger sister called to say, "Barb, we don't think it's fair that you rent your house and live in ours."

I felt as if I had been hit in the stomach. I could only stammer, "But it's my land, too. How am I supposed to use it?" Adding plaintively, "Do you all think that?"

"Yes," she answered, blunting my hope that it was just her. "You can have picnics there," she added. I thought about how I had sat on Mummy's bed with her shortly after Desie died and she had told me she wanted to sell The Point, because she had been happiest there with Desie.

"It's the one place they couldn't get him," she said. "When he was there he was really with me, not on call, not at work, and they didn't bother him."

"Mummy," I answered, "I understand, but it's not worth much and I know Des and Joan and Frankie love it, and I love it."

She turned and looked at me, saying, "I'll give it to you and then you and Des, Joan, and Frankie can build a house on it."

I thought, too quickly, and blurted back, feeling again unworthy of this gift, "No, don't give it just to me, that will make the others angry."

"All right," she replied. "I'll give it to the four of you."

Now I thought, How stupid I have been. I hadn't had the money to build a house with the others, all I had was my share of the land, and now I was being told I couldn't even use that. I thought about how I'd tried to work on the house and land, planting, making a pathway to the house like a long Japanese garden. I was too hurt to fight. I told my brother and sisters that if I couldn't use the property, I would sell it to them. I could hardly bear the pain of losing something I loved more than anything in my life except my children. But I turned my back on my sisters and brother, and on the land. I didn't drive down the road past their driveway for more than ten years. When I did so again, I could only accept the tears and sadness that followed me. Only when I was freeing myself from my marriage was I able to go back to the house and the land. Even today, when I think about this time in my life, I cannot quell the tears, and they flow up from a well so deep in me I have not yet found the source. Worst, perhaps, of all was something I did not understand then. In further isolating myself from my family, I was almost totally cut off from any balancing weight in my life; I was standing on one side of the scale with Tom, and we were sinking. Years later when my brother and older sister and I had reconciled and become friends, they told me how difficult it was for them to share the house with Tom, that they found him arrogant and controlling and they resented his intrusion into their lives.

★ ★ ★

We were, however, beginning to have some success in real estate. We sold a piece of land to a friend in Northeast Harbor,
then our first house to a young couple, Chuck and Gloria, and
quite quickly after that, a shorefront house in Northeast Harbor.
Tom seemed to enjoy putting people together with property and
had a very good eye for seeing what could be done with a piece
of land or a house that needed remodeling. We began to buy
small pieces of land or houses ourselves and work on them, selling them and doing well with the projects, a sidecar to brokerage that we developed later into a much more substantial and
profitable business.

The spring of the first year we worked as real-estate brokers was
my twentieth reunion from boarding school. I looked forward to
the three-day celebration because I had had many very good
friends in the class, substitutes even then for my family. I hadn't
spoken to any of them in many years, but they still meant a great
deal to me. Perhaps that was the reason Tom said, "But you can't
go to that. You have to stay for Chuck and Gloria's wedding. It's
going to be very important for business that you are there. How
can you go when you're just starting out in real estate? You need
to be at that party." He nagged at me until I backed down, in part
because it was easier not to go to the reunion by myself; the iso-
lation of my life had worn down my thin layer of confidence. So
we went to the party, where we knew hardly anyone. As we
drifted around the edge of the crowd of people, Tom seemed
pasted to me. I tried to disengage from him so I could get into
conversations with other people and "work the crowd," which
was, he had said, the reason we were there. But he was like a
limpet and I never talked with anyone else. Later we learned that
Gloria was studying for her real-estate license, and all her relatives
we had hoped to cultivate would be her customers.

A few years later we gave a big party in August for summer
people we knew from the other side of the island and a few ac-

quaintances we had made where we now lived. We knew it was a trek from the other side—the fashionable side of the island—so Tom agreed to offer dinner in addition to drinks to make it worth the trip. We invited everyone we knew. I loved mixing people from different parts of my life, people I thought wouldn't know each other but might find a common thread. The party was a great success even though many of the people we asked did not come. The next day, when I was showering at the club, I overheard one of our guests talking to a friend.

"I went to the most amazing party. It really was fun; you would have been amused. I was talking to the nicest man and he turned out to be my plumber! I had never met him before."

I had prepared enough food so that I felt comfortable that we were "spreading" an elegant "board." There was more than enough for people and they seemed to enjoy eating what I had cooked. But Tom was angry that there were leftovers and told me I had been wasteful. Over the years it became harder and harder to give a party. At the last party we gave, when we had moved to the pond, we assembled many of our clients, and Tom noted afterward that we had brought together more wealth than the GNP of many countries in the world. Many of our clients were rich and famous. Tom seemed to soak up confidence from them and delighted in counting the millionaires and even a billionaire sitting together in our living room. At one point, when they had eaten all the salad, I had to run up to the garden, half a mile away, and pluck lettuce from the soil, jamming it into a garbage bag, trying to shake off the surprised slugs, and racing back to wash it hastily and throw it in the salad bowl, because I had skimped on food to placate Tom. But that was the last party, and it was really just for business. After that we gave a small party each year at Christmas for the people who worked with us, and then none at all, taking them instead to a local restaurant for lunch.

I had begun to realize that we weren't being asked out as much as we had been when we first moved to the island. I understood that in winter people just didn't give as many parties—but in summer? One day I was talking to a summer acquaintance who said, "I'm so sorry you couldn't come to the party last night. We really had fun. I think you would have liked talking with a man there who is a sociologist interested in island culture."

"I'm sorry. I didn't know you were having a party. I would have loved to come," I responded.

"But I called Tom," she replied. "I asked him and he said you were busy."

"Oh," I answered, trying to cover for him, "I guess maybe he thought we had plans, he must have gotten mixed up."

When I asked Tom for an explanation, he said, "I'm sorry, I just forgot," which I accepted. But then I thought about other times people had said they missed us at a party and I realized he must have thrown out invitations, refused them when people called, and not given me messages from friends he thought were going to ask us out.

"Tom," I said, "I think we got an invitation to the MacHenrys. I would have liked to go. What happened to it?"

"Why would you want to go to their house?" he replied, frowning. "That is a hideous house. I don't know how the town can allow someone to build such an ugly house." He turned to me, laughing, and added, "It should be zoned commercial—it looks like a row of stores."

"Tom, that's not the point, " I said with irritation. "They invited us and I never saw the invitation."

"They probably sent it to the office and I threw it out with the junk mail," he replied.

If I answered the phone when someone called, I learned quickly that I had to say I would check and get back to him or her because if I accepted an invitation, Tom would get so upset. "How can you do that? How do you know I want to go? I don't want to go to their house. How am I going to go running? I don't want to sit around with a bunch of silly people and make small talk." He would get red in the face and stomp around the house, pouting. But perhaps most difficult of all were the times we did go to parties.

We rarely went anywhere unless Tom thought it was necessary for business. And if, after all Tom's complaints, we actually went to a party, increasingly he followed me, hovering by my shoulder, a shadow I could not evade. If I managed to slip away for a moment, he followed me with his eyes. He looked at me whenever he talked with someone else, so that the joy I might have felt in going was leeched away before we got there. Increasingly, he criticized what I ate or drank, making me feel ashamed and embarrassed to be with him, and I wondered how much he was drinking, because his nose and face often became very red.

Once, as we drove down a quiet street in Northeast Harbor to a party, I looked at the elegant Victorian houses lining the road, houses and their occupants I had known since childhood. There was the parsonage of the Episcopalian church named Magnum Donum. A big gift, yes indeed, bought recently by a family from Washington. Then the dark, almost forbidding house set back from the road, where my friend and her family had summered for many years after her father was killed in an avalanche. Then the surprisingly Teutonic house now owned by an equally Teutonic man and his wife who was rumored to serve at her dinner parties roadkill that she scraped from the highway in front of her house. How very strange were all the rumors flooding through this town, regardless of the season. We parked near a handsome yellow Victorian with white trim owned by some acquaintances, the newly appointed head of a major company who would, over the years, pull it out of a deep financial morass, and his always elegant and kind wife. I thought how much I liked and respected these people and hoped we would have a good time at their party.

"Hi, Ben, hi, Brenda. Oh, you look so beautiful. I brought you some lilies from the garden. There are so many, but you have so many here, too."

"Welcome," they both said, smiling. "How great you could come. Just come on in. The flowers are wonderful. You grew those? Barbara, you're a genius. Now go get a drink and something to eat." As we passed into the living room, I watched the lights gleaming off the women's jewelry, the silver vases, and photograph frames. The flashing colors in paintings and crystal reminded me of the times I had sat in the summer church watching the light playing through the rose window, rivaled by the light reflected back from the diamonds and sapphires, rubies and emeralds of the parishioners.

"What do you want to drink?" Tom asked. "A glass of Chardonnay, please," I replied. Tom edged through the guests and came back with the glass. I was talking to three sisters I had known since we played together as children. We were talking about children and their parents, tennis and sailing, and I wished Tom would go join someone else, but he wouldn't leave me. After a while I said, "I'm going to talk to Jonathan and Betsy over there. I haven't seen them for years," and cautiously I moved away.

"Barbara," Jonathan said, "how are you? I heard you were living here year-round. What's it like? Oh, you've finished your drink. What can I get you?"

"Chardonnay," I answered. He came back quickly to join us and handed me the glass. Suddenly Tom was there again, hovering by my side,

"Isn't that enough? You already had one glass," he growled. He frowned at me and pursed his lips, and I felt like a little child who had just been chastised. I could see Jonathan's eyes tighten and Betsy was staring down at her feet.

"Oh, really, Tom, don't be silly," I replied. "I've only had one glass. I don't think that's a problem. Here, do you want half?" I asked, and I poured out some of my wine and turned away again, trying to find another group to join.

Just then a waitress passed the hors d'oeuvres. I knew her from town, Betty, a woman my age with beautiful blue eyes but a lined face, a face telling of long hours cleaning houses and coping with a painful marriage. "Betty, how great to see you." Here we were no longer equals, though I tried to make it seem we were.

"Baabra," she said, "try the shrimp and bacon. Some good that. Mary made them this morning." As I reached for a canapé, Tom was there glaring at me.

"Haven't you had enough of those things? They're just fat, you know."

I withdrew my hand as if bitten by a snake and blushed. "I'm sorry, Betty, I guess I won't just now," I muttered, and backed away from the tray. At this point I gave up trying to get away from Tom and realized it was just easier to leave the party.

I began to feel as if I were playing a game, at parties and at home. How many hors d'oeuvres could I sneak before he caught me, how many glasses of wine could I drink? But when I realized I was eating and drinking more than I wanted to only as a way of subverting Tom, I was able to swallow my self-destructive pride and stop. Sometimes when he "caught" me and said something that humiliated me in front of other guests, I laughed and tried to deflect the pain and embarrassment with a joke, absorbing the hurt as I had learned to do when I was a child. Sometimes I told him in the car going home how he had hurt and embarrassed me, sometimes I even got him to say he was sorry and that he wouldn't do it again. But he always did and I always swallowed my hurt and anger because I feared a humiliation even more public.

Though staying at a party was painful, it was also awkward when Tom wanted to leave early. "But you haven't had dessert yet," the hostess would remonstrate.

"Sorry, Tom has to get up early. I'm so sorry we have to leave," I'd say, and yet it was also a relief to leave. Sometimes we simply backed out of a cocktail party, not thanking the host and hostess because it seemed so rude to leave that early. But why, I asked myself, why does he have to get up so early? Why does he have to go to bed by eight-thirty? Why does he have to be home? And slowly it dawned on me that the pattern of his day, the way in which he used the time in a day, was essentially one of avoidance. If he got up very early, he could have hours of the morning to himself. If he went to the office early, he could read the paper and write letters to friends for hours before anyone else showed up for work. If he left the office at two-thirty to go running, he had the rest of the afternoon and early evening to himself before I came home from work.

I realized Tom was retreating into his own time and space, making it difficult for me to have any life with friends or family, to have any relationships with people that were not based on business. My own fears and insecurities made me vulnerable, and I began to feel as if I had no role or value for people except as a broker. There was no one to whom I could turn and honestly say how frightened and miserable I was, so it was a relief to realize eventually that we simply weren't being asked anywhere.

After living in the big house on the ocean for two years, we began to dislike its coldness. I am a very good gardener but I could not fight the wind that beat against the house and land, I could not escape its inevitability. One night, during a particularly loud gale, the house felt like a bellows, pumping air in and out. The walls shook and creaked and I could feel the headboard moving as the house breathed hard. Though we planted twelve large spruce to buffer the house and gardens, the wind sucked the moisture out of everything. I loved looking out the windows, but not cleaning the salt spray that traced patterns like dried snowflakes across them. I loved watching the few birds, seagulls and occasionally osprey and eagles, but it seemed the birds and animals, like year-round people, knew enough not to live on the ocean. It was a hard place—and I began to feel the moisture and life being pulled out of me—much as I had when driving through the desert in Israel, a palpable desiccation.

We decided to sell the house and move into town and were lucky to accomplish this easily. We bought two properties with the proceeds: one a small house in the town, which we began to fix up, the other a large summer house in Northeast Harbor. Pat, the broker who had sold us our first house, had called one day, saying, "Hey, kids, there's a real opportunity down the street from you. A man who is the black sheep of his wealthy family just wants to dump his house because his neighbor, you know who I mean, well, she is nosy and nasty and she sits there all day with binoculars and stares at him. And now he's bought a semi. Can you imagine— a semi in Northeast Harbor? It's parked in his driveway and she is really pissed. So he wants to sell. It's a great house. Can you come see it?"

"We'll be there in five minutes," we answered. The house was a large white Victorian, sitting next to the Fleet parking lot. Pat was right; we knew it was a tremendous opportunity—so we bought it that afternoon, moved our furniture, inherited from Mummy and Desie, into it like a setting for a play, and sold it that summer for twice what we had paid. We called it "Flying Cloud," not only because it rather looked like one but because an ancestor of Tom's had commissioned the clipper ship *Flying Cloud* and doubled his money when he sold it while it was sitting on the ways.

As my brother-in-law once said, "Any fool could make money in this market," and we proved him to be right.

That fall we moved into a little house on a central street in the village which was fun at first. The kids could walk to school and seemed to enjoy their new proximity to friends. Living in a less pretentious house seemed easier because it was less offensive to our neighbors and the children in Stephen and Katherine's school. But living in a town where Tom was doing his running was difficult. Everyone recognized him and his bizarre way of dressing, particularly when he was exercising. Too soon, when he walked down the main street, teenagers would yell out as he passed, "Hey there Tommy," and laugh. Sometimes they mumbled things under their breath, which I tried to ignore. When Tom had substituted at the high school and had a hard time teaching adolescents who were not interested in writing well or reading, he had the courage to give them the grades they deserved, but that didn't make him a popular teacher. The catcalls upset and embarrassed me and I worried about their effect on the children. I began to think that even here, in this little town, where people tolerated and accepted eccentricity, still, even here, we could not escape reaction to Tom's behavior. Again I thought about leaving him and taking the children to live somewhere else, but I didn't know where to go; I had cut loose the mooring I had, however fragile, in Greenwich, and I was drifting.

I don't remember if Tom was still seeing the therapist he had found after we moved to Maine, a kind man who counseled people from his tiny home office off the island. Perhaps Tom had already stopped going for his weekly sessions by the time we bought the house in town. As I look back, I realize that Tom drifted in and out of therapy, moving in reaction to currents within and around him. And perhaps because his therapy seemed to accomplish so little to change his behavior, I did not mark the times he was seeing a therapist. Living in town meant that more people saw Tom, and saw him as strange. There were certainly other people in the village and on the island who were considered to be eccentric and it hurt me to feel that Tom was one of them.

Then it seemed that every day Stephen was coming home from school with his chin wobbling. The school had put him in eighth-grade classes, though he should only have been in the sixth grade, and chronologically he should have been in the fifth. One day he said, tears shining in his eyes, "I can't ask questions in school anymore."

"Why?" I asked.

"Well, Sammy asked Mr. Clark how Indians shaved their beards. Mr. Clark told us that they filed down clamshells to a sharp edge and used them. But I know that's wrong. So I raised my hand and I said, 'But, Mr. Clark, Indians didn't have beards.' He was really mad at me."

I thought of all the books he had read—books I used when I taught classes about Native Americans in Greenwich, books he had picked up and enjoyed ever since he was a small child. One time, when he was in the first grade, I saw him carrying around *One Flew Over the Cuckoo's Nest,* and I thought about taking it away from him. But one of the best things Mummy ever did for me was to let me read whatever I wanted, even though her friends criticized her for it. She gave me the freedom to absorb what I could. I read *Andersonville* when I was in the sixth grade, horrified by the conditions the prisoners of war suffered. How could you wash a sheet in a cup of water? How could you endure the cold and heat, the lack of food and water, the lack of privacy? I wondered. I remember her friends talking with her while they played bridge, "I really don't think it is appropriate for a girl her age to read such books. She's going to have nightmares." But Mummy had stood up to them and I was grateful. I let Stephen read his book, and a week later when I noticed he was reading *Life on the Mississippi,* I asked him why he stopped reading Ken Kesey's classic about the mental institution.

"I thought it was a bird book," he replied, and I sighed, relieved that Stephen had edited his own reading.

But again, we were isolated. As Stephen once said, "What am I, Mom? I'm not a year-round person, and I am not a summer person."

"You are a year-round summer person," I answered, because that was, in fact, what we were called, but in many ways life on Mount Desert Island was a no-man's-land. We were not part of any community, and increasingly lived unto ourselves. One day, as I was running along the road that paralleled the sea, the road I learned was the most expensive to maintain in the state because it was so frequently washed over with boulders deposited by a jesting sea, a man I knew slowed his car and stopped to talk with me.

After a while he said, "Surprised to see you out here alone. Seems your husband is so jealous he never lets you out of his sight."

"Oh, I don't think so," I replied, feeling confused and defensive. "I certainly never give him reason to be jealous," and I wondered what the man meant.

I was more and more worried that Stephen was being hurt by being placed so far ahead of his class and by the comments he heard about Tom. Stephen's best friend, a thin blond boy who was a genius at math, moved when his father, who was head of the local coast guard base, was transferred. There were a few other boys he liked to fish or catch frogs with, who lived in the nearby trailer park. But too many others we later read about in "Police Beat"— caught driving drunk, using and selling drugs, driving to endanger, wrecking cars, abusing their spouses, stealing, and committing fraud. It was an extraordinary record for a class from a small town. I didn't know why Katherine seemed less vulnerable, perhaps because there were many more children in her class with whom she became friends.

I called the head of admissions at the only boarding school we knew that accepted eighth-graders. "I have a problem," I said. "It's a wonderful problem in some ways. We have a son who is very bright and the local school doesn't really know what to do with him. He's only in the sixth grade but we want to think ahead."

"Why don't you come and see us?" the man suggested.

When, soon after, Tom and I waited outside the admissions office, sitting in the deep chairs, I thought about how much I hoped that boarding school would be for Stephen the reprieve that it had been for me. After at least an hour Stephen and Mr. Gray, the man I had spoken to, emerged from his office; Stephen's face was bright pink and his eyes were shining. I was afraid the interview had not gone well, but Mr. Gray turned to us, saying, "You might think about sending Stephen here next year. We'll talk soon," and soon afterward we received a letter accepting Stephen into the eighth grade. I cried from a mixture of relief and sadness when I read the letter. I never wanted to send my children to boarding school, but I gave up being a part of Stephen's daily life because I hoped that being in a school with intellectual peers could give him the same warmth and delight I had felt when I went to boarding school and escaped my own cold house.

With Stephen going to boarding school we knew we needed a steady income, and somewhat resigned, we also realized that we were real-estate agents not teachers and had better try to work for the best firm we could. We left Bob and Francine and moved to the most prestigious firm on the island, a firm that had been in business for over a hundred years serving the affluent summer community, the one from which we had bought our first house. After a few months the head of the company offered us a chance to do the summer rentals, which coincidentally was expected to bring in about the same amount of money as Stephen's tuition, so we accepted the offer, which gave us a steady income and, more important, a steady supply of new clients.

Although we had been brought up in the same way as many of our clients, serving their prejudices and pretensions was a strain for me. I remember sitting at lunch with a Mrs. Holliston, the plump first wife of a Southern executive who had traded her in for a more recent edition. "Barbara," she said, "it's so good to work with you. You know just what I like, we have just the same taste." "Thank you, Gladys," I replied. "I love what you've done with the house. It's so light and cheerful—not like some of the old cottages that are so dark you can't appreciate them." "You know, Barbara, I wanted to do that for the tenants so they would have a lovely month in the house. But I worry sometimes about who might be there. What would you do if you had unsuitable people, people who couldn't join the club? I wouldn't want anyone un-suitable." I knew who she meant by people who might not feel comfortable at the club—Jews, blacks, and Catholics—and I hated her automatic assumption that I agreed with her. It made me angry and frustrated when people called who were rude and abrupt to our secretary and then unctuous or sticky-sweet with us. So many times I wanted to say, "You hopelessly insensitive bigot, what do you mean by insulting people like that, including me?" and then turn on my heel and never look back. But I had to make the money for Stephen's tuition, and I could not afford to tell them what I felt about them. We had made money selling our own houses, but real estate was a precarious business, and as we had more money, we only seemed to spend more.

Over the years I began to see our business as a yoke around my neck. Tom didn't worry about spending money; he seemed to think it would always appear when we needed it. I was always worried about money and was reassured by his nonchalance. We were two poles standing far apart, neither grounded in a secure foundation. We lived from closing to closing, from project to pro-ject.

As time went by, Tom became increasingly conscious of his social connections, trading on his father's well-established real-estate business in Georgetown, and on connections to Princeton. Years ago he had angrily told the *Social Register* they had no right to put us in their book, but now we needed them for business. Tom asked me to write a letter telling them that my progenitors had donated the nails to build the original Yale College, were colonial governors of Connecticut, that one was Yankee Doodle Dandy himself, and that Tom's ancestors included a congressman from Kansas and the great theologian Jonathan Edwards. He decided I should leave out Jesse James.

Increasingly he seemed to think that his connections to rich and famous people gave him status, and so many times he would include references to such people in his conversations, dropping so many names I thought he seemed ridiculous. Of course, to many of the people we dealt with, this gave assurance that they were in good hands, but to others, particularly people not so "well connected," it must have seemed insensitive and offensive. Worst of all, I could hear myself doing the same thing.

I was not sorry to leave the big house on the water, or the houses we bought from the profits. I was excited to have found a place I really thought could be home—Blagdon Pond Farm, encompassing 28.9 acres of land with 1,792 feet on a mile-long pond, the opposite shore owned and protected by the national park. No one else lived on the pond year-round and the land was so varied that it offered many habitats for birds and animals, and for plants I could grow. I fell in love with it immediately.

One day, just before we moved to the farm, I was talking with our neighbor in Southwest Harbor. Though she had never been a close friend, we were from the same summer community and she had lived on the island year-round for many years. She had been a guide for us when we first moved to the island. Now she said, "I don't know how you can stand moving so much. Isn't it bad for the kids?"

"No," I replied. "I don't think so. I don't think it is the place that matters so." Besides, I thought to myself later, we'd made a lot of money and now we could pay to send Stephen to one of the best schools in the country. But I also realized that Stephen had lived in nine houses and he was only twelve.

I grew to love the land on Blagdon Pond, feeling I knew it like my own body. I can today recall the names of birds, animals, and flowers I saw and the places where I found them, all the things I loved, now gone from my life except in memory: hairy avens with their rose bell flowers tucked between ferns on the path to the beech grove, the fox denning some years above the driveway, and others on the hill overlooking the little bait pond, a birch and poplar woods where the pileated woodpecker gouged enormous holes in the rotting wood; the upper field where once, driving home at night in a snowstorm, we saw a gigantic stag, poised with his head raised, his antlers glowing in our headlights. I found places where the deer had been scared and left the scent of musk from their hooves to warn other deer of danger. I planted trout lily on the path I cut through the woods, lady slipper in the woods near the little stream, Wapato duck potato and wild rice in the marsh around the little pond, wild rhododendrons and azalea in the woods. Was it there that Katadhin found the family of skunks on parade through the woods, or over there that one afternoon I heard rustling in the fall leaves and stopped still as the sound came closer and closer, louder and louder, thinking a hunter or large animal was headed my way? Suddenly I saw a raccoon out looking for food, so intent that he didn't detect me, and finally when he was only three feet away, I said, "Well, good afternoon. Are you out for a walk, too?" in a conversational tone because I was afraid if he bumped into me, he would be so frightened he would attack.

On the hill paralleling the driveway I planted thousands of daffodils and snowdrops and squills, and in winter skied over them. One time, while I was watching the pond from this vantage point, a dark vole walked over my skis and stopped to look at the view from this perspective. The eagles and osprey soared over us, and in our first spring we saw a cloud of tree swallows swooping overhead. The Soil Conservation Service sent out a man who helped me devise a plan for caring for the land, and I planted wild plums, olive, and other berry-bearing bushes and trees to provide cover and food for birds and animals. It was my own little paradise. The work consumed me, particularly after Katherine also went to boarding school—so each weekend instead of going out or having dinner with friends, I worked on the property. I rarely spent money on myself, but I spent a great deal on my land.

One day the phone rang and a man who said he was the CEO of a major real-estate development company, owned by the family of a summer resident I had heard of, told me he was interested in having us start our own development company on the island. I was shocked. They wanted us? We would have our own office, have all the advice and support of their huge resources? I felt like Adam being touched by the hand of God. It was an extraordinary opportunity, one we were thrilled to take. Over the next two years we worked with this man, a very kind and generous person, but as the real-estate market and the economy declined, tensions developed between us and eventually we parted ways. But the parting only helped us to stand more firmly on our own feet, and we decided to work through our own company in real-estate brokerage, rentals, and construction. The pressures Tom and I had felt as our relationship with the developer deteriorated, and the problems created by a poor economy, made our life difficult. We had very little experience running a business and relied on our young bookkeeper so heavily that it was not until too late that we realized she had given us bad advice and we were in debt. Fortunately we could pay what we owed by taking out a line of credit on the farm, but the pressure at times seemed almost unbearable to me. Early one morning during the time when I thought we might go bankrupt, I walked down our long driveway, wrapping my arms around my chest to hold in my sobs, wanting to scream and howl like the rabbit I had heard a few nights before, caught by an owl or coyote.

During the years we lived on Mount Desert Island the toe Tom had broken in Greenwich became increasingly painful for him.

Over time it turned inward and his foot was hobbled so he stumbled. The foot developed calluses and hurt him a great deal and he couldn't run or play tennis well anymore. A specialist he went to in Bangor told him he needed an operation, which would mean that he couldn't exercise for six weeks. Tom's fear of losing control over his body was worse than the daily pain, or the threat that the foot would further deteriorate, and he refused the operation. Instead, he began soaking his foot throughout the day, filling the gray wastebasket at his office desk with cool water, and sitting with his foot in the bucket, or at home, bathing the foot in the living room and soaking it. Then, as the foot developed calluses to protect tender places not designed to bear weight, he had to file the calluses every night. Soon the coffee table in front of the television was piled with metal files with blue plastic handles, sometimes ten or twenty of them, piled like a cairn to mark his pain. As his foot deteriorated further, and he withdrew into himself, he lost more weight and became physically weak. When he crossed a room or an open space, he hugged the walls. In a pathetic shuffle he moved along the wall, holding door frames and chair backs, hobbling to his destination like a very old man. The big toe had grown completely over the second toe and the foot was red and purple.

Sometimes I felt as if I were watching an overloaded truck struggling up a steep hill, seeing it slide back, rev its motor and regain ground but inevitably failing, dragged back down by the weight of its burden. I had tried so hard to convince Tom to see a doctor when he first broke the toe, and then over the years watched him suffer. I had thought I understood how important running was to him because it was the only way he could deal with his circulatory problem. But I hadn't really. I hadn't acknowledged that running was just one symptom of an overwhelming obsession that controlled him and made him try to control everything and everyone around him. Now, as I watched him hobble around the office, or stumble slowly down the driveway in a pathetic mockery of his former athleticism, I felt deeply sad, not only for myself but for him, for the accumulated devastation he had wrought on his own body.

Over the years we had grown more distant from each other physically. I felt increasingly self-conscious around him, feeling always that he was critical of my body and didn't want to touch me, and I was relieved he didn't. I could always feel myself contracting, literally holding myself in when he touched me, because I thought he would think I was fat. We fell into a pattern of almost ritualized and infrequent sex—which often ended abruptly. The prelude was always a dinner during which I could eat as much as I wanted to, and drink more than I wanted, without fearing Tom's criticism. Sometimes the liquor washed away my revulsion, sometimes it could not.

After Katherine left for boarding school we gave up any attempts to eat together and fell into a routine of cooking and eating separately. I struggled to prepare small but good meals for myself and tried not to notice the little bowls of scraps of cheese and vegetables covered in ketchup that Tom ate. Inured to his daily habits of spitting, chewing ice, leaving a trail of ketchup on the kitchen cabinets, doorframes, and upholstery, and spending interminable amounts of time in the bathroom, I hardly noticed the grotesquerie of our life together. I only knew I hated being by myself with him. Perhaps strangest of all Tom's habits was that he constantly ran his hands into his ears or put his hands in his crotch and then ran them under his nose—perhaps a desperate affirmation of his humanity. I didn't understand, but felt repulsed every time I saw him do it surreptitiously, in stolen moments that, if they had to happen at all, should have happened in private. And yet here he was, in the office, at meetings with clients, touching and then smelling himself.

Before the children went to boarding school, Tom liked to

work in the woods as he had done in the Adirondacks with his own father, hacking at underbrush until he had created great piles of debris, and slashing at limbs of trees with a Woodsman's Pal, a combination ax and machete that he liked. During the years we spent at the farm he worked less and less on the property as he became increasingly consumed by running and taking saunas, and as his physical strength deteriorated, the gardens became my refuge. In winter I spent hours planning, comparing catalogs, making long lists on yellow legal pads, and then creating elaborate overlays on transparent paper showing the bloom time for different seasons, even developing a computerized way of tracking the plants I had purchased, where they were planted, what care they needed, and when to divide or fertilize them. In spring and summer I spent whatever time I had on weekends and after work pruning, planting, weeding, collecting plastic bags full of slugs I threw to the delighted frogs and fish in the little ponds, and glorying in the abundant flowers the cutting garden produced.

One afternoon I planned to plant blueflag Iris and wild rice in the boggy marshland near a little pond. As I was leaving the house, Tom told me he wanted to work with me. I was surprised but not pleased; he didn't know much about gardening, and the gardens were a place where I could get away from him. But I knew he was making an effort, and I didn't feel I could refuse him. I suggested he fill the Garden Way cart with brush, rocks, and detritus from another area I was clearing. After working there for a while he called out asking me to help him because the cart had sunk into the dirt and he could not move it. I walked over and pulled against it with one arm to test how heavy it was. The cart moved easily. I thought of pretending I couldn't move it to save him from the shame, but his weakness, his self-inflicted weakness, disgusted me so much I pulled the cart, one-handed, out of the mud.

"There, I've done it. It wasn't heavy." I turned my back on him and strode back to where I had been planting. It was hard to admit to myself that I was stronger than he was. A man should, at least, be physically stronger than his wife. But he wasn't, and it made me feel sick and ashamed of him. I remembered the time when we had just moved to the farm and borrowed the battered truck of a young man who was helping us. Tom parked it on a slope and forgot to put on the hand brake. I heard the truck move and realized it was slipping slowly toward the pond. Horrified that the truck might get damaged, or hurt one of the children, I raced to it, flung myself into the cab on the wrong side, and jammed on the brake, bumping my head hard in the process. Tom had been standing nearby also, but I had seen him running toward the woods. Now I thought about how scared he had been and how weak he had become, and I felt frightened.

Tom was also drinking even more, I think, than he had before; at least it was more obviously an important part of his life. When the children were home, we would eat dinner at a restaurant because it was easier. "Can we go to a restaurant sometime where you don't have to drink?" Stephen once asked Tom.

One evening, as I sat in a restaurant, staring out at the tide coming in, the seagulls bobbing in the gentle waves, and a sandpiper snipping at the sand, I thought to myself, Why, when we go to a restaurant, do you have a double rum, two shots, one dark Myers rum, one Bacardi light, followed by wine and then a double brandy Alexander? It scares me when you insist on driving us home. I dared not complain but I said I wanted to drive when we got up to leave. "That's ridiculous. What do you think I am, drunk?" he said as he stormed to the car, jammed it back out of the parking space, lurched it toward the main road, and then careened home. Thank God there's no one else on this road now, I thought. I remembered coming home in the early hours of the morning from a debutante party in Virginia when I was eighteen. A friend of Kevin's, an alcoholic and a son of alcoholic parents, who eventually killed himself drinking Listerine, was driving. As

I nestled against Kevin, I watched trees blur past on the country road until I looked up and saw a tree coming at us, but in slow motion, and the wheels mired in mud, avoiding a collision. Now I felt suspended in time and loosened my grip on the car door only as we slid into the garage and stopped with a jerk before hitting the back wall.

I always tried to deny how important drinking was to Tom, but one time when Katherine was home from boarding school and after Tom was asleep, she said, "You know, Mom, he has liquor hidden away all over the house." I knew she was right. I had found bottles of wine in his bathroom closet when I was cleaning, or in the gym in the garage, but I replied, "Oh, no, Kit, I don't think so," out of a numbed sense of loyalty and a hope of protecting her. She answered, "I'll show you," and jumped up from the couch. She led me to the bathroom and pulled a bottle of wine from the closet, hidden under a pile of dirty clothes. She walked into the kitchen and pulled another from behind the mops and broom, and then another from the hall closet.

"All right, yes, yes, you're right. I'll talk to him about it." But I knew talking would make very little difference, because I had tried to talk to him so many times and I couldn't think of anything else to do. I knew I had failed my daughter again, and that in many ways she was more grown up and confident than I was.

I began to think about all the bottles that had vanished—bottles of champagne we were given as a present at Christmas by my sister, bottles of liquor we had bought on a trip, bottles of fine wine given to us by clients. "What happened to the Grand Marnier?" I asked Tom one evening when I wanted some after dinner and it was gone.

"Oh, I was pouring a glass and the bottle slipped. It just broke on the tile floor," he replied, adding, "I'm sorry."

Another time, when I asked, "What happened to the wine Des gave us?," he had answered laughing to convince me it was a joke,

"You know, it had gone bad. It was an old bottle and the cork must have dried up. That's the risk with old wine." I started marking the bottles surreptitiously in the liquor cabinet with a thin line of pencil, and checked each morning to find the level of the liquid had fallen, like a reservoir drying up in a drought.

Tom liked to buy wine in large casks with a spigot because it was easier he said than opening a bottle, and cheaper. The carton was so big it took up a large segment of the icebox. But gradually, as I watched the empty cartons pile up in the woodshed, I realized that neither of us could tell how much was left, or how fast we were drinking the wine.

I wonder now why I tried so hard to ignore Tom's drinking, why I tried to excuse it and believe his excuses. I can look back and see so many clues, but so many times I turned away from knowing what I knew. Why did it take me so long to admit that he drank because he needed to, because his sense of self was so fragile, like the skulls of syphilis victims I once saw on shelves in a glass case in the Smithsonian. The bone had turned to gauze, so porous that if the skulls were not protected by glass, the whisper of a draft would cause them implode into dust.

I look back and again, now, I see that I should have left then, but I was too scared. I had two children in boarding school and I had to make a lot of money to cover their tuitions. I had fallen into a deep trap: a big house, a big mortgage, big financial responsibilities, and I couldn't see a way out. Sometimes I felt as if I lived on a roller coaster, sometimes as if I were inside a bellows with the air pumping tight around me then suddenly releasing if I burst out and confronted Tom. I could still ignore the way Tom treated me unless he did it in front of other people, particularly the children.

Sometimes I tried to protest. "Damn it, I am so fed up with scraping ketchup off the kitchen cabinets. Can't you just wash your hands instead of smearing the damn stuff everywhere," I lashed out.

"Oh, I'm sorry. I guess I just don't notice," he responded.

"Well, that's the whole point. You just don't notice and it's a total pain in the ass to have to clean up after you." Another time, sitting on the couch in front of the television, I tried to be reasonable. "The kids are coming home. I want to do some of the cooking," I said. "I just want to have a nice meal, sitting together and talking. Not you pouting and frowning at the end of the table. I don't want to go out."

"We have a good time when we go out for dinner," he answered, sounding puzzled. "No, we don't." I replied. "You drink two double rums before the meal comes, and then wine, and then you want a brandy Alexander. That's a hell of a lot of liquor." He stared at his hands and rubbed the palms together, but said nothing. "I am scared to get in the car with you. You've drunk too much and the kids say it's scary, too. And you just laugh and say you're fine and then we weave home. I hate it."

By then we had given up having Thanksgiving dinner at home and tried going to a restaurant, hoping it would be neutral turf. But as we sat in a formal dining room in the elegant "function" room, I thought about how far we had come from the ideal in my mind—a large extended family, sitting around together in a house, enjoying a huge meal they had all helped prepare, and loving their time together. Tom sat at the head of the table, the children between us, and I sat at the other end. The table was so large it made us feel even more self-conscious, and I wondered what the waitress and waiter thought about our stilted conversation and Tom's silence. One Christmas it occurred to me that if we had fondue Tom wouldn't be able to monitor what we were eating. I bought two fondue pots and prepared meat, shrimp, vegetables, and sauces. This compromise allowed us to escape some measure of his control, and even Tom seemed to be more relaxed.

But the worst thing was that the children and I couldn't laugh together anymore. I began to notice this when they came home from boarding school for vacation. We would be sitting on the couch together, talking about school and laughing as we did when they were children. They would laugh and tell stories to each other, and when I joined in, I could feel Tom glowering, getting red in the face, almost literally heating up until suddenly he would burst out, "Stop that. You sound ridiculous. What are you, some kind of adolescent giggling?" "I'm just joking with Kit about her imitation of Mr. T. at school," I said, stunned into submission. "Well, you sound stupid laughing like that," he barked. One night I read a book about adult children of alcoholics and learned that they fear laughter because when they were children it was a prelude to their parents' drunken outbursts. I began to understand the gloom that hung around Tom and enveloped me in its gray mist, and I pitied him. I told him what I had read, and though on an intellectual level it helped us both, the fears of his childhood held him, and us, in an implacable embrace.

Often, when we visited our children at boarding school, we stayed with my close friend Faith, who lived nearby. Faith tried many times to break through the walls I threw up around me. "Tee, why don't you come sit awhile in my room before we go to bed? It seems we never get a chance to talk." But I was scared. She would hint sometimes that she found Tom controlling, just a tiny hint, but I knew what she was thinking. "You can't be sleepy this early, Tee. You won't wake him up if you go through that room while he's sleeping." "Oh," I replied. "I'd love to talk, but one time he didn't run and he said he gained fourteen pounds of water; he looked like a watermelon. It's the Reynaud's. You know, the condition that killed his mother." Sometimes we talked for just a few minutes before Tom stormed out of the bedroom and stood in the hall shouting, "Aren't you coming to bed? You said you were coming to bed now." "I'll be very quiet," I replied, hoping to placate him, embarrassed by his outburst in front of Faith. "You're going to wake me up if you come in later. I don't care how quiet you try to be, you are going to wake me up," he said, unaware, it seemed, of how outrageous he was being. And I would capitulate to stop him, and say to Faith, "Well, another time," and then go quietly to the back room to keep the fragile peace and because I really didn't want to think about all the things that talking with her would have forced me to face.

The only time I saw friends, acquaintances really, was during summers at the swimming club. I began to hate going there with Tom, but he told me we had to go, that it was good for business, and sometimes it was. But most of the time we would park in the graveled lot and walk across the street to the large shingled club while I watched out of the corner of my eye for anyone I knew, hoping we would be invited to join someone and not have to sit alone together again. In summer Tom's madras pants looked almost acceptable because so many of the men wore similar pants. But Tom's were stained and too short. "Hello, Mrs. Sargent," I said to the woman who sat at the desk in the front lobby, screening everyone who came in. I walked over the gray canvas that lined the walkways, wondering how long it would be before a child got lockjaw scraping a toe against the rusting staples that stuck up like pins from the canvas, and admiring the geraniums and lobelias growing in planters along the railings. Occasionally I pulled off dead stems and blooms that the crew had missed, thinking I was almost one of them now and had to help keep up the illusion of perfection for the summer people. At first, when we went, I changed into a bathing suit so I looked more at ease, but I stopped pretending because I didn't much like swimming, and Tom looked so gaunt in a suit and polo shirt. Too often we sat by ourselves because we went to the club too early, when young mothers and their children and nannies were eating. Tom didn't want to wait until after one when people our age could eat in relative peace, because he had eaten breakfast so early.

One day I was sitting on the bench eating chicken salad, staring out at the beach in front of the dining deck, watching little blond boys throw pebbles into the water and little blond girls digging their colorful plastic shovels into the sand. I watched as people circled their beach chairs around the new heated pool and lay back sunning themselves and telling each other stories. Tom was eating crab salad, and licking his fingers. I looked at the young families laughing together and I wondered if they felt sorry for us, as I did. I thought we had become like the old couples in restaurants who are there out of some sense of duty but stare at their plates because they have nothing to say and nowhere else to go.

9

THE VASE

December 1989

Slowly I recognized patterns that had been etching themselves into our lives for years. It was harder now not to see them because my children were away at school so much of the time. There was no one to hide behind, nothing except myself to separate me from reality. I would go to do errands on a Saturday and find I had no cash. "Oh, I'm so sorry. I know I cashed a check yesterday. Maybe my husband took the money for something else, or my children borrowed it. I'll pick up my loafers next week," I lied. I could feel the warmth creeping up my chest and hoped I could get out of the cobbler shop before it reddened my face. Bart, the shoemaker, smiled behind the old black cash register, the bags of shoes stacked behind him like unborn bees in their cells. The shop smelled sweet, of leather and polish, and I wanted to talk with him as I sometimes did about his collection of "specialty" knives with inlaid handles of pearl and onyx arrayed in the glass cases and about his travels to the unfamiliar world of knife shows. But the sign above his scarred wooden workbench that suggested one HIRE A TEENAGER WHILE THEY STILL KNOW EVERYTHING reminded me that it hadn't been mine who had taken the money.

"Please," I said to Tom when I got home, "if you want me to cash a check for you on Friday, I will. It is really a pain to open my wallet and find it empty. I felt like Old Mother Hubbard."

But it happened again and again. I buried my money under my bras and underpants or deep in my brown Coach briefcase, but he'd find it anyway. At first I didn't think of it as stealing. When I asked Tom about taking my money, he said he was just borrowing the money and he was going to put it back, and besides, what was his was mine and vice versa.

At first, I agreed with him, but over the years, after I had begged him many times to tell me when he borrowed from me, I began to see his habit of taking money from my purse as stealing; and to understand that it was another symptom of his illness, another way in which he tried to control and upset me.

When we used to go shopping for food together and I wanted to buy Ben & Jerry's Heath Bar Crunch frozen yogurt, or brownie mix, I would stop the cart in front of it in the aisle and say as casually as I could, "Oh, I think I'll get some of this. Shall I get enough for you, too?" When I turned toward him I would see the blood rushing to his face, tightness pulling it into a gargoyle mask.

"No, we don't need that shit. No one needs that shit."

"Okay," I'd reply. I'll just get one for me." But then a few days later, when I looked in the toffee-brown carton, it would be almost empty and often there were traces of other food, mustard or ketchup, around the upper edge. When I wanted to make brownies, I'd find the box was open and the mix, moistened with spit, clumped around the edges. His teeth scored the butter and tore the French bread; his fingers gouged a trench through soft cheese, pudding, and mayonnaise in the jar. "Damn it, Tom. I just don't get it. You said you didn't want any of that stuff. Why do you eat the whole thing?"

"I got hungry," he answered.

"Fine," I yelled at his back as he walked out of the kitchen, "but you make everything so gross I don't want to touch it."

I now believe that having food in the house that Tom craved but considered defiling was a source of constant torment for him which he struggled to resist. Torn between his need to deny himself to achieve a purity he thought would make him acceptable and even lovable, and his need for nurture, he fought himself until beaten, and took some of his anger out on the offending food.

The people who worked with us had complained for a long time about sharing a kitchenette with him. "Please, Barbara," Pam and Greta both pleaded, "can you just get him to use his own dishes and cutlery. He never washes anything properly, so there is ketchup on the plates and spoons, and he keeps the dirty stuff in his desk drawer so there isn't anything for us to use. The cutlery drawer is disgusting. I just won't use it and I'll bring my own things to eat with. It's just so gross, I don't understand what's wrong with him."

"Please, Tom," I'd ask again. "Please. Greta and Pam are really ticked off about the way you take the spoons and leave your dishes in the sink for someone else to wash. It's such a small office, we really need everyone to take care of their own stuff."

"Sorry, I just don't think about it," he replied.

"I know, that's what you always say. But you've got to think about it. You're really irritating everyone here. They aren't going to put up with it."

I couldn't deny the evidence that confronted me every time I went into the office bathroom and found his dirty dishes soaking in the sink, making it impossible to wash my hands. I resented washing up after him, and I didn't want Pam or Greta to do it. But I could deny that he was stealing from them, even though they told me that someone was taking their food: leftovers they brought for lunch, rich chocolate homemade brownies with macadamia nuts for afternoon tea, salads from the deli in the market next door. It was embarrassing and awkward to cover for Tom when they suggested he had been taking their food.

"Barbara, I hate to bother you with this again, but I think Tom took some of my shrimp-and-pasta salad. I would give him some if he just asked, but I hate it that he takes food from me. It seems so strange, he just has to go to the market next door. That's where I went," Pam would say.

"I'm so sorry, Pam. I don't know why he would do that. I'll ask him about it," I'd reply. I could see disgust spread over her face, because I had said this to her so many times before and Tom always denied the thefts.

"Tom," I'd say, "Pam seems to be missing some of the shrimp salad she bought for lunch. By any chance did you take some from her?"

"Why would I do that?" he'd reply, "I can just buy it in the market."

Relieved, I would answer, "Of course that's what I told her."

But seeping out from somewhere inside me was the knowledge that he was stealing. I tried to talk to him about it many times and asked him to get help, but no one seemed to be able to help him. I thought again about all the doctors and therapists Tom had seen over the years, but that their treatment never really seemed to dig below the surface or help Tom improve even the outward manifestations of his illness. Today it still amazes me that none of these people helped Tom to see that he was re-playing his childhood relationship with his mother on the stage of his adulthood. Perhaps because he was smart and articulate Tom was able to fool not only himself but the professionals who were trying to help him.

When he stopped seeing a therapist he said the reason was that he was much better, or that the therapy was a waste of time, but I began to wonder if he left when it became uncomfortable for him, just when it might have been most useful. Some time after Tom stopped seeing the man he had first gone to after we moved to Maine, he started seeing a gentle middle-aged woman who lived about an hour away. At first he said she was warm and accepting, even motherly, and that he liked the fact that she didn't push him. She kept stuffed animals in her office for her patients to hug or punch, which amused but never engaged Tom, and sometimes he said that he found her limited intellectually and a little boring. I never met this therapist, which suggests to me that I was more comfortable on the sideline as well.

Now I worried that again Tom did not seem to be getting better and his symptoms were, in fact, more severe. One morning when I walked into our office, Greta told me she had to talk to me in private. She was almost rigid with anger, her face flushed and her eyes fiery. I knew something was very wrong. We went into the conference room and she told me that she had known for a long time that Tom had been stealing her food. "I've told you again and again," she added, "but you always take his side and you don't believe me. He's just lying to you. He steals our food and today I caught him."

"What do you mean?" I asked.

"I had a sandwich in the icebox. I had put it in a brown bag and written my name on the bag. Then I taped it closed with Scotch tape. He went in there and he took the bag, unfastened the tape, took out the sandwich, unwrapped the aluminum foil, and took the meat out of the sandwich. Then he put it all back together. What does he think, that I won't notice? He is sick, Barbara. I can't stand it anymore."

I looked at her face. She was a young woman, a natural strawberry blond with blue eyes, normally quiet and composed, serious and diligent. Now her face glowed red with anger and she was almost in tears. "I can't stand it, Barbara. You have to do something," she said again.

There was no denying her anger, and what Tom had done to her now, after denying stealing so many times, felt more like a kind of rape to me. I was horrified that he would do this to a young woman who worked for us and whom, I knew, it had been my responsibility to protect. I had failed her. I had failed the other people in our office who had complained to me over the years about his behavior and I was determined not to fail them again. Suddenly, like lightning flashing over a dark field, I saw all the moments when he had lied to me, all the times I had protected him by wanting to believe him.

Greta returned to her desk and I called Tom into the conference room and confronted him with her story. "No, I didn't take the meat from her sandwich. That is ridiculous. Why would I do that?" he asked.

"I don't know why you would do it, I just know that you did," I fired back. "Did you steal the meat out of her sandwich?"

"No, no, I didn't do that." He looked at me, backing into the corner behind the door. At first he tried to stare me down, but then his eyes weakened and he looked at the floor.

"Did you take the meat out of her sandwich?" I asked again. He studied the floor. "Did you take the meat out of her sandwich?" I repeated.

For the first time I was as relentless as he, pushing him because I knew I had to until finally—*finally*—he said, "Yes. I don't know why," and I wheeled out of the room, too disgusted to stay. I apologized to Greta, told her I was very, very sorry, and that he had admitted he had stolen from her then and before and that I would try again to make him get real help.

All that day I thought about how angry I was, angry about the lying, angry about his stealing and the ways in which he had fooled me, ways in which I had acted like a fool by believing him because

I was too scared to admit he was lying. When I got home from the office that evening, I told Tom I was moving out of our bedroom because I couldn't stand to share a room with him anymore. "Tom," I said, "I know I have to work with you, but I don't have to stay in the bedroom with you. I'm moving into the middle bedroom." He didn't argue. I moved out of the large bedroom we had built as an addition to the house a year or so before, and I lived from then on in the small middle bedroom. But the stealing didn't stop.

I knew Greta would leave us, and that nothing could prevent her from telling people in the small island community about Tom's bizarre behavior. It scared me to think about having other people know our secret because I was still complicit, still too ashamed to admit the severity of Tom's illness. After Greta left, we hired another young woman, Inge, who also ran the office very competently. I had hoped Tom would change his behavior after his embarrassment with Greta, but now here was Inge, looking at me, her eyes wide, and her hand trembling. I saw the pulse on her wrist pumping and wondered what was coming.

"Barbara, this is awkward. I'm not sure how to say this."

"It's all right, just say it and we'll work it out," I replied.

"Barbara, I think we shouldn't have a petty-cash box. I've asked him so many times just to fill out the form, to tell me what he's taking. But he won't, and I can't keep track."

"Oh, don't worry," I responded. "It isn't much—it'll be okay. Could you hide the box? Just don't keep much money in it. Would it be okay if you just got a little at the bank each day—or could we get by not having petty cash?" I heard her words and my response and thought how pathetic it was that we had to hide the cash box from one of the owners of the company.

"Well, yes. But it seems he ought to be able to fill out the form like everyone else." I had to admit this was reasonable, but I knew Tom was incapable of doing it.

We used to go to the market together, but this finally became too difficult. At first I didn't notice that Tom was eating the grapes before they were weighed, but then I realized he was continually taking something without paying for it.

"That doesn't seem fair. That seems like stealing to me—we haven't paid for those yet," I admonished him.

"But it's only a few. Just one or two. They wouldn't weigh anything anyhow."

Finally I just looked away, trying to pretend it wasn't happening, that I hadn't seen what I had seen. Then I stopped trying to go to the market with him or buying food I liked to eat.

None of his symptoms ever went entirely away. Rather, like artifacts mired in permafrost that continuously rotate, pulled from the surface down to the level below frost, then are finally churned upward again, Tom's infantile behaviors would sink away only to resurface when internal pressures forced them out. For a while he wouldn't seem to drink so much, or be so negative and curt with people, but after a day of so he would start to chew ice again and fill all the sinks in the house with ice water while he went running. For a while, usually when the children were home, or after I had exploded in anger and desperation, he would struggle to be cheerful, try to make jokes, not talk about food, but then again he would become irritated, drink so his nose and cheeks were florid red, and sink into the implacable grasp of his illness.

Other people had tried to tell me I needed help, but I'd turn away when I sensed what they were about to say. But when, almost accidentally, I had tea with Nan and Abby, my roommates from boarding school, for some reason I was able to listen to them. Perhaps they read through me and knew what to ask, perhaps I was more comfortable with them than with any other two people I knew, even though I had not seen them for years, and so desperate that I knew they were my last chance. I began to tell them about my life, about how scared I was and how lonely. They listened to me with such patience and love that I was able to accept it when Nan turned and said, "Barbara, I want to give you a hundred dollars to go to a therapist. Please, you need help."

I could easily have afforded therapy, but I hadn't been able to admit to myself that I needed it. I had always struggled to deal with problems myself, and besides, Tom was the one who was sick, not me. I thought I was all right because I was coping well, on the surface, at least. But I listened to Nan because I knew she knew me and loved me, and I allowed myself to take her money, knowing that then I would have to make myself see a therapist, and worrying how I would find someone in our small community.

When the children came home for vacation, we tried to think of things to do. We had given up trying to eat together, and it was no fun to go out to dinner anywhere. For a time we still tried that, but it was too discouraging. One Sunday we decided to play miniature golf. There was nothing else we could do together that would permit Tom to run and take a sauna in the morning, eat at eleven, and then run again by three. We couldn't go climb a mountain, as we used to, we couldn't go sailing, or even to a movie. There was nothing we could to do conform to his schedule except play a round of miniature golf at the new course on the outskirts of Bar Harbor. Perhaps it'll be fun, I wished. We drove in two cars so Stephen and Katherine could go to the town afterward. I was relieved because I hoped Tom would vent his irritation at me, like the putrid exhaust from his drying sweatclothes, not against the children. Sometimes when I came in the front door of the house, the cloud of smell caught me unexpectedly and I wished I had thought of this when we built the house.

When we got to the golf course there was a line of people waiting to play. I hoped we wouldn't have to wait long because I was worried Tom might complain. We stood in the line and finally it was our turn—but even this game was no fun. The kids were tense, waiting for their father to be angry with us or the people around us, waiting for him to be rude and gruff. He moved slowly, like an old man. He was the center of our attention and effort. We catered to him, we deferred to him, he dominated us. I realized how careful Stephen and Katherine were with him, how they tried to buffer him against the rest of the world just as I did. "Dad, it's your turn now. Here, try this club. Oh, great shot, Dad, well done." They were buoying him up just as one would a fragile child.

We made the rounds, through the beached rowboat, a wicked left and over to the Pirate's Cove, watched out for the water slide, and then jumped the logs and barrels. What, I wondered, are we doing here? Here on this magnificent island, with its deep woods, mountains with spectacular views of the outer islands, this island with streams, lakes, and bays for kayaking, with the blue ocean beckoning for sailing, ospreys and eagles soaring overhead, and warblers hiding in the beech groves. Here on this amazing island that greets over two million visitors a year to its national park, to its museums, restaurants, libraries, boutiques, whale watches, deep-sea fishing, mountain biking over fifty miles of carriage roads— here on this island where I have friends from childhood whom I haven't seen for years, haven't eaten a meal with, haven't invited to my house, or been invited to theirs, haven't gone to their parties or invited them and their children to a barbecue, a picnic on the beach, a lobster feed, what are we doing with the time we will spend together this summer as a family? We are playing miniature golf.

Stephen hit a hole in one, which entitled us to a free round, but we were exhausted, worn down by trying to be happy and cheer-ful, by doing our duty to each other, by pretending to have fun. I could not talk to my children about their father, I could not admit to them how sick he was, because I could not admit it to myself. He had caught the three of us in an unwritten agreement not to betray him by talking about his illness, not to admit even that he was sick.

The kids asked if I'd like to go for an ice cream cone and I realized I wanted nothing more in the entire world than to be with my children, without Tom forbidding us to have fun, to laugh, to enjoy each other's company, to talk honestly and openly and with love about our fears, what we wanted for ourselves and each other—in short, to be a family. Tom was angry with me for wanting to stay with them, but I was more determined than I had ever been before. I began to see that all the times I had tried to make his life, and my own, easier by acceding to his will, by putting his needs above my own and even my children's, had only made him more fragile. Now I began to think that I could pull away from him and that we would both survive.

Stephen and Katherine suggested we go to Carlo's Pizza, a place I had never been to before. And when we sat in the darkened restaurant, I ordered an individual pizza with everything— double cheese, mushrooms, pepperoni, peppers, and onions. I knew I couldn't eat that much, but I was having so much fun trying, sucking in the hot cheese as it dripped over the side of the redolent crust, catching the falling mushrooms in my hands and putting them on top of the slice, swirling the peppers and pepperoni together in my mouth, reveling in the orgy of tastes. It was a small act of defiance and Tom was not there to see it, but I had not eaten pizza in years and it felt great. Then we walked down the street to the ice cream shop. There was a long line of people because the ice cream was all homemade, even better than Ben & Jerry's. I had never been to this place either and I felt our roles reverse; my children were introducing me to places I should have been taking them to for years. The ice cream was amazing. I was glad there was a wait because it allowed time to read the list of what was available: Rocky Road, Old Cow, Chocolate Frenzy, Lobster . . . *Lobster*? I settled on BB+B, a velvet cloud of vanilla ice cream, brandy, Benedictine, and bourbon, a powerful brew.

When I was in second grade, our class went on a field trip to an ice cream factory. I remember watching the wave of vanilla ice cream slowly turning in the room-size vat and thinking I had just seen heaven. If I could, I would have dived into the vat and turned slowly with the ice cream, eating and absorbing it until I was satiated. Now I thought about why I had denied myself so many things I liked, and I knew that Tom was making me see life the way he saw it. I was excising the things I loved because he told me they were bad, bad for me, bad because I wanted them, bad because to deny oneself was good. I knew it was easier to live with him if I did not transgress his rules. I saw that when my children were away at school I had given up many things I might have fought for if they were home. But what really scared me was that I was so used to living this way that I had begun to believe him and think he made sense.

"You know you'll bloat if you drink water." So I didn't drink much water.

"The sauna is really good for you. It cleans out the impurities, gets rid of all the bad chemicals in the junk you eat." So I took saunas, though never more than one a day.

"You're looking bloated, you're looking fat, you're getting heavy." Again and again and again he had said this until I had believed him. What I didn't understand was that not drinking water made my sinuses block and get infected, taking saunas was bad for my skin because I have acne rosacea and am not supposed to get overheated, and the tension I felt constantly from living with Tom was making me ill.

When we designed the office at home, I didn't know I would be spending so much time in that little room. I thought a small window would be adequate so I would not be distracted by watching for hawks circling the marsh, or the fox hunting for voles. But later, when I spent so much time secluded there, I wished I could open the wall to the air and sky. Instead, I sat huddled in front of the screen of the tiny Kaypro computer I bought in 1985. I enjoyed deciphering it by myself, rather like working on a puzzle or game. With it, I designed a program for tracking what I planted on the farm—how much the plants cost, how to care for them, when they would need fertilizing and splitting—made lists of people to whom we sent Christmas cards, and figured out a way of tracking tenants at our rental cottages. But I was frittering away my ideas and energy, struggling to find something that would give me some joy and pleasure.

I began to grope for ways to connect to people. I didn't feel I could confide in friends; to do so seemed too threatening then. I could not admit to myself that I was miserable, so how could I tell a friend? But other people saw me and knew better than I did how I was feeling. A wealthy client, who had been through two divorces and lost her parents when she was very young, talked to me about what I needed to do. "Barbara, you need to work on yourself," she said. The very concept baffled me.

She gave me a book—Gloria Steinem's *Revolution from Within*. At the end of the book, Steinem asks her reader to envision a child walking toward her. I saw a thin little girl with brown hair and eyes, dressed in the slate-blue Potomac School uniform, walking slowly down the dark hall of Mummy and Desie's house. She had just left the dinner table and was going upstairs to her room. Before I recognized the child, I saw how lonely she was and reached out to enfold her in my arms. Then I suddenly recognized her as myself, a self I had not been able to protect as a child, but could love and care for as an adult. Next Steinem asked me to envision an old woman walking toward me, and I saw a lavender-gray-haired woman in gardening clothes, a woman with a rounded, welcoming body, walking toward me across a sunlit field of wildflowers, bending and blowing in the breeze, the surrounding mountains holding us as in the palm of their hands. She was smiling. I realized I was seeing my neighbor Terry, a generous, large-spirited, and loving person whom I admired. "That is who I want to be when I am older," I thought, and then I had to ask myself how I could become that person.

During the moments when I was able to admit my unhappiness to myself, I had thought about leaving, but always put it off to a distant time when my children had graduated from college, when I would have no responsibility for their tuition, and when I thought it would be acceptable to leave. But the time crept closer and closer, and after another bitter fight I told Tom I was going to leave him after Katherine graduated from college and we had no more tuition to pay. As I look back, I doubt I could have lasted another year without getting sick again. For years, driving myself through fifteen-hour days and seven-day weeks and having nothing that mattered to me except my children, whom I rarely saw, I felt as if I were always pushing against currents rushing over me.

An avowed atheist, or at least agnostic, as an adolescent, I had stared at the visiting preachers as they led us in prayer at mandatory chapel services. I didn't need God, and besides, there wasn't one. But as my marriage and life congealed I started going to church, telling myself I just wanted to sing in the choir. No, I don't need to think about the service or the sermons, I just want to be in the quiet of this church, this church I have gone to since I was a child, I said to myself. I sat in the same choir stalls I had sat in as a child and listened to the same organ wheezing and the same uneven sound of untrained voices with too little practice but confident in singing familiar hymns. I just want to sing with friends and be in this quiet place. "I will meet and remeet lots of summer people," I told myself and Tom. I justified my longing for connection, the need to fill the void inside me, by saying I loved to sing, and I justified it to Tom by saying that singing in the choir would be good for business.

I enjoyed my tentative steps to pull away from Tom but I tried not to upset him. I told him half truths—that I was going to sing because I would meet summer people I had known when I was a child and their friends, that it would be good for business. I knew he felt threatened by my absence and I thought about how, over the years, because we spent more and more time together, we had seemed to draw closer but that really, we had moved far apart. I wanted to be gentle but the anger growing inside me often made me curt and sarcastic, and the best I could do was avoid Tom as much as was possible given that we shared the same office and house.

I sang with the choir throughout the summer, and then as we moved to the tiny white wooden winter church, I moved, too, drawn by my need for communion with other people, but still just singing, not absorbing or listening. Slowly the words and the Word seeped into me. Slowly I found myself listening, just a little, and then I found that if I listened each Sunday, somewhere in the service, suddenly and without warning, a phrase pierced through me. Sometimes I gasped from the pain of recognizing myself in a story, or worse, at the recognition of who I wanted to be and how sad I had become. I began to feel the power of the hurt, as if my tears, like droplets of spray, betrayed the presence of roaring water behind a dam. I began to cry more often and more easily, and that scared me. Then I felt as if I couldn't go to church, at least not to sing with the choir, because I had to stand in front of the congregation and I was afraid of crying. Finally I had to admit to myself that I just needed to be in church and I began to go and sit in the back pew. Sometimes I couldn't stop the tears, and once I had to leave because they were streaming down my face and I was starting to sob. I rose from the pew quickly, hung my head, and walked out the door as quietly as I could, hoping people had not noticed. But if they did notice, they never said anything to me and I was grateful for their silence.

But one morning, after the service, a woman I knew only slightly asked me if we could go back to my office and talk about her house. "Of course," I answered, not really wanting to work on Sunday but not able to refuse the possibility of new business. When we sat down at the polished oak conference table in the office, she looked at me and said, "Barbara, there was something about you today, something that told me I have to say this to you. You look so unhappy. I just wondered if there was anything I can do to help."

I was so shocked I burst into tears, tears that surged out of me in sobs so strong I could hardly breathe.

"Oh, my God, Polly. Oh, no. No, I don't know what to say." I felt trapped. Trapped because I had never trusted the woman. She seemed the consummate gossip. She had been married for years to a man who drank too much, though she defended him always. He had left her for another woman, and she had struggled through therapy, and now, twenty pounds lighter, she looked vibrant. But I was beyond caring; she had pulled my finger from the dam and pain was flooding out of me.

"I know it must be difficult for you to trust me," she said, "but I've been in a group for the past two years and I have learned how important it is to be discreet. If you talk to me, I won't tell anyone. I promise you that."

God works in mysterious ways. Of all the people I might have thought he would send as a messenger, Polly seemed the most unlikely.

"Polly, I don't know what to do. Tom is so awful to live with. I hate my life. I feel trapped. We never go out. I've lost all my friends. I don't do anything but work. I don't know how long I can stand it," I blurted out, and then I put my head down on the table and I cried while she sat there saying, "It's all right, just cry, it's all right, it has to come out."

We talked for over an hour, or rather I talked and cried and she listened. When she left I sat at the table and stared at my hands, rubbing one over the other over the other again and again. The rhythm calmed me down and I started to wonder how I could have trusted Polly with my secret. I became afraid, though not sure what was most frightening—that Polly would tell all her friends, that our business would suffer, that Tom would be angry. But she never told anyone and I will always be grateful to her.

Finally I decided I needed to talk to Paul, my minister, about my changing relationship with God. I left a message for him with the parish secretary, immediately regretting that I had told her I needed to speak with him. Maybe she'll think it's about the summer fair, I hoped. When I walked into his sunlit study, I sat uneasily in the armchair facing him, scared to say anything, but he started, saying, "Barbara, I've missed your voice in the choir, and I've watched you from the pulpit, seen you always sitting in the back pew. I've been thinking about you."

I was so raw I started crying because he was so kind. "Paul, I don't know what to do. I've felt pulled toward believing in God, but when I was a child and a teenager, I didn't. Now I think maybe there might be a God," I tried to joke. I could hardly stand the idea that God might know I existed, let alone think I was worthy of loving. The first time Paul and I met, we talked just about God, but the next time, meeting in his little office, he asked me about Tom. "It's hard," I replied. "I don't really feel very happy, but I don't know what to do."

Paul said to me, "I don't know how you've stood it all these years with Tom. Enough is enough," and I felt enormous relief as his sanction of my feelings allowed me to forgive myself for feeling them. Later he told me, "Of course you couldn't believe in a heavenly Father when you never had an earthly one." I felt my guilt begin to drip away like melting wax. "But, Barbara," he added, "I can only help you so much, only talk to you about how this relates to your feelings about God. You need someone else to talk with. I think you need a therapist to help you with this."

Damn, that again, I thought. I didn't want to go to a therapist. I had always tried to handle problems by myself. I was ashamed of needing help. I'm smart, I had told myself. I should be able to figure this out and know what to do. I read once about a character who viewed life as a test and forced himself to stand in a wind tunnel. Now I saw that I, too, had taken an odd pride in withstanding the pressures of my own "wind tunnel." But I began to admit that I had no idea how to deal with what I perceived as Tom's illness. I had tried everything I could think of: patience, support, kindness, covering up for him—but nothing had helped. Now I realized I was becoming angry and nasty, and I didn't like seeing that in myself. I knew Polly had been seeing a therapist and I asked her for the woman's name. "Debra," she told me. "She's wonderful, very smart and sympathetic. You'll like her a lot, and she is in Ellsworth, so it isn't like being right here, but it isn't too far away either."

I called Debra, but I was scared, and I tried to cover my fear with bravado; I wasn't the one who was sick, I just lived with someone who was sick. We arranged to meet the next week. When I walked toward the office, I could feel my stomach turning. I looked around the street and wondered who was watching me enter the building, who would know I was seeing a therapist. I looked at the heavy brown door for names of other agencies or people I could pretend I was seeing. I walked up the stairs as if I were climbing the gallows, turned in to the waiting room, sat down, and hid behind a copy of *Smithsonian* I had read a year before.

"Hi, I'm Debra. I'm so happy to meet you." She was tall, about my height, a bit younger, dressed comfortably in black pants and a purple shirt. Most remarkable was her wildly thick long brown hair that radiated around her face, most important were her deep brown eyes that looked at me intently, but with balance and humor. I thought, I think I'm going to like this person.

After a minute, perhaps two, of pleasantries she looked at me and said, "So, what are you here for?" I wasn't prepared for the question, but the answer blurted out, "I want a divorce, a doctorate, and singing lessons." There it was. That was what I wanted. I hadn't known before.

In early spring 1993, Tom told me he wanted to go to the Adirondacks to celebrate his fiftieth birthday. It was a place in which he found respite and comfort, and I hoped that being with his brother Michael and sister-in-law Becky would help him. I also hoped it would help me. Michael, the youngest child of his alcoholic mother, seemed the least touched by her drunken outbursts, though he, too, could withdraw into himself. Michael once helped run day-care centers for Cesar Chavez and now, with Becky, had created a day-care center for children in the county where they lived. Many of these children had what was euphemistically referred to as "special needs."

We rented a house in the valley near them, the only house that had its own sauna, because Tom would not travel anywhere without having a sauna available to him. The long drive across Maine, New Hampshire, and Vermont was difficult. We occasionally tried to make small talk, but mostly we were silent. I stared out of the window at the passing scenery and thought about what I would say to Becky and Michael, what they would say to me, and whether or not they could help me understand what was happening to Tom.

Tom was usually irritable and curt with the people in gas stations. "Fill it up," he'd say when the man approached the car window—never "How are you? Good to see you." Never "please" or "thank you."

But I was used to this and tried to soften his abrasiveness with my own greating, "Good morning, how are you, thanks so much," which seemed so obvious and stupid when sent on its mission from the other side of the car.

I felt as if I were traveling with an invalid. He held on to the car as he eased himself into the seat, held on to the door frame when he wanted to rise. He was so thin, as thin as I had ever seen him. His veins rested just under the skin, exposed because there was no fat to enfold them. Watching him hobble away from me, seeing his gaunt frame shadowed by the sun against his pale shirt, I was scared to realize how frail he had become.

We passed the little towns of Maine and then the mountains of New Hampshire, going through Gorham, where somehow something bad happened whenever we traveled to or from the Adirondacks. Once a bee had flown in the open car window and stung Tom, another time his brother Jonathan, going twenty miles per hour, was arrested for passing a truck at four in the morning and Tom, too, had been stopped for speeding there. This time we drove through unscathed, and by the time we stepped onto the ferry to cross Lake Champlain, I was hopeful the trip would go well and Tom would feel regenerated.

The house we rented smelled of its owners; the decor was motel modern with vivid oranges blaring against the beautiful blues and greens of the mountains and sky, but at least there was a sauna, the only sauna in a house available for rental. It smelled so strongly of old bodies and dried sweat that I had to force myself to enter it. The damp moldy air grabbed my throat. I stepped on mouse droppings. The wood was black with grime and I knew there was no point trying to clean it. But I also knew that the consequences of not taking a sauna would have been worse because Tom would get so irritable, and so I forced myself to spend an hour each evening in this unpleasant little box. "I hate that sauna," I told him. "It stinks and it's so dark I can hardly see to read." "If you don't take a sauna, you're going to bloat and get fat," he warned me. I knew I would have to put up with him pouting the whole time we were there, so I took the saunas so he would have nothing to hold against me.

Even though we no longer really lived together, I feared his criticisms. I feared being with him in public, even though the public was just his brother and sister-in-law. I knew he would criticize me for talking to people I met, for being friendly, for laughing. I knew he'd tell me I was looking fat. I knew he'd say insulting and rude things that were thinly disguised by awkward humor. But I was so used to living this way, so used to the tension, that I hardly felt it anymore.

But now, when we were away from home, I saw him more clearly than I did when we were in familiar surroundings. I saw the look on people's faces who had known him since childhood— such as the elderly man and his daughter who ran the real-estate office and rented us the house. This man, now in his eighties, looked more vigorous than Tom at fifty. The daughter was cheerful and welcoming, but I could see shadows in her eyes when she looked at Tom and she seemed puzzled and sad.

We drove to Michael and Becky's house. They had expanded the log cabin Tom's father and stepmother had built to get away from Tom and now the place was full of children's drawings and toys, books, and craft projects. It was a warm, welcoming house overlooking the valley, standing just above the lawn and the huge white pine under which Tom and I had been married.

"Hello, great to see you," they called out to us when we drove up. Tom slowly got out of the car and I saw the sharpness of his legs against the faded madras pants. They looked like sticks, the pants seemed empty, flapping. I had not seen him naked since I moved from our bedroom after Tom stole from Greta, and now, though I tried to push the thought out of my mind, I could see the corpses at Auschwitz piled in hideous stacks, and shocked myself thinking he looked like one of them. Now he looked as frail as the newborn mice I once found in a nest in my closet. Their hips were so thin the light shone through them; translucent, they were so fragile and I knew I had to try to save them. They died, strangled by the Easter grass I used for their nest, soaked by the milk I tried to give them but that ended up gluing the green cellophane to their skin.

Tom climbed the little rise to the house, but slowly and painfully. He grabbed onto the tree branches for support, balancing himself carefully and painfully, putting one foot ahead of the other. I paused to look at a mushroom sprouting next to the path to give him time to catch up, so his slowness would not be so obvious. Finally we were at the house and I saw Michael and Becky looking at him, and through their eyes I saw him, too. He was so emaciated that his ears seemed larger, like the ears of a rat. His eyes were wide, the whites circling the iris as if his face was pulled back away from itself. And the sweet smell like sewage and self-destruction that had followed him for years was so strong it made me dizzy. So many times when I had smelled it, I hoped I was the only person to do so, but now I saw Becky and Michael recoil slightly when they went to hug him. I thought again about the superb athlete he had been, about how his body now was like a desecrated temple, and sadness swept over me. I thought about how he was his own casualty and then I wondered, just for an instant, if I weren't complicit in the damage. I wondered if he had lived his life with anyone else if perhaps she would have been more help to him than I had been.

Tom's weight moved up and down, responding to his own pressures. So many times throughout our marriage, the pressure would build and his behavior would become so bizarre that I'd finally burst out, "Tom, this has gotten awful. I can't stand the smell. I don't know what it is, but it's like this miasmic cloud. I can't share this little office with you. I can't breathe." And then for a while he'd eat and the smell would dissipate and I would forget. Or I would get so sick of finding the pots ruined by ice, or listening to him crunching ice, or cleaning up the ketchup on the kitchen cupboards and doorjambs, that I would yell at him, and for a little while, a day or two, perhaps longer, he'd make an effort to change his behavior. Once Inge told me he left ice cubes on the new computer, which melted and almost destroyed it, and I berated him so he vowed to be more careful. But he couldn't stand to change for long, and soon he'd be sucked back into the dark swamp of his sickness. Now I watched him against the backdrop of the valley and mountains that he loved, watched him in the place in which he should have felt content and secure, watched and saw him more clearly than I ever had before, and sadness swept over me. He was an old man, a walking wreck of a man.

We stayed only a few minutes with Becky and Michael, leaving soon to go to the club so Tom could run the road to the lake as he had during so many summers, and so I could take a walk. When we got there he hobbled off into the woods, and I remembered the first time I went there with him, when he turned before loping away down the dirt road and said, "Just watch out for the bears." In twenty-five years I still had not seen a bear, and I thought of the toll of the years of self-abuse on Tom's mind and body. Now he could hardly walk, let alone run, so often I pretended I, too, was moving at a slow pace, as if I had turned the camera to slow motion to equalize our steps.

I remember walking down the long driveway to a client's house for a party, one of the very few to which we were invited at the time. The driveway was covered in crushed pink gravel, embraced on either side by lush ferns and moss, and there was lots for me to admire. "There is kinnicinuck—Indians used it for tobacco. We call it bearberry." I pretended to be looking at the plants, but really I was just giving him time to keep up with me. Other times he seemed so pathetic that I couldn't stop myself from walking at a normal pace, as if by moving away from him I could disassociate myself and escape.

When we returned to the rental cabin, Tom went to take a

sauna. While he was gone, Michael called to ask if we would come to dinner. He said that Jack Cleland, a former student, was there and wanted to see us. I was pleased because Jack had been one of our students when we taught in Connecticut, and he had married the daughter of an old friend of Tom's. "This will be good," I said to myself, hopeful that Tom would enjoy this little group of old friends and family.

When he came back from the sauna, I said, "Hey, Michael called. They've asked Jack and his wife for supper and they want us to come."

But he lashed back, "I don't see what gives him the right to go ahead with plans without asking me. It's my birthday, my vacation, and what if I don't want to do that?"

"Tom, I think he was just asking people to his house for supper and he asked us, too."

I had so hoped Tom would welcome this chance to see people who might feel "safe" to him. It had been so long since we went out, or asked anyone to the house. I tried to placate him—but then I added, finding some safety in this familiar place myself and in being with Michael and Becky, "You know, you don't have to go if you don't want to. I can go by myself."

"Well, how are you going to get there? What if I want to use the car to go somewhere else?"

"I'm sure Jack or Michael would pick me up. Don't worry. Just do what you want to do," I added, realizing that I didn't care what he did and that it would be a relief to go without him. He was grumpy and angry. He said that going to Michael's and being with Jack and the others was an imposition, but finally he called Michael and instead of flaring at him the way he had with me, he just asked what time they wanted us to arrive.

When we got to the house, I was very happy to see Jack and his wife, who had also spent her summers in the Adirondacks. "Hey, Barbara, I can call you that now, right?" he asked. "Right,"

I replied, giving him a hug. Jack had been one of my favorite students, not always my most successful, but one who struggled, and had energy and a sense of humor. Now, as we sat on the couches in Michael and Becky's cabin, he told us he loved his life, living in the Adirondacks near his parents' summer home, to which they had retired, and running his own contracting business. He had two sons about whom he talked with joy and pride. I was listening so intently to him talk that it was a while before I noticed Tom.

He had withered into the couch, pressing himself into the pillows. He sat head down, staring at the rug on the floor and at his hands. He looked numb. He said nothing. He emanated hostility and anger. Jack said, "So, Mr. R., have you played any tennis yet this summer?" Tom shriveled even farther away, mumbling a response we could barely hear, volunteering nothing. "It's still too cold in Maine," I replied. "What about you, Jack? Do you still play?" Becky said, "Tom, it's great to have you here, great that you wanted to be here on your fiftieth birthday. We're so happy to see you. I made a cake for you." Oh, God, I thought to myself, how could you do that, Becky? Don't you know how he'll take this? Tom looked at her briefly, and then down again at his hands. "I don't want cake," he said.

Finally we all gave up trying to get him to respond and seemed to have agreed to talk around him, almost as if he were not in the room. As we sat around the table singing "Happy Birthday" while Becky brought in a huge chocolate cake covered with thick, gooey icing, I looked at him and at his brother and sister-in-law looking at him and I saw him, though their eyes, as a truly ill man—a man incapable of relating to those around him, so withdrawn he was not there except as a ghost of himself.

The next day I called Michael and he asked if I wanted to talk to Becky in her office. She had been trained as a clinical social worker and had recently established a counseling practice in a larger town nearby. I told him I would call her to make an appointment for the next day during a time Tom would be running. I told Tom that Becky and I were going for a walk but instead I went to her office.

Becky's office was a large room with comfortable couches and chairs with many pillows covered in the warm and inviting colors of the earth. I sat on the couch and Becky faced me, sitting in her chair. I didn't know where to begin, so I asked her what she had seen and what she thought I should do. This was such a different situation for her as well as for me. I was not a regular client—we would only meet this once and we both felt we had to cover as much ground as we could.

I was grateful that she began to talk. "Barbara," she said, looking straight at me, her deep brown eyes meeting mine. "He's really sick. He is so sick. I think he is the sickest, most withdrawn person I have ever seen. He can't react to anyone around him. He just sits there. He can't respond to anyone."

"Yes," I answered, too sad to say more.

"Barbara, damn it, he looks like someone in a death camp. That's what he is making of his life—a death camp. You know," she added, "people die of this. Anorexia will kill him. It kills brain cells. And with the drinking on top of that—he isn't getting food, he's living on sugar. Of course his mind blanks; he's destroying his brain and, oh, God, it's just pathetic. You have to get him to go for help."

She talked about Tom's mother, the mother neither of us had met, who was also the mother of his brother, her husband. She said she must have been horrible to the kids, that Michael had told her stories about the drunken screaming and the way she used to wake them in the middle of the night telling them to clean their rooms, laughing and yelling hysterically. Becky made me see that what I had almost become inured to was intolerable, and was destroying me, too. She helped me see that I had to stand up for myself. Talking with her helped me see how dangerously far we had slid into a chasm of control, irrational behavior, and self-deprivation.

During the long drive home to Maine, Tom and I were almost silent. I was thinking the whole time about my talk with Becky. I worried that I had betrayed Tom by talking about him, but I knew Becky was right and I was relieved to hear her say he was terribly ill. I felt torn apart, pulled in one direction because I wanted to share my fears and have him say, "That's ridiculous, of course I'm all right, I just was feeling down because I turned fifty," but dragged in the opposite direction because I knew that he was not all right, and that I must stand apart from him and act for him in what I thought was our best interest. I felt lonely and disengaged from my own life—as if again I were acting in a play with a bad script, hearing my own voice speaking while I listened to it self-consciously, wondering if this could all be happening to me and my children.

When we got home I waited a few days and finally I told Tom that I had talked with Becky, that she had said anorexia could kill him, that he was depriving his body of nourishment and killing the cells of his brain.

"How much do you weigh?" I forced myself to ask.

"Oh, I've gained some weight," he answered. "I'm about one thirty now."

I thought he was lying and mentally I deducted ten pounds.

"What was the lowest you ever weighed?" I asked, not really expecting him to tell me, and wondering again if he would pad the figure.

"I guess I was at one sixteen, but I'm much heavier now."

I thought about the fact that he didn't look better—that he looked about as bad as he had ever looked. He seemed like an old man, the folds of flesh drooping from his face like a basset hound, his shoulders hunched and thin like a bird's wings. I remembered the many times he couldn't finish a thought, lost it midway, or couldn't connect to his own experience or repeat strategies he had used many times in business. I thought about the many times he asked me where something was kept, a form for a purchase-and-sales agreement, thumbtacks, a thermos, so many things he had used so many times but couldn't place. I had thought he was just lazy, or forgetful. Now I began to wonder if his brain was collapsing.

I thought about the therapist he was seeing. Now Tom was saying that she wasn't helping him, that he could work on the problems himself, that he just needed more willpower. I thought about all the doctors and therapists he had seen since he was hospitalized. It seemed that when he got close the edge of his problems with each, he backed away, blaming his retreat on the ineptitudes of the people treating him, rather than looking directly down into his fears. I began to see that his self-destructive behavior was affecting each part of his life: his relationship with me and his children, his relationship with the people at work, his effectiveness in doing his job; in short, his physical, emotional, and psychological health. I also began to acknowledge that covering up for him, as I had done for so many years, was not helping him either.

"You know, Barbara," Pam once told me, "I'm really glad we have good liability insurance; someday he's going to do something really bad that he can't buy his way out of." Sometimes when he was on the phone with a customer, I would write notes to prompt him when he couldn't seem to remember what he needed to say. "Dad's brain-farts," the children called it when he couldn't put thoughts together.

Now I realize I was just hiding from myself. But I told Debra about my conversation with Becky and how ill she and Michael thought Tom was when they saw him in the Adirondacks. Debra said I had to get Tom into more intensive treatment, that he was literally killing himself. She was very clear and firm about this and suggested several places to go for help. But I found it so hard to hear her; I wanted to block out her words. I remembered what it was like to have Tom in the hospital in Washington, how scared he was of losing control, but I knew I had to try to make him get help before he collapsed again. Debra suggested a hospital in Portland that cared for anorexics—but rarely for men.

Debra called Tom's therapist, the woman he had been seeing reluctantly who had the stuffed animals, after he had given permission for them to share information. Somehow together we all convinced Tom that he should go to the Portland hospital for an evaluation. He was nervous and kept saying he wasn't going to go if he had to stay overnight in the hospital. But he was told the evaluation could take place during the day if he arrived early in the morning, and by afternoon he'd be free to go. I offered to go with him but he insisted on going by himself. He drove to Portland, spent the night at the hotel, and went for the evaluation the next day. All day I wondered how it was going and when he came home that night he seemed elated.

"Guess what?" he said. "I don't have to go for inpatient treatment. They said I just need to see my GP, my therapist, and a nutritionist. That's all. I don't have to go to the hospital." He seemed so relieved that I, too, felt better. If the doctors in Portland at the center for anorexics didn't think he needed more help than that, then why should Andrea and I be concerned?

So Tom called Lee, his GP, and set up an appointment and after he had seen Lee he told me he was going to meet with a nutritionist. I was surprised after he met with her to find that she prescribed at least one drink a day, which Tom suggested was a remedy she must have learned in her childhood in Scotland. I wondered if she knew he was an alcoholic.

A couple of weeks later, when I next saw Debra, I told her

about the plan for Tom's treatment. She frowned almost imperceptibly and looked at me with questions in her eyes. When I told her about the nutritionist's prescription of a glass of wine a day, she seemed angry, though she controlled it well. "That's terrible. She has no right to do that—he's an alcoholic, you don't prescribe alcohol to an alcoholic."

Then she looked at me again and asked, "Didn't he tell you?"

"Tell me what?"

"Barbara, the treatment center in Portland didn't think he was so healthy that he just needed to be an outpatient, they thought he was too ill for them to treat. His therapist told me that they diagnosed him as alcoholic and anorexic, and they can only treat one disease at a time. They told him to go home and get cured of alcoholism or they couldn't help him with anorexia. They can't deal with a double diagnosis. He has two very serious illnesses."

Later, at home, I talked with Tom about my meeting with Debra. "Tom, what did they tell you about the evaluation?" I asked him.

"What do you mean?" he replied, looking startled. "They just said I didn't have to be an inpatient."

"No, I mean, what did they tell you about treatment?" I clarified.

"Just that I would see Lee and the nutritionist and the therapist. That I don't have to go to the hospital," he responded.

"But, Tom, what did they tell you about why they decided that?"

"I don't see what you're talking about. I'm following the diet the nutritionist gave me. I have to write out everything I eat in a day. You know that," he answered, sounding defensive.

"Tom, Debra said that your therapist said the hospital can't deal with two illnesses—they can't see you if you're an alcoholic as well as anorexic. Didn't she tell you that?" I asked, incredulous.

"Well, no, I was just happy I didn't have to stay at the hospital."

He seemed not to understand. I never figured out if that was because he had completely blocked what he was told by the doctors in Portland, or because he couldn't admit to me what he knew about his diagnosis. I only knew that he continued to see Lee and the nutritionist for a while. For several months he filled out the forms listing all the food he had eaten and gave them to the nutritionist, though I had no idea what was on them or how accurately he complied with her instructions. But then he stopped, though he continued to drink, and justified this by saying the nutritionist told him alcohol was good for him.

Lee told Tom a psychiatrist had just moved to the area who had trained at Harvard and specialized in eating disorders, and that he recommended her highly. By this time Tom was irritated with the therapist he had been seeing and decided to change. I knew of this doctor because she and her husband had worked with one of our brokers in looking for a house. Our broker had told me they were some of the strangest people she had ever worked with and that the husband was the most difficult, obnoxious man she had ever met. It didn't seem an auspicious beginning.

In 1993, we had been married for twenty-five years. About three months before our anniversary, Tom said, "Let's have a twenty-fifth wedding anniversary party." I was shocked. We had been getting along badly for a long time, had not slept in the same bed in several years. We hadn't asked anyone over for years and we certainly hadn't had a party in years. Now he wanted to celebrate?

I thought about the idea—but only for a minute or two. In those minutes scenes of a party flashed through my mind. I would have loved to give a party. I thought about whom I would ask— everyone I liked, perhaps friends would come from far away who meant a great deal to me. Perhaps we could put them up in our three rental cottages. I thought about a wonderful weekend with people I loved, and then I stopped and thought about how hypocritical this was. Tom wanted a party to celebrate, but it didn't feel like a celebration to me; rather, it felt as if he was claiming ownership, trying to show people we were happily married. I could not do that, there was nothing to celebrate, and I told him I didn't want to have a party.

In July my friend Faith called. "Tee," she said, "there's something I think you have to know. Remember you told me that you had been married twenty-five years this summer?"

"Yes," I replied.

"I know you've been miserable for so long. It seemed odd to me that I just got an invitation in the mail to a surprise anniversary party for you that Tom has planned."

"Oh, no, Faith. I can't believe this," I stammered.

"I called Katherine to see if you knew about this party and she said she didn't think so and that she didn't know what to do. I didn't want to put her in the middle of it. A surprise anniversary party, it just seemed so strange."

"Oh, my God, Faith, I feel like throwing up," I said. "You mean he sent out invitations? He asked me months ago if I wanted to have a party and I told him no, I didn't. We just got an invitation from friends for a party that night in a café in the village. You mean that party is really for us?"

"Yes, I think so. I'm so sorry. I thought I had to gamble and let you know in case it was something you really didn't want to do."

"Thank you for doing that. Thank you, I know that was hard. Oh, damn him, damn him. This is just nuts. He told me that he wanted to have a party. I told him no, there was nothing to celebrate and I didn't want to do anything." The words and anger spilled out of me. "I know I hurt him," I continued, "but it just would make me feel dreadful to pretend through the whole thing that we're happy. Oh, God, I don't know what to do."

Faith suggested I talk to Debra, and that seemed to make sense. I couldn't see her for a couple of days, and by the time I did I had made up my mind that I couldn't go to the party. I realized that Tom was playing another power game, making another desperate attempt to control me and our life together by saying publicly that everything was fine in hopes he could pretend that it was. I talked over my decision with Debra, who supported me fully, but I was still upset. Driving home through Ellsworth after seeing her I realized my mind was wandering when a siren startled me and I saw a policeman commanding me to pull over. I stopped and an older man hopped out of the police van. "You're not keeping within your lane, lady," he said. "But—but there aren't any lines on the road," I replied. "Yep, they're painting the lines, but you've got to keep in lane anyhow. Let's see your license. Seal Cove, huh? Guess they don't let you off the island too often." His joke cracked the veneer I had shellacked over my pain and it broke through. I started crying and alternatively laughing at myself. "I am so sorry," I kept saying. "I don't mean to cry, I don't mean to use that old ploy, sorry," and then I'd burst into tears again.

"Something happen to you, lady?" he said, with what seemed sincere concern in his blue eyes.

"Yes, yes, I guess it did," I answered. "But I don't mean to cry and I'm sorry."

"Hey, it's okay, just keep between the lines, you know, like crayoning," he replied, smiling, and he let me go.

When I got home Tom was sitting in the living room in front of the television, filing a callus on his foot. I sat down on the couch and said, "Tom, I know about the party." He looked over at me. "I don't understand how you could have done that without asking me. I told you I didn't want a party," I continued.

"I just thought it would be a nice surprise for you," he said blandly. "You never said you didn't want a party."

"Tom," I replied, clenching my hands in front of me in exasperation, "you asked me months ago and I said no, there wasn't much to celebrate and I didn't want to have a party. Don't you remember? We talked about it."

"No. I just thought it would be a nice surprise. Everything is set up. You can't cancel now," he said, looking at me smugly.

I guess this was my first real act of defiance. I had gone along with so many things, but I knew I couldn't go to this party and I knew he couldn't make me. So I said, "Okay, you have the party, but I'm not going," and I stood up and walked into the kitchen. Immediately I felt enormous relief. Later I told him I wouldn't help undo the party, that it was his responsibility to get us out of the problem he had created. Tom canceled the invitations and no one said much about it. Perhaps they had wondered all along why he was planning a surprise anniversary party.

Tom's new psychiatrist was a woman of about thirty-five or forty, tall and willowy, with very short-cropped brown hair. The first time I heard her speak I was dumbfounded. She sounded like a child; a thin wispy voice wafted from her mouth, as if it were a floating cloud. The doctor said she wanted to talk with me, so we arranged to meet in her office in the medical center in the village where Tom and I worked. It was a plain, small, one-story building, well lighted through large windows. But when I think of her office now, I see only dark walls and dim lights. She sat on a chair to my left, Tom on a small couch to my right.

"Well, Barbara," she whispered, "I just wanted to meet you and get your ideas about what's happening here."

"I'm certainly glad to be of help. What do you want to know?"

"Well, I just want to know what you think is going on," she whispered from her seat next to the heavily curtained window.

It was surreal. I sat in the darkened room and talked about Tom. I tried to keep my voice even, my frustration and anger concealed, but they leaked out at times. I said, "Things have been bad for quite a while. I don't blame Tom. His mother was a cold woman, and an alcoholic."

"Yes," she whispered again, her voice a thin shred of sound. As I continued I began to feel defensive, hiding behind a wall of detachment, as if I were trying to protect myself by being dispassionate and clinical.

"Well," I said, "the way Tom behaves sometimes makes me think he just wasn't nurtured as a child, that he just craves the kind of attention an infant wants."

"What do you mean?" she asked again, and added that she thought he was making so much progress in the short time they had seen each other. I began to think he had pulled her in, disguising, perhaps unintentionally, the depth of his illness from her.

And so I said, "I'm talking about stealing food from the people who work with us, and eating nothing but ice." I saw her raise her eyebrows involuntarily, and I added, "I moved out of our bedroom several years ago because he was stealing from our employees and because the room smelled so bad. I think his body is eating itself and produces a horrible smell." She sat silently, but her mouth opened and then closed. Finally I said, "I'm really sick of stepping into his spit. I've asked him so many times not to spit on the floor so that I won't step in it, and to flush the toilet and zip up his fly."

Her eyes widened, she looked shocked, and turning her long neck, she looked at Tom and said, "Tom, aren't you ashamed?"

Now it was my turn to be shocked. *Ashamed?* I thought psychiatrists were never supposed to say the word "shame" to their patients.

Tom looked at his hands, and in a very low voice he replied, "Yes."

I thought to myself that I had more sympathy for him than this psychiatrist did, and I wondered why she had held up shame and "ought to" in front of a man who was torturing himself to death because he felt so ashamed of his "self" and his own body. I decided not to share anything more with her then, though later I would ask for her help again, and again I was to feel let down.

Finally, finally I was ready to feel my own pain. Patiently, Debra had waited for me to be strong enough to face my loneliness, my feeling of self-doubt and worthlessness. I had also started taking singing lessons with an ebullient redheaded singer and actress, named Hannah, who was worried about her second marriage. Singing the bittersweet songs of love helped me touch my own sadness, and sometimes in the middle of a lesson I broke down. Standing in a cramped room at the high school, with only a plywood door to shield us from intrusion, Hannah persuaded me to make an appalling range of sound in vocal exercises that quite literally helped me find my own voice and the courage to use it.

In 1954, when I was twelve years old, I spent a year in Japan. Desie was posted there as the director of overseas operations for the CIA in the Far East. We moved to Kamakura, an ancient village, once the seat of the shogun, and now interlaced with extraordinary orange red Torii soaring into the air, streets filled with women in exquisite silk kimonos that swayed at their feet as they walked under parasols, teetering slightly on high getas. I wondered at the contrast between them and younger Japanese men and women, who wore Western dress, their sense of color somehow evaporating in the transition, so that the colors they had chosen seemed to clash and they looked uncomfortable. I marveled at the huge bronze Buddha that towered above me on my walk home and delighted in going inside it to see how the metal plates were sutured together, the scars like keloids.

We lived in a gigantic Tudor house, built for a Japanese prince by a German architect and then owned by a Chinese general who had three concubines. The living room was eighty feet long and there were two huge marble fireplaces covering the central heating ducts. A picture of Mount Fuji done entirely in sequins hung over one mantel, and two alabaster lamps held up by naked ladies with polished bottoms stood at the far end of the room. My bedroom had heavy red velvet curtains, a palatial bed, and an enormous marble mantelpiece on which I displayed my growing shell collection. I was told my bedroom had been reserved for the general's favorite concubine and I tried to conjure up what went on there.

I felt immersed in this foreign life and comfortable, particularly as my Japanese improved. I would go to the little stores on my way home—the lacquer shop where the men turned out bowls and boxes in rich deep red, shining and richly decorated, or the wood shop where they made intricately worked utensils, or the lantern shop where workers pasted brightly colored rice paper over arched bamboo struts twisted into undulating shapes. The owner was an opium smoker I learned, when I asked why his eyes were so red and unfocused.

My favorite was the antique shop that Desie and I used to visit. Many times he and I went to the shop together to talk with its old owner, because we liked talking to him and because it seemed he enjoyed being with us. Perhaps he and Desie were old friends or accomplices in the spy business, but to me our expeditions were innocent delights.

The shop was dark enough that I had to wait for my eyes to adjust to the lack of light. Slowly I began to see the room lined with vitrines of highly polished dark wood, the doors inset with handmade glass, the irregularities refracting light subtly. Behind the glass, resting on silk brocade in peach, persimmon, the blues of aquamarine and tourmalines or hand-softened ivory, like well-loved temptresses, lay artifacts that evoked a past stretching over centuries. Green jade snuff bottles with tiny long-stemmed spoons so delicate they looked like the stem of an orchid, netsuke polished by countless hands, gold and tortoiseshell ornaments for the hair that likely had graced favored courtesans, small porcelain cups and bowls of celadon and bull's blood, and Han bronzes, their elegant surfaces an intricate mosaic of greens and grays. The old lacquer fascinated me because I could see similarities between the antique pieces and the new ones made lovingly by my friend the lacquer maker. The antique shop smelled of sweet dust, tea, and years, and I treasured the time I was there with Desie and felt honored that he had chosen me to accompany him.

We sat on tatami mats on a raised dais and drank tea from thin deep red porcelain cups, so thin that light filtering through them made them look like the petals of a rose. The old man and Desie talked for a long time while I watched them and looked at the wonderful objects in the shop, making up stories, trying to sense where they had been and who had touched them before. Then the old man would say that he had something he especially favored and would like Mr. Williamson-san to see—because he would appreciate its grace and importance. He would then disappear into the mysterious recesses of the shop and bring out an object swaddled in thick white cotton, and put it within a circle of light on the mat in front of us. Slowly, so slowly, he unwrapped the cotton bands, to reveal a figurine or bowl, a carving, or once, a Tang horse.

When my stepfather said I could help him buy one thing, my eyes flew to the porcelain vase. It had a rich cream glaze and fading green, blue, and red flowers and circling black clouds, though once they might have had a touch of silver. I realized later the piece was not particularly beautiful, but I loved being the one who had chosen it and that my stepfather bought it on my recommendation, not for me, but for our house. After his death, and then, later, my mother's, I took the vase to my house. I thought of Desie many times when I looked at it, sitting on the marble-topped pine cabinet I had bought from another antique dealer I grew to trust and admire.

★   ★   ★

In the final years of our marriage, I would come home, finally, after a long day, a day extended because I wanted both to hide from Tom and to feel I was useful. During those years, when I got home, I walked upstairs to the living room and found Tom on the couch. I knew he had been drinking, but somehow at first I denied what I knew. One night when I walked into the dark living room, he was sitting on the chair next to the television watching the news, only he was not really watching. He was waiting for me. The tension knotted inside me as if I were walking into a trap.

"Well, you sure are home late. Did you leave the icebox door open this morning? I think you did. It wasn't working properly. Some of the food might have spoiled. You must be more careful."

As always, his accusations were trivial and stupid. But I was tired and I felt wronged and I couldn't understand what he was talking about. I tried to defend myself, but instead I just got sucked into the stupidity of an argument based on old anger not logic. I had a glass of wine myself and I started to feel angry, too. Instead of recognizing that he was baiting me, trying to get me to argue, I started screaming back at him.

"How dare you accuse me of being lazy and incompetent? Look at you. You leave work at two in the afternoon. You go there and pretend you are working in the morning, but you're just reading the paper and writing your friend Carlos. You are pathetic. Pam and Inge and I cover your mistakes. You are horrible to live with, here and at work."

He cowered in front of me like a broken child, and when he looked up at me I realized he was turning me into his drunken mother, who in her fits had cursed him for his existence until he no longer wanted to exist. Making me yell at him took him back to his childhood, to a familiar place. I became so furious I picked up the vase Desie had bought in Japan and started to throw it on the ground, but then hesitated, knowing I would destroy it. In that instant I remembered my mother's story of Bobby Kennedy, that he had toasted his primary victory by putting his crystal champagne glass down and picking up a cheap glass to throw into the fireplace, having carefully prepared for the moment. I knew I had to find the courage to break the vase. I knew I had to mark the moment for myself with something so precious that I would forever remember how angry I had been. And so I threw the vase and it smashed on the oak floor. So many times I have thought of that moment, a moment I will not return to, just as I will not return to that marriage or to the ugly, screaming harridan I almost became.

10

SHARDS

February 1993

The last years were the worst. It wasn't just that we were estranged, living in separate rooms, that I was trying to create a separate life and that we were alone together because our children were at school. When they were home, it was harder to stand up to Tom because I was afraid he would get angry. When they were away I had no one to hide behind. No, the worst thing was that I was always reacting to him. I timed my life by his comings and goings, trying always to be going when he was coming, coming when he was going.

Usually I worked late at the office, arriving home about seven-thirty when I knew Tom was taking a sauna. I parked the car and moved quickly through the dark garage, past the small gym in the back of the garage, and into the house. I walked up the stairs to my home office, my refuge, relieved that he was not there. I dropped my work for the evening on the burnt-orange desktop over the filing cabinets that held my life: courses I had taken, birth certificates, pedigrees for cats, children's grades, inoculation records, comments from teachers, warranties on appliances, copies of leases for rental cottages, comments from tenants. Usually I had calls to make in the evening to rental customers or clients. Often people called late at night because they couldn't do business during the day—they were busy with their own work—and only had time to think about their vacation in the evening. To someone else the calls might have been an intrusion, to me they were a relief.

I looked at the photographs on the walls, my mother as the ingenue curving against Paderewski, hero of *Moonlight Sonata,* my stepfather surrounded by paunchy Chinese military men on Quemoy, or drinking bullshots, his version of a Bloody Mary made with bouillon. I looked at the picture of him and me at my debutante party, the one I didn't want but didn't refuse to let them give. I saw again the lines of eligible bachelors parading in front of me. Too bad their eyes were breast height, too bad they didn't seem to have chins and all looked alike to me. I stared at pictures of my children at a lake in the Adirondacks, the hills bleached by acid rain, and at another of my favorite tide pool in Maine hung beside a photograph of my sister and me at the same pool, and at about the same ages, dipping mussels out of the sand so we could tear the seed pearls from their flesh and collect them in matchboxes throughout the summer. Years later, when I returned to the spot, I wondered if our careless destruction was responsible for the paucity of mussels remaining in the pools.

I got ready to exercise and take my own sauna, knowing that soon Tom would be coming back into the house. The minute I got home I was supposed to go to the gym right as he was leaving it so I would finish working out and he could take another sauna before going to bed. I could not allow time for it to air out, so the thick sweet smell of wine sweat in the gym cloyed in my throat; I dreaded the way Tom's smell and rigid schedule imprisoned and controlled me.

I walked to our gym in the garage and began to exercise; sometimes I did aerobics on the small oak floor we had built, sometimes I lifted weights, used a StairMaster or a NordicTrack. I wonder now why I dropped my membership at the health club in Trenton, where I saw other people, to hide myself even more. I didn't like driving forty-five minutes there from the office to work out for an hour and then driving another thirty-five minutes home. I didn't like being The Realtor, cornered by people with questions about their houses, and I disliked feeling that I had to listen so I could make money. But even more than that, I couldn't stand to be around women who loved their husbands.

At the club there was a woman who had survived breast cancer. As she walked around the locker room, a towel draping her ample body, she seemed to have accepted its destruction and reconstruction. She talked about her husband, how much he loved and supported her. I wanted to be her friend but I couldn't reciprocate; I couldn't talk about my life or my husband honestly. I couldn't watch people who were happy and talked with love about their husbands; I couldn't interact with them. It hurt to pretend I was happy and so I had withdrawn deeply into myself. Now, as I walked to my own little gym, I thought about how isolated I was, and how spare my life seemed beside the lives of the other women and how, in my fiftieth year, I had created such a loveless life.

One morning I woke up an hour earlier than usual and let my cats out of the house. A few minutes later I heard angry barking, not that of a dog but a harsh and wilder voice. I realized it must have been the vixen that denned on our driveway and I walked down the gravel driveway in my old flowered bathrobe to see what was happening. The cats were standing at attention, puffballs of white-and-brown fur, looking from the driveway up the hillside, where, between granite outcroppings, a glacier once shoveled sand. Shaded by birch and hatmatack, the den had been the home of many tenants—weasels, groundhogs, and for the past ten years foxes. Now this vixen stared at my cats defiantly and I realized that by letting them out of the house so early I had encroached on "her time"; I had upset a system for sharing space that she, like me, had so carefully followed in order to survive.

Other events forced me to think about my life, or perhaps I was just ready to read the signs. I learned that the husband of a summer acquaintance had shot himself in their New York apartment, going into the back hall so his children would not stumble over his splattered head, but also so his wife would find him when she went to dump the garbage. I was not a close friend of this woman, but I became obsessed with what had happened, feeling I had to be useful to her, getting her summer house cleaned and open, buying flowers, making sure that everything was in order for her and her children when they arrived at their refuge. I wished I was her; I envied her release from a crazy life, a crazy husband, a man who lay in bed eating vanilla ice cream while recovering from a liposuction he could not afford to have done, having just lost another job. People at the club had joked about him for years when he blustered his way through the lunch line, or wore the wrong shoes to play tennis, or got drunk and smashed his boat, injuring a friend. But now I saw him as someone who was sick and I began to wonder what people thought of Tom and of me.

I often dreamed Tom was dead. I would sit in the office at home at night, my mind wandering, thinking about how to find some release. In my mind I heard a sound like backfiring, but I knew it was a gun. I had listened to hunters during the fall, poaching

deer in the woods across the pond, or sometimes closer. Now—
shotgun or rifle? Sounds more like a pistol, and so close, I commented to myself. In my mind I rushed out the front door, but the
woods were still, the animals and birds shocked into silence. I
walked, hesitating, toward the garage, opened the gym door, and
there he was, sprawled out of the sauna, dying, blood streaming
down his temple, his face white. I worried that he was so weak his
emaciated body could hardly function and I sometimes found myself fantasizing that he would catch pneumonia from running in the
winter, the way he once got pleurisy. I thought his protruding belly
betrayed that he had developed cirrhosis of the liver like Mrs. Mu-
ñoz, my client on welfare who died three days after I first met her,
complaining that she "just had the gas" and her belly hurt but she
would be fine. I thought about how much he looked like the skeletal figures in the Giacometti lithographs he loved.

Sometimes, when I thought about the way he had abused his
body, anger pulsed through my own as if a powerful force had
gripped me. Before my mother and stepfather bought their own
farm, they rented a house from close friends who owned a large
working farm. One day, as I walked to their house, I stopped to
watch Larry, one of the farmers, as he worked to catch a black
snake. Larry was a huge gentle man, so strong he had pulled his
house on rollers from its first foundation about a half mile away to
a new and better spot overlooking the herds of Herefords. Larry
caught the snake, an enormous writhing black snake that was stealing eggs from the henhouse, and killed it by snatching it up by the
tail and cracking it like a whip until its back broke and its head
snapped off. I watched in awe and then turned to walk away, and
Larry, in a moment of careless cruelty, flipped the snake so that in
its dying convulsion it wrapped its headless body around my bare
legs. I jumped and screamed, frozen in shock, until he came to
peel it off my legs and throw it into a nearby gully.

Now, in torturing nightmares and daydreams, I saw Tom floating through space. Sometimes I was suddenly overcome by such vivid feelings of revulsion and disgust at the thought of my husband, committing his slow suicide, that I saw his body as a clutch of dry stalks. In my mind I picked him up, cracked him like a whip, and then flung the dry husk of his body into a gully as hard as I could, and watched as it fell slowly into the darkness. I had lost my friends and my family, and now I felt I was losing my mind and my soul.

In the gym I worked the pain out of my mind. Sweat purged the day that had passed and the night to come from my mind and body. When I finished I moved quickly to the house, trying to walk silently on the pink gravel, carefully closing the front door behind me, hoping Tom would not hear me so I could have a few extra moments alone. Usually, he came right out the front door as I closed the door to the gym and I thought he must have been watching and waiting for me in the front hall, waiting for the faint click of the garage door as I left the gym. We passed on the driveway, our shoes crunching across the gravel. Sometimes he said someone had called and I needed to call them back, but usually there was nothing to say, and so we passed, shadows illuminated by the faint moon.

I took a hurried shower, snatching a towel to drape over my body. I had a Jacuzzi in my bathroom but I never used it because it took too long. I felt time at my back, and as I pulled the ugly old dressing gown over my head, I wondered why women at the health club smoothed their bodies with creams and lotions. I never took such care of myself, hoping the roughness of my skin would guard me against being touched. I scurried to the little kitchen to cook the same meal each night every night, month after month after month, a meal I knew I could make before Tom came in from the sauna. I put ready-made tabouleh in the thick brown onion-soup crock, covered it with shredded mozzarella, and zapped it for two minutes in the microwave. I heard Tom come in the door and go to his bathroom to take an ice-cold bath, plunging his body into the water, and pushing his gaunt pelvis along the bottom of the tub so that it made a sound like knuckles on a washboard. I walked quickly to the office, closed the door. It didn't close well, but if I pushed up against it, I could almost shut it, and if Tom wanted to open it, he had to tug and the door would make a scratching noise that warned me of his presence.

As I gulped the food, looking at the framed photographs, I wondered how I could have so diminished my life that it took place within these walls. I felt grateful for the spaces in my mind the photographs created, but I lived within a tiny emotional space circumscribed by Tom's illness, and my own vulnerabilities. I could no longer cook if Tom was anywhere near me; I could not eat if he looked at my food. I worked in the office until he went to bed, and then sometimes I came out to read, sitting in the living room, embraced by the comfortable blue velvet couch. Sometimes, as I sat there, I had a glass of wine by myself and I cried, wrapping my arms around a pillow as I held it close to me and buried my head in its folds. But it was a brief, unsatisfying acknowledgment of loneliness, and mostly I did not cry because I did not want Tom or anyone else to see the signs of my tears in the morning.

Tom and I passed in the halls, at home and at work. When I heard him coming toward me, I shuddered away from him. At work, if he asked, I passed him a paper, or the car keys, a pencil or pen, but so carefully that I would not have to touch his cold thin fingers, thin as the crazy-eyed aye-aye, a lemur that uses its gaunt middle finger to poke into bark in search of grubs. I felt the cold of his hands creep down the pencil into my hands and I feared the cold would kill me.

My soul and mind were falling away. I thought about how my mother died from grief when she was fifty-three because when she lost Desie seven years before, stress turned her body against her. I thought about how my father died just before my mother, the stresses of his childhood cornering him in alcoholism and the smoke of too many cigarettes. I had learned my own body's vulnerabilities and I knew sometimes my mind was too strong for my body and that my body would collapse first as I neared my fiftieth birthday. I began to see that if I wanted to live, I must break this life and create a new one from the shards.

I disliked myself. I hated being the nasty harping wife and, though we were nominally partners at work, hated being the boss of an ineffectual employee I couldn't fire. I hated always looking for what was wrong not what was right. I hated delighting in Tom's failures, cutting him to slivers like tissue vivisected to examine under a microscope. I hated my words, Barbara's barbs, destructive as ninja weapons, hurled in anger. I knew I helped cripple Tom, helped make even ordinary functioning impossible for him. In some way, now contorted by anger I enjoyed watching him hobble around the office, clutching at doorjambs and chair backs, moving haltingly through the rooms. I enjoyed his mistakes because they heightened my sense of my own competence.

"Oh, Tom," I started to say innocently. "Joannie just called to say she told you she wanted the windows in the kitchen changed so they are twice the width they are shown in the plan. But she just looked at the video we sent and they're still the same single windows."

He looked up at me and focused as if he were coming out of a haze. "Huh? I don't remember talking to her," he replied.

"But she said she talked to you a couple of weeks ago after they were up here to look. She said you told her you would talk with Bill, and his guys could change the windows easily because they hadn't finished closing in," I added. He sat at his desk while I gloated. I knew I was right. I knew he had screwed up again. I could feel myself thinking of him as a pathetic, sick child, that he didn't pay any attention to details and relied on me and the others in our office to bail him out time and time again. Where in the past I had felt sorry for him, and so often sympthized and tried to correct his mistake, now I was getting angry and bitter.

"Oh shit, I guess I just went too fast, too much to do," he added to cover himself.

"So what are you going to do about it?" I asked.

"I guess we just won't charge a fee on that piece of work, that will cover it," he suggested.

"Tom, how are we going to stay in business if we don't charge a fee? It's not just your time—you can waste that if you want— but think of the phone bill, the rent, Inge's time, the postage. Damn it, all that adds up and you don't seem to care. You come in here and read the paper and write letters, and then you leave at two-thirty to go run and you spend half your time here soaking your foot, cooking disgusting messes in the microwave. It is just so totally gross no one can stand sharing this office with you!" I stood up and walked out of the room, almost unable to control my anger, worried the other people in the office would hear be- cause the walls and the door were so thin. I walked through the office as quickly as I could and went out into the parking lot, out onto the street, walking and walking, clenching and unclenching my fists. When I had walked out my anger, I shook myself and walked back slowly to the office, resigned.

I had stopped drinking alcohol when Tom was around and, later completely, I realized that I was being pulled into his web of fantasy and hurt, when I realized that I was becoming like a spider waiting to trap him, and that I was learning the part too well. When I didn't drink around him, I felt safer; I could keep my guard up. I no longer had to scream at him to make him leave me alone as he seemed to want me to. I heard a minister say recently that if we stay uninvolved in anger, if we back off, we do not feed someone else's anger with our own energy, and their anger withers. One night when I came home, Tom lashed out at me about wasting money and I took a step back, away from him. "If that's what you think, fine. I don't want to talk about it," I said.

"Don't want to talk about it? Why don't you want to talk about it?" he yelled.

"I just don't want to get into another argument," I replied calmly, turning to walk into my office to put my briefcase down.

"Well, it's important. We have to talk . . ." But I closed the door and left him sitting on the couch, nursing a glass of wine. I see now that when I backed away, I left Tom's anger and hurt to die because I didn't feed it with my own. It was a useful strategy I stumbled onto, and only much later, when I was with friends I could trust, would I let myself drink wine again.

Debra often asked me to talk about myself. "This is your therapy," she'd say. "I know the problems with Tom are intense, but let's think about you." But I couldn't do this, at least not for long. Sometimes I could talk about my father, or about growing up in a house where I felt like Cinderella without her prince, but always I brought the conversation back to Tom. I see now that this was safe ground for me, as if I were saying, "I must be all right if I am coping with such a difficult situation. He is sick. I am much healthier, so I must be all right."

Debra was patient with me. Several times she asked me if I ever thought about being with another man, having a new life. "No," I answered. "That's over for me. I mean, I haven't had sex for several years now. It really isn't a big deal. I don't miss it."

One time she asked, "If you were going to get involved with someone, what kind of shoes would he have?"

"Shoes?" I replied, mystified. "What kind of shoes?"

"Shoes, just think about the shoes," she suggested. I sat looking out of her office. The room was too hot, even though the windows were wide open, because the radiator functioned on its own rhythms and couldn't be turned off. I stared out the window, looking at people shopping on the street below, and I struggled to answer her.

"Okay," I said tentatively, "I think he would have desert boots, or some kind of good strong work shoes. Nothing fancy, no shined Brooks Brothers black leather, just plain, simple shoes, a bit beat-up and worn, but very comfortable. Sort of used but not used up," I joked. It seemed safe, as she hoped it would be, to think about shoes, but it was a long time before I let my mind creep up to deal with anything more threatening.

As I tried to reconstitute the person I had been before I was married, I thought about what had given me pleasure, what I enjoyed doing, and when in my life I had felt most involved. But I didn't know that was what I was looking for, only that I had to find the broken pieces of myself and try to glue them together again, much as I had done when I worked for the Smithsonian Institution or the Peabody Museum, taking the shards of pottery and slowly building a vase from the debris that archaeologists had excavated. Piece by piece I had to find those things in myself that had mattered to me, and rebuild my life.

First was my love for my children, which kept me from breaking into pieces so small they could not be put back together. But what else? I realized I no longer wanted to live through and only for my children; that was too big a burden to place on them. What else matters? I asked myself. I remembered walking the streets of Harlem and the South Bronx, being a welfare worker, clutching my black casebook and walking into tenements, nodding at the heroin addicts in the front halls who nodded back to me in congenial unison. I remembered my client Miss Jones, who had two small children. I went to see her before I had read her case file because I liked forming my own opinions about my clients. She lived in a dingy second-floor apartment, her pudgy face bore scars and bruises, and the bags under her eyes suggested that she drank too much and too often. I thought she was about forty, certainly much older than I was. When I read her file I was shocked to discover that she was eighteen, that her children were born when she was fourteen and sixteen, and that she had been raped when she was a child by her father and thrown out of the house into a snowbank. To stay alive she sold the only thing she had, her body.

Shortly after I met her, I went home for Christmas, and while I was away I sent each of my clients a card. When I returned to New York I got a call from Miss Jones. She was sobbing, sobbing so heavily I could hardly understand her. "Miss Lorenz, I never got no card before. You sent me a card. I did a present for you. I painted my apartment. Come over and see it." Her words were fuzzy but her meaning clear and I went to see her the next day. She had painted the apartment pink, florid, flamingo pink. Everything was pink—radiators, doors, trim, baseboard, walls, some of the floor, the ceiling. It made me feel as if I were inside a cow's belly. But I knew how hard she had worked and what it meant to her to change her environment, and I felt happy to have been a part of that.

I knew I could not return again to the mean streets of Harlem and the South Bronx; the times had changed and so had I. Now I would be scared because I had things to lose—my children— and as a result, I would be less effective. So what else? My love of using my mind, being with people, being useful. "Where have I found that before?" I asked myself. I searched over my life looking for the times I felt connected, and found them when I was teaching. I remembered the times I thought I made a difference in students' lives and when I knew they had made a difference in mine. I thought about former students. Chris, the young man who was dyslexic, I thought, but whose parents had always told him he was lazy and stupid. I remembered telling him that I wore contact lenses because I could not see without them. I told him that like me, he had inherited a slight miswiring in his circuitry and needed help to deal with it, but that it was no more his fault than my myopia was mine, just a question of biology. I remembered seeing him sit up straighter when I told him that, as if a heavy burden had been lifted from his shoulders. I remembered the young woman in Greenwich who with tears in rivulets down her cheeks told me that she didn't want another car, she just wanted her father to be home with her and her mother, but that her father thought he had to provide for them in material ways and so didn't give her his time and love. So many faces stood in line before me, walking toward me, and reaching out to me to pull me back to them. Like a dream sequence I saw them, marching up to me and then smiling and turning where I was standing like a tree in darkness.

I asked myself what I wanted to do with the rest of my life. I thought about being an old woman and looking back over my life. What if all I saw was a woman who made money and had a big house. Did I want to look at my life when I was eighty-five and say, "I sold a lot of overpriced houses to people who didn't need them"? Once I put it to myself that way I could not escape, I could not turn my back on the thought. I knew I must pull up the roots that grew through my feet into the earth below me—roots clawing down, burying themselves in fear of change, fear of not being able to support myself and my children who were in college, fear of being disgraced, and perhaps most terrifying, the fear of failing at marriage, something I had vowed I would not do.

Did I want to be a welfare worker again? No. Did I want to teach again? Yes. How can I do that? I thought. How can I leave my real-estate business and still earn the money to pay the children's tuition? I can't. How can I begin to move my life back to what I love? The answer was that I could go back to school myself. If I couldn't be in a classroom where I was the teacher, I could at least be in a classroom where I was a student. I got the catalog for courses at the College of the Atlantic in nearby Bar Harbor, and going through it, I found courses in education that I could take. I found that the college offered residents of the island a reduced tuition rate. And I thought about how to tell Tom.

For days I tried to think of ways to make my plan to return to school most palatable to him. I thought about the wife of our former boss, who left their real-estate business to earn a degree in nursing and emergency medicine, something she had longed to do. Perhaps having that model would help Tom, but then I thought better of the idea as I realized that would make him think I was planning to leave the business entirely. I knew any change in our routine would be threatening to him and I was afraid of displeasing him, but finally I just told him. We were sitting at our desks in the office, and I turned to face him.

"Tom, I've been thinking about taking a course at the college. I think it would be fun and it's easier than going to the university in Orono."

"Why do you want to do that? You don't have time. You can't just take off from work," he snarled.

"Well, there's a class called Secondary Methods that seems good and it just meets once a week, on Wednesdays, in the afternoon. I can get Pam to cover the office for me and I'll come back and work late," I answered, prepared and consciously modulating my voice so it was even, cheerful, and determined. I could feel the blood rushing into my face and my stomach turning, but I knew it was crucial that I stand up to him. I thought about all the hours he exercised, how he always left the office hours before I did, and it made me angry.

"I don't know. I don't see how you can do that and all the other . . ." His voice trailed off and then he shot back, "I've wanted to do something like that for a long time, but I just couldn't take the time out from work for it. It seems pretty selfish, if you ask me."

I had chosen to have this conversation in the office to protect myself from his anger, and now I realized it was also protecting me from my own. I turned back to my desk, facing the Rolodex, the phone, the *Social Register*—all the tools of our trade.

"It's good for me to get out, and besides, I may meet people who will be interested in having us do something for them in real estate."

"The people at the college don't have the money to buy anything."

"You just don't know that," I replied curtly. "Remember, Paul Newman's daughter was a student there, and those people who bought the big farm on Beech Hill. I bet I'll meet people I can do some work for."

So I disguised my need to find a way out to Tom and perhaps a bit to myself, covering it in a cloak of business and the intention of finding clients.

I was twenty-five years older than the other students in the class, but they and the teacher seemed to welcome me. I worked hard not to say too much in class, as if I were sitting on my hands, using energy to repress what I wanted to say so I wouldn't dominate the discussion because I had so many more years of experience from which to draw. Taking the class didn't detract from my work in our real-estate business as the class only met one a week and I could do the homework at night, but Tom still resented my absence.

After several months, when we had settled into the new routine, he said he thought he would like to go back to seminary and he began to investigate several programs. I thought he was doing it in part to spite me and I wondered about the sincerity of his refound interest in the ministry, but that really didn't matter. I was pleased and relieved because I thought he might meet other people and become less isolated, and because it seemed less likely he would criticize me for going back to school.

That spring, after taking two courses, I could not get into a class because of a conflict in my schedule at work and, it turned out, because students who did not know me feared competing with me. I was touched that two students who did know me came to my defense, but in a meeting held without my knowledge, I was voted out of the class.

When the professor told me, I felt the earth caving in on me, sucking me into a mucky void. I had nowhere to go, nothing I wanted to do. I walked out of the turreted Bar Harbor cottage that housed the offices of the college, stumbled across the grass, and got into my old blue Toyota truck. For hours I drove around and around the island. I cried so deeply I was beyond control, sobbing and sobbing convulsively as I clutched the steering wheel. When I couldn't see clearly, I stopped and stared at the ocean, watching the cold, gray waves breaking over the granite rocks, feeling the cold seep into me, watching the seagulls lined up along the tarmac, watching the water as the fishermen also liked to do in the early morning and late afternoon. Around and around the island I drove for hours, held only by the arms of familiar places I had loved since I was a child.

I purged so much pain out of me that day that I felt cleansed, fresh and powerful, though those were fleeting feelings, too. Soon, coincidentally, I learned about a graduate program at Boston University School of Education, and buoyed by the support that reached out to me from the catalog, I applied. I was accepted as a doctoral student and began the program in the fall of 1993.

I began commuting weekly to take classes at BU in education and anthropology. On the plane trip back and forth, as I began to meet new people and redefine myself. As I sat on the plane, my engagement and wedding rings began to feel heavy and tight. I could feel them literally dragging my hand down, and hurting my finger. The slight fracture in the sapphire, barely visible when Tom gave me the ring, had grown so that I wondered if the stone had split. Years earlier, when I had mentioned my concern to Tom, he had laughed and replied, "I hope it isn't a metaphor for our marriage," but now I knew it was. Finally I took the rings off and put them on my other hand, replacing them as I sat in the plane on the way back to Maine. After several months of taking them on and off, changing my persona as I went back and forth between Maine and Boston, I laid them in a drawer and replaced them with two rings Grannie had given me just before she died. They were mine, and it felt more honest to wear them than the rings from Tom's family. Finally my hands felt as if they belonged to me again. I knew Tom was hurt when I took off the rings he had given me, but by that time I was focused on gathering the remnants of my self and he couldn't deflect me. One day, in the office, he said to me, "I see you aren't wearing your rings anymore."

"No," I replied. "They started to feel heavy and I feel better wearing the ones Grannie left me. I'm sorry, but I just can't wear the other ones anymore."

He didn't push me to explain anything more. We both retreated to the safer ground of talking only about business and our children. The friendship we had once had based on our ability to talk about our families, books, politics, and a wide range of subjects had eroded, leaving us on either side of a widening gully. Where once I had come to his defense if anyone criticized him, taken his part when he felt slighted or hurt, now I began to defend myself and in doing so, felt like a traitor to him. When I had told my father I didn't want to see him I felt I had told him to go to hell, and he had. Now I felt as if I was doing the same thing to Tom.

My commute from rural Maine to Boston became a lifeline, a means of reaching my self. At first I used my married name, but as I began to feel stronger, I used my maiden name at school. In a required course called Group Problem Solving I had to describe a conflict and plan a resolution. I tried to make up a problem in education, but finally I went to the professor and told him my problem was that I was in a miserable marriage and I didn't know what to do. I asked him if I could write about that instead of a problem in education, and he gave me permission to do so. The students in the class worked together in small groups—mine included four other women who listened sympathetically when I described my problem and thought about possible resolutions. Then the professor came over to listen to our discussion and finally said, "It seems to me that you need a sabbatical from all this. It really is crushing you." A sabbatical—time off! I realized I had felt as if my life had piled stones on top of me; now someone had shown me a way to take some of them off. But I was still frightened, worried that if I left Tom I would have no way to earn the money to pay my children's college tuition.

I enrolled in a seminar that met for a week in Washington, D.C., an experience that left me exhilarated and exhausted. The night it was over I went to the airport to fly first to Boston, then to Maine. I walked down the aisle of the plane, feeling frumpy, my blue-and-green batik printed cotton dress wrinkled and a little dirty. I sank into the cramped seat, regretting it was in the middle, relieved there was no one sitting next to me. When a large, equally rumpled sandy-haired man sat down in the aisle seat, I offered to move over so we could have more room, but he told me the flight would be full because it always was on a Friday night. Just before the stewardess closed the cabin door, a man with black hair curling around a thin face walked fast into the plane, and then joked with the man on the aisle about having to climb over us to get to his window seat. I talked amiably with my sandy-haired companion about nothing and then my other seat mate started to tell me about the fancy new computer he had on his lap.

We talked about our trips, mine for school, his for business, and where we lived. I took off my glasses as casually as I could, wishing I had worn my contacts. Gradually we began to talk about our lives with the openness of people who do not expect to meet again. "I am so beat right now," I said, turning in the small seat to look at him, "but it's a good kind of tired, not the deep, hopeless tired I feel when I'm in Maine." He had brown eyes, which sparkled with light, though I noticed deep circles almost like bruises under them.

"Yes, I'm beat, too," he said, and laid his head back on the seat. "Too much traveling. I sold my business to a company in Boston, but they're screwing it up, screwing up the vision I had for it." As we talked I realized I had began to measure his body against mine and look at his hands, wondering how they would feel on my skin. I realized I was flirting for the first time in many, many years and enjoying my awareness that he was interested in me. We walked from the plane together and stood in the Delta terminal, I heading to catch the plane to Maine, he to his apartment in Boston.

As we stood next to each other to say good-bye, I wished he were taller. I leaned toward him to kiss him good-bye because I was grateful he had flirted with me, but then pushed the thought away and put out my hand. "Good-bye," I said. "I enjoyed talking with you."

As we shook hands he said, "I'd like to see you again," adding, "When you come to Boston, we could have a drink."

"Oh," I replied, stunned.

"Do you use E-mail?" he asked.

"Yes. Well, I guess so—I have an account at BU but I'm not sure really how to—"

"Well, give me your address and we can see if it works. Here's my card." I gave him what I thought was the address and smiled as I turned away from him and walked to catch the bus to the other terminal. It had been a pleasant diversion, I thought, but I never expected to see him again.

I didn't hear from him for three weeks and then, by the time I had forgotten about him, there was a message in the computer saying I had given him the wrong address, but he had used some computer wizardy to find me. I was flattered that he had made the effort, but I didn't know what to do. I hadn't thought about meeting someone new. Though I had played and replayed old loves in my head for years, I had never betrayed my marriage vow—at least not the one about forsaking all others. But it seemed harmless to write—so I did. For months we wrote, and the long letters drew me in. I learned Robert was nine years younger than I was, single—never married—Jewish, raised in California, a high-powered computer "nerd" who had been in a doctoral program at Yale until he dropped out to start his own company.

"Why don't you come stay with me sometime when you're here? I have a condominium," he wrote. "There are two bedrooms, so you are quite safe."

"I guess it would be cheaper than staying at the Howard Johnson," I answered, "and more fun, but I'm not coming back until the summer is almost over." I decided to call Faith to ask her to look up his address, though I felt like a schoolgirl when I did. "His name is Robert Wahl," I said.

"Well, spell his last name for me," she told me, and when I did she said, "That's amazing, he lives a block from my office. He must have some money if he owns a place there."

Having a man to flirt with at a distance helped me distance myself from Tom. We worked together, we lived in the same house, but in different worlds and realities. I had thought many times about leaving Tom, and had even told Robert I would leave when Kit graduated from college, but it was more of a threat than a plan for action. I knew the stress of the way Tom and I were living had been affecting not only his health but my own for years. But I had let myself become so isolated, that I couldn't leave because there was nowhere I wanted to go, no one I wanted to be with. I couldn't leave Tom because I would be completely alone. My parents and grandparents were dead, I was estranged from my sisters and brother, I had pushed myself away from friends, and not made new ones. I couldn't leave my old life because I was too scared to do so. At least I knew where I was—I didn't know then where I could be. I could only leave when I thought I saw a fragile net hanging below me—thin as a spider's silk, but enough of another illusion to let me hurl myself into black space, much as I had once done on an Outward Bound ropes course—leaping into the air from a tree limb thiry-five feet above packed earth, knowing there was a man standing below who would catch the weight of my falling body with the ropes twisted around his own.

For years I had taken a perverse pride in disguising myself and my life from everyone around us; now as I began to open my life to other people, I closed it even more firmly to Tom, telling him nothing about what I was doing or thinking, and yet missing the times we had spoken honestly in the past because now it felt as if there was no one I could talk with, except perhaps Faith.

Reassured by our continuing correspondence, I told Robert I would like to stay with him when I came down to start classes at the end of the summer. The afternoon I flew down I took a cab from the airport because I didn't want to get hot and sweaty on the T— and I got into a wonderful conversation with the driver, who was from Kenya, about his family and his country. As we drove down Beacon Street looking for Robert's house, I started thinking seriously about what I was doing. "Now, when you come to Kenya," the driver said as he got out of the car to get my bag, a wide grin splitting his face. "When you come to Kenya, we are going to give a big feast for you. My family will all be there and we are going to dress you in a lion's skin as our honored guest." I smiled back at him, thinking if I walk into this house, I may never walk out.

I suddenly remembered the way the Mbuti pygmy in the Ituri Forest talk about death, describing levels of partial death until one is absolutely and completely dead. I am already partially dead, I thought, and the risk that Robert will hit me over the head is worth taking. It is better than the reality I live in. As I stood on the street talking to my new friend from Kenya, I could feel Robert's eyes on me through his window. I stood there, prolonging my exit from what I knew before entering territory that was as yet unknowable, finding refuge in word games, "terra incognita, terror cognita," in a moment I knew would change my life, and then I thanked the driver, walked up the steps, and rang Robert's doorbell.

"So. You're here," he said. He looked much younger than I remembered him, perhaps because he was wearing a T-shirt and blue jeans, not an elegant suit.

"Yes, yes, I am," I answered, feeling awkward and self-conscious. "I had a good flight, a great cab ride. I'm kind of sweaty and disgusting, but I'm here. How are you?"

He put his arm across my back gently and opened the front door. "We're in here. I bought this place when I moved from Connecticut. Haven't really got any furniture yet. Let me show you around." I dropped my bag on the stairs and we walked around. He showed me the little office he had made in the hall, the grand living room up a flight of stairs with dark wood paneling and extraordinary antique wallpaper of seminaked ladies gamboling and cavorting. Now I know what that means, I said to myself.

"It's pretty wild, isn't it?" he said. "Grover Cleveland was supposed to have lived here and I guess he chose the wallpaper." There was a huge television in a modern teak cabinet and a mattress on the floor. In the kitchen were a Sub-Zero, a Gagenau range, an elegant pink granite countertop and island, and two black-leather-covered stools. "My sister and mother bought the stuff for the kitchen," he explained. "Otherwise there probably wouldn't be anything here. I'm not much on furniture. Maybe you can help me choose some."

We walked down the stairs and sat at the bottom step talking. That night we went for dinner and walked with the crowds of couples on the streets of Back Bay, Robert pointing out places he liked, I craning to look up at the skyscrapers as though I had never been in a city before. We passed a fortune-teller sitting on a red plastic crate on the sidewalk and she looked at us hopefully, saying, "You, you need your fortune told."

"You want to?" he asked.

Then the woman said, as if to entice us, "I see love in your future."

I was so startled I cried out, "No, no," and ran down the street away from her. Robert laughed at me, and then leaned against the jamb of a doorway into a store and said he wanted to get some ice cream.

"Good night," he said when we got back to his house. "I hope you sleep well. I'll see you in the morning." I went to take a shower in the guest bathroom and stood by the bed fingering the new white cotton nightgown I had bought the day before. I had gone into all the little shops in the village, looking for something new to wear, because I couldn't bear the thought of wearing one from my old life. I had felt like a young girl, hoping I would find something pretty and sexy, but there was nothing to choose from and I had bought a simple white cotton sleeveless gown with an embroidered yoke. I look like a fifty-three-year-old virgin, I told myself.

I lay on top of Robert's guest bed, feeling the rough wool of an afghan he said someone in his family had made and staring at the ceiling, thinking, Some seduction scene this. I wished he would come in to say good night. I heard the television playing through his open door and I imagined him lying on his bed. I began to feel how lonely I was, and finally, I got up and walked to the door of his room. He was lying on his bed wearing a T-shirt and shorts, just as I had pictured him.

"Hi," he said, turning his face from the television to look at me.

"Can I just come in for a little while and watch television with you?" I asked. "I don't like being by myself. It makes me feel lonely. Just for a little while?"

"Of course, come over here, just for a little while," he said, a little laugh playing around his mouth. I lay down on the bed next to him and he put his arm around me and we just lay there like two old friends at a slumber party. The next morning, as I lay next to him, listening to the rhythm of his breathing, scratching my face against his beard, he stroked my hair softly and then eased my hand between his legs. "Just to give you something to think about," he explained when I hastily pulled away. Much later, after I had stayed with him several times, I asked him why he didn't try to make love to me that first night, and he replied, "What would you have done if I had?"

"I would have run away," I said.

"I know," he answered.

11

SECOND CHANCES

October 1994

Robert gave me the excuse I needed to leave, but that's all it was, an excuse I had been looking for without knowing it, for many years. But after I stayed with him, I could no longer share the house with Tom. Sometimes, well after Tom had gone to bed, I would be writing Robert an E-mail and Tom would come upstairs to get a glass of wine. Hurriedly, I would terminate the message and go back to writing a paper for class. Often I would creep upstairs in the early mornings to see if I had gotten an E-mail message from Robert, fearing Tom would wake up. I didn't like living in this deceit, and so I knew I had to move.

And I knew I would have to be the one to leave the house. I was afraid that Tom was simply too weak, both emotionally and physically, to be able to move anywhere else. I felt as if I were abandoning an invalid and that I had to at least give him the comfort of a place he knew and where he had a sauna and gym.

Secretly, I rented a small apartment over our office through my friend who owned the building, and I planned my escape. I packed an emergency bag with a change of clothes, something I could grab if I had to run, an extra pair of shoes, my hair dryer, and my jewelry. I packed a larger bag with more clothes, including the heavy red Yugoslav sweater with colorful embroidered flowers that always makes me feel happy. I tucked the suitcases into the closet in the little guest room I had been using since I moved out of my own large bedroom with its cathedral ceiling and my sewing loft. Then I packed a box of things I treasured, photographs, the strange rock I found in Maine when I was a child that looks so much like a human face, as well as some of my silver and other valuables. And I packed the elegant ivory carving of the goddess of war brandishing a sword in one hand and a shield in another that Desie had bought in Japan. "You will need a warrior goddess," Nan had told me. "You need to believe in the warrior goddess within you to get through this." I was afraid Tom might notice that a few things were missing in the living room, but he didn't.

I thought if I told Tom Friday morning, just before I left for Boston, it would be easiest. But then, thinking about my children, and the awkwardness of being at Robert's place if Tom called them looking for me, I knew I would have to tell him I was leaving a few days before I moved out to give him time, and to be with him. I worried he might hurt himself, though I think now that was in my own mind more than his, because I had for so many years wished him dead, wished I were the grieving widow everyone felt sorry for. That Sunday, as he was watching television, I told him.

"Tom, I've rented an apartment and I'm moving there this weekend."

He turned red and buried his face in his hands. He looked like a balloon deflating, the air and life going out of him.

"But I thought I had eight months. You told me you would stay until Katherine graduates from Harvard, until spring. You can't go before then."

He was crying now, and I looked away from him. I could see the anguish in his face, feel his sense of failure turning in my own gut. I looked at the wreck of a person I had helped create and I almost lost my nerve. But I knew I had to gamble—to bet on his and my ability to survive.

I reminded him that we had not slept in the same room for more than three years. I did not tell him that for years before I had dreamed of old boyfriends, holding them in my hands, until the pain of my loneliness shut out all feeling.

"That's not such a long time," he said, and then he asked what I had known he would ask. "Is it another man?"

I had thought about this question. If I told him about Robert, he would have hidden behind that rather than face the real reasons I had to leave. And so I said no, because it was the truth.

"Good," he replied. "Because if it were, I would have done what O. J. Simpson did."

I shivered, afraid for myself for the first time, realizing that though he was weak and emaciated, he had been a marine and could hurt me if he wanted to. That night I pushed a chair under the handle of my bedroom door and opened the sliding-glass door in a feeble attempt to give myself time to run to my kayak on the shore of the pond and paddle away to safety. It seemed pathetically melodramatic, but I couldn't think of anything else to do.

The next few days were very difficult, but we tried to be kind and civil to each other. When I went to Boston, I called Robert but he wasn't home, so I left a message that I would stay at the Howard Johnson. I thought he'd call, but he didn't. That night I was woken by a male voice pounding on the sliding door to the balcony of my sixth-floor room. "Wanna fuck?" he asked, before he drifted away into the night. The second time he pounded on the glass, I went to the door, and when he saw a middle-aged woman instead of a coed, he climbed quickly over the balcony wall to the next balcony a few feet away, so quickly, I thought he might fall.

When I returned to Maine, Stan, who is my friend as well as caretaker, and his son Chris moved me and my things to the new apartment. I was touched by their kindness and grateful for their warm, strong arms. Tom refused to let me have my cats, but after a few days he got tired of caring for them and I went to bring them to the little apartment that would have fit into the living room of the house, worrying that they would feel cramped.

Living in the apartment over the office, I felt as if I had severed one tentacle that only made me feel the grip of others. I was connected to Tom by the business, through our children, property we owned, a life of twenty-seven years. Tom lived in a house I owned, in a community of people and places I had known and loved since I was five years old. I could not bear to leave them all at once, and besides, I had nowhere to go. My identity was so tied to Tom, that I had to sever the strands one by one. We tried to be gentle with each other, but each day was a strange torture, like a child wiggling a tooth, slowly letting it work its way out to allow room for the new one. Though at the time I thought I was pulling away slowly to give Tom time to adjust, I realize now I was also protecting myself.

I joked about having a short commute to work, but the oddness of our situation wore at me. I could hear Tom when he arrived early in the morning, and I never felt entirely free from him because he always had a right to be in the office, just beneath my feet, and could show up at any time. What would I do, I wondered, if Robert wanted to stay with me? Before I went to stay with him the first time, he had E-mailed that he would come up in his white horse, a Cherokee Laredo, to rescue me if he just knew where I was.

A week after I moved out of my house Robert E-mailed to say

he didn't think we should see each other anymore. How can he do that to me? I thought, he knows how vulnerable I am now, he knows I'm here by myself. I couldn't even cry because my face would betray me, and so I put back the mask and went to work, walking down into the office from my apartment each morning, walking back up to have lunch for relief, forcing myself to return, forcing the tears inside. But a month later there was Robert again in my computer, saying he missed me.

I began to hate going to the office, spent more time in the apartment, had to force myself to go back to my desk. I sneaked out the back door of the office, up to my apartment, just to check my E-mail to see if Robert had written. I made lunch, read the paper. I told myself I would work late, had to work late. I worked on schoolwork, checked my E-mail again, anything to avoid the office. I paid less attention to my real-estate work and hid in my schoolwork. I became bored and disengaged, the tooth was almost out.

With Debra's help I was finally able to begin thinking about why I had stayed so long in a marriage that intensified my unhappiness. Although it has taken me many years since then to come to terms with my own complicity in that marriage, I began at that time at least to think about why I had to leave Tom. I remembered times I had to fire people who worked for me. It was always a difficult process, something I delayed for too long, but which I was finally able to do, in part, because I knew the person was unhappy in the job and that doing the job poorly was contributing to his or her misery. I thought about the ways that being with me must be making Tom miserable as well, and that the only chance either of us had for a better life, for a second chance, was for me to leave completely. I began to see that to save myself I had to divorce Tom, leave our business, and leave the island, but that in doing so I would give him a chance to rediscover his own strengths and find a new life as well. I thought about my children and realized that I wanted very much to show them that we always have a second chance if we have the courage to look at ourselves and try to change.

One Saturday night there was going to be a dance and supper at the Neighborhood House in town, and everyone was going. I talked to Arthur, my landlord and friend who owned the market adjacent to our office, and asked if I could sit with him and his girlfriend Mindy. Because he had been divorced just two years before, he understood how nervous I was and how hard it was for me to go to a party alone. That night I dressed carefully in casual clothes and walked down the street to the Neighborhood House. I paid my money and had my hand stamped, cracked a nervous joke, and walked into the large hall.

It was totally dark. I couldn't see anyone, just heads outlined against the stage lights. I couldn't see Arthur and Mindy. I panicked. Fear, of what or whom I did not know, punched at my stomach and left me struggling for breath. You know most of the people in the room, I said to myself, trying to calm down. But seeing them in the dark as a congealed mass terrified me. I turned on my heel and ran out, crying before I reached the door. I ran down the darkened street and up the stairs to my apartment, collapsed on the blue futon couch, and held the pillows against me, sobbing until I couldn't breathe, for the first time completely overwhelmed and out of control, finally feeling pain. I am such a coward. I will never be able to handle going out, I berated myself. But when I calmed down, I told myself I had to have time, that I couldn't expect to feel comfortable so soon, particularly when I hadn't had any practice going out at all for so long, and I determined to forgive myself.

I began to think about the child I had seen coming toward me as Steinhem had suggested. I began to realize that as an adult I could take her in my arms, forgive her for not defending herself when she was a child, and, most important, begin to love her. I realized I had stayed in a marriage to a deeply ill person because I, too, was ill. I was unused to love administered in doses larger than the ones I had known as a child. Wasn't that, in fact, why I had married Tom in the first place: In my own way, like Tom, I, too, was paying penance, recreating my childhood.

I believe that only by leaving and looking at how I was formed in childhood was I able to create a new life, finding the pieces I enjoyed in myself, and reshaping the ones that fit only old patterns. I think of the times I thought about leaving—and there were always reasons not to. The easy explanations sufficed for so long. At first I couldn't leave, I had a child. Then two. I didn't want my children to have a stepfather. I didn't want them to feel like displaced or misplaced persons. I didn't want them to feel unworthy or unloved, ashamed and guilty. Then I couldn't leave because I was running the company, because I was making the money. I had to pay tuitions. I had to keep the house going, I had employees, responsibilities. I had to stay for everyone else.

Though I mourn the time lost and the lies I believed, I realize I could not be who I am now without having been the child or woman I was. I would not trade gifts I have of sensitivity and kindness for a sense of entitlement which can so easily drift into arrogance. Now the definition my mother and father, and other people in my family, had thrust on me because of their own insecurities, seem like ill-fitting clothes, and I can cast them off. I wished I had had the strength to reject them before, but it is only very recently that I have found in myself what friends have seen and loved.

Now I know I stayed because I felt guilty. In my own way, like Tom, I, too, was starving myself, denying myself the fundamental sustenance God has given us to nurture ourselves, His love and the love of each other. I, too, thought I was finding my salvation in deprivation. Now I see that like an anorexic, I thought I could control my destiny by denying myself what I most wanted. Perhaps it was too hard to live with people and easier to block them from my life. Like the child at my stepfather's table, the child who didn't have the name or the money or the love, as an adult I felt it was too painful to try for what I most wanted, a loving marriage with a man who would cherish and nurture me, a partner with whom to enjoy life, and a warm, loving home, full of laughter for my children and family.

But the real reason—the reason at the bottom of the pile of reasons—is that I didn't feel worthy of leaving. I thought my life was my punishment. I played the messages of childhood over and over and I believed them. I didn't think I had a right to a better life. I short-circuited success because I didn't think I "deserved" it. Certainly, I short-circuited any chance of success in love by marrying someone who met needs based on my weaknesses instead of on my strengths. I had defined my worth as a woman in the ways I felt my father and mother defined me. I didn't think I was good enough to marry a stable, loving man who would be my friend and who would allow me to grow into the person I wanted to be. I began to see that I had married the negative potentials in myself rather than what was best, and then I realized that Tom had done so as well. It seemed simplistic but true when I finally said to myself, I married my father. Tom married his mother but neither of us wanted to be that other person.

One morning, when I was just about to leave for Boston, Arthur called to say he had to talk to me immediately. I walked down the stairs of our office, down the delivery ramp to the back entrance of the market. Arthur met me at the door and motioned with his hand that we should go into the storage basement so no one would see us. While I stood in the musty gloom in the middle of the crates of oranges and toilet paper, Campbell's soup cans and rotting lettuce, Arthur told me that all summer he and the cashiers had thought Tom was stealing from the market. Now he had hard evidence. Caught on the cameras, Tom had paid for groceries and then stopped in the liquor aisle to adjust the package, and slip a bottle into the bag.

"I don't know what to do. Does he need money? What's wrong? Joan knows, and I can't keep it quiet if he keeps doing it. Joan felt so embarrassed telling me, but she checks him out and knows he doesn't pay for everything. I watched him go down the aisle and stop at the liquor." I heard the words but I could only moan slightly and Arthur continued. "Is he just afraid to buy more liquor? I went over to him and started talking; he wouldn't look at me. He fidgeted and then I could see his face turning red. I watched him put the bag in his car, and when he went into your office, I opened the car door—I'm sorry, but I checked the bag. There's a bottle of liquor in it and it's not on the checkout slip. If he does it again, I'll have to prosecute."

"Oh, no. No, not again," I said, first to myself and then Arthur. Suddenly I realized it was again—again and again. Stealing. Stealing from my pocketbook, from the money we saved, from petty cash, stealing grapes from the market, stealing food from Greta, Inge, and Pam, stealing towels from the club.

"Does he want to be caught?" Steve asked.

"Yes," I answered the question, "perhaps that's why he does it." And then I saw the circle was widening as he threw pebbles, then stones, now boulders. How do I stop him? I asked myself. And I realized I couldn't. I couldn't save him from himself, or his childhood. Only he could do that.

But Arthur had caught me as I have been caught so many times, right in the middle.

"I'll talk to him Arthur, but will you talk to him, too? So many times I've been in the middle and I just can't do it now, not by myself. I'll call his doctor because I think she'll want to know, and maybe he will see her. I have to catch the three o'clock plane to Boston. I don't have much time. But I will go talk to him now.

Thank you. I know this is hard for you, too. Thank you for handling it this way."

I walked up the steps to the office, very slowly. At each step my body felt heavier, and I was angrier. By the time I reached the door, I knew that I had to get a divorce before Tom's illness dragged me down any deeper.

"Tom," I said. He was sitting at his desk with his back to me. "Arthur wants to talk with you about something. You have to go do it now."

"Oh, what about? I don't have time right now."

"I think you had better call him and talk."

"But what is it about? I don't want to talk to him right now." His eyes narrowed and his face got red.

"Well," and then suddenly it rushed out of me—I couldn't control my anger anymore, couldn't see him as a sick man. I was just hurt, angry, and so ashamed. "Well, they caught you on the monitors stealing. Stealing from the market. Tom, I have known Arthur since I was a child. How dare you? How dare you defile my relationship with him? Do you want to be caught? Do you want everyone to know you steal cans of soda and bottles of beer from the market? That is just pathetic, like poor old Nicholas, who was caught and told he could never go back. Is that what you want?"

Now he looked shocked. Shocked into silence. He stared at his hands, and then he looked up at me and said, "I will call him."

I walked out to give him privacy, and when he came out of the room he said he was going to meet Arthur. He looked like a child, an abashed, ashamed child, but there was a forcefulness to his walk I had only seen when he had been crushed to a place from which he could rebound. How many times he had said he would win a tennis match after being down two sets to love. How far down now must he go? I wondered.

While he was gone I called Will, my lawyer. "Will, something awful has happened."

"What, Barbara?" he asked, and I could see him sitting at his large desk in the office overlooking the village, his eyes squinting in concern for me. I could not have found a better man to help me now, I thought.

"Tom's been caught stealing from the market," I told him. "I am scared, Will. I wanted to give him time to get used to the idea of divorce. But now I feel scared he is going to drag me into something awful. I feel responsible for what he is doing but there is nothing I can do to stop him. I've begged him for years not to take things, from me, from the market, from the office. I just can't stop him."

The words were pouring out of me and Will interjected, "Barbara, I am so sorry. No, you can't do anything to stop him; you can only protect yourself. What do you want me to do?"

"I have to catch the plane to Boston to get to school, but would you prepare the papers so I can get him to sign them when I get back?" I asked.

"Of course," Will said.

Tom and Arthur worked out an agreement for repayment and Steve allowed him to continue to use the market. The next Monday I called Will. He had the papers ready for Tom to sign, papers in which Tom agreed not to contest the divorce. I walked down the village street to pick them up, thinking about how Tom had betrayed me and Arthur, and feeling angry and responsible because I had brought him to this place and these people I treasured. As I climbed up the stairs to Will's office, I thought about what I was about to do—file for divorce, admit defeat. But I was finally so angry that I didn't care about hurting Tom, I just knew I had to pull myself away from him like an animal trying to escape quicksand, whose only hope is to move carefully and deliberately, inch by inch, to escape being sucked down.

"Barbara," Will said. "You understand that if Tom doesn't sign these papers, then he will be contesting the divorce and you'll have to go to court."

"And if he signs them," I responded, "then we just go before a judge and it saves a lot of time and money?"

"That's right, it is really a lot less painful for everyone."

I walked fast down the street back to the office, past the little shops, most of which had been there since I was a child—the pharmacy, now a store; Mrs. Stacy's shop offering antiques, yarn, and crafts made by local people; past the market—my mind and heart hardening as I walked.

I walked into the office, back to the room I shared with Tom. He was sitting at his desk, and as I sat in the chair at my own desk, I turned to face him and said, "Tom, I have an agreement Will drafted. I want you to sign it."

"What does it say?"

"It says we are getting divorced and you are not going to contest it."

"Well, I don't think I want to sign that. I don't believe in divorce. I don't want to give you a divorce," he said, sounding determined and a bit triumphant.

I felt sick. There was nothing to save here—except myself—so I played the trump card.

"Tom, if you don't sign it, I am going to tell people about the stealing." I didn't like myself when I did this; I knew I was kicking him like an injured dog groveling at my feet, but I didn't know what else to do.

He was quiet for a long time and then he turned and said, "All right."

I put the paper on his desk, he signed it, and I picked it up and walked quickly to Will's office. I couldn't quite believe what I was doing; again, there was too much drama. I was in another movie with a bad plot. But I said to Will, "I think I've done it. He signed the paper."

"Okay, Barbara," Will responded. "Now we just have to get a court date and then you two will go to court and the judge will grant the divorce." And four months later that is what happened. We stood in front of the judge, I in a proper dress, Tom in a blue wool jacket and madras pants, both of us feeling awkward and self-conscious, but determinedly polite, separated, and represented only by Will, and told the judge we wanted to end twenty-seven years of marriage because we had irreparable and irreconcilable differences. I thought I saw the judge look at us and decide instantly that there was no reason to prolong our marriage, no reason to suggest counseling.

I had spent so many years isolating myself further and further away from love, loving only my children, denying the best parts of myself because I felt guilty that I had sent my father to hell, that my parents had divorced, that I was a stepchild, that I was not worth loving. I had found another person with whom to share that guilt and pain, with whom to nurture and feed it until it was a roaring flame that almost consumed us. I left Tom because I knew I was going to die if I stayed and because I had to show my children that we do always have another chance at life. I thank God for giving me that chance, and I apologize to myself, to Tom and to my family for staying so long in a marriage built on pain and guilt.

A year later I moved to Boston to finish my doctoral degree, reversing my commute and returning to the office in Maine once a week where I stayed with a friend, Brook, who had been widowed two years before and was raising her two children. One evening when Brook and I were having supper, she told me that Tom had a girlfriend, Rachel, another widow who lived on the island, and was a teacher. I was surprised but relieved.

When I went to the office the next morning, I found a love letter from Tom's friend mixed in with the bills I had to pay and I wondered if Tom had put it there for me to find. People in the office told me he seemed to have new life in his step and to be much happier than they had seen him in a long time. Later that day Rachel called and he darted out of the room we still shared to take the call, laughing and talking in whispers. When he returned I said to him, "Brook told me you were seeing Rachel. That's wonderful, I am really happy for you." He seemed relieved. "I met her in church," he said. "She is a wonderful woman, kind and sensitive." Several months later Tom moved in with Rachel. Once he told me that she loved him unconditionally and I said to myself, That is something I could never do for you. Perhaps that is exactly what you need.

PROLOGUE

I could hear the music before I saw where it was coming from. It floated over the water from Southwest Harbor to the elegant cottages of Northeast that line the shore like ancient ladies with lorgnettes and cascading pearls that hold up their necks. I drove from dinner with the chatelaine of such a cottage around the harbor filled with Hinckley yachts. Driving up Sergeant's Drive along Somes Sound, I left this world, watching phosphorus catch the moonglow, hearing the tinkle of glasses and the slap of halyards against wooden masts, until I traveled around the island to Southwest Harbor, to the dance at the marina wharf. Now the music was loud and thumped against me.

There were people of all ages at this dance: people in jeans and faded jackets standing in groups drinking sodas and munching po-

tato chips, toddlers sleeping in their mothers' arms, children dancing well and wildly, adolescents standing back against the fence of
lights surveying the scene, older married couples, gay and lesbian
couples, dancers with rhythm, dancers without, dancers who had
glided together for years, dancers who had just bumped into each
other and performed an impromptu celebration. The wharf was
full of people, highlighted by the stars and the lights of Northeast
Harbor shining together.

Like Sand Hill cranes, the dancers worked their necks up and
down in an elaborate ritual that spanned seasons, sexuality, and
culture. I would not have been at this dance, my first as a single
woman in twenty-seven years, if my friend Brook, a widow too
young for her life, had not brought me and her friend Jim. Somehow she had found courage to keep looking for joy. As the music
caught us by the arm and dragged us into the circle, everyone
danced, and so did I. Brook led us in single file, Jim following and
drawing me along. How kind this is of them, I thought.

When I looked at the crowd, I began to distinguish people I
knew. I saw Richard and Karen, newly married, whirling and
whirling, writing a symphony in their touching and turning, for-
getting for a moment his child, whom they had left in the hospital,
hoping for the miracle of donor marrow to work its strength in
his blood. I watched Brook and Jim as they twisted against the
music and each other, she always a little ahead of him. One young
man, an extraordinary, original dancer, was a joy to watch as he
invented steps and reacted to the beat of the music.

So we all danced, turning misery out of our minds. In the final
dance I felt wild and free and danced with rhythm and invention,
flying lightly over the wharf, turning and twisting, a woman re-
born. We were joined by a young man who could not see in the
half-light that I was twice his age. He liked the way I danced and
I liked it, too. And so I danced, absorbing the salt night air and
the throbbing sound of the drums and guitar, letting the moment

envelop me. For a while I danced, letting the music pour through me like waves of cleansing water, and feeling the motion of my own body again, acting and reacting in a dance of second chances.

Turning my life around was an act of desperation, will, and luck. I feel the weight of that turning now like a heavily encumbered old freighter, rust staining her sides where the paint has flaked from rivets and portholes, burdened with an unbalanced cargo of lies and fears, dusty baggage, and heavy anchors. Slowly her engines push through the current, and if she doesn't waver, the going seems almost easy, the destination predestined. The pressure of the water moving past keeps her on course, so that turning requires a complete redefinition of her journey, enormous effort in defying the churning waters, the help of tugboats, and felicitous weather and tides. Changing the direction of our lives is so difficult in part because we cannot even imagine reasons to look for a new harbor; our childhoods have conditioned us to the port we find as adults. I see now the changes I made, compass point by compass point, until by degrees I redefined my course. Sometimes I think it is not surprising that it took me so long, it is surprising that I was able to do it at all—surprising I was able to push through the turgid self-doubt and reach clear, open water.

One bright fall morning, just after I had moved from my house to the apartment over the office, I walked across the main street of the village over to the post office. I picked up my mail, which included two letters from friends asking how I was doing, and I realized I was doing surprisingly well. I felt richer than I had ever in my life, rich in friends and family, rich in loving and being loved. And I looked up at the blue sky over the village street and I saw an image of myself in the clouds, borne aloft by people, each a brightly colored helium-filled balloon—purple, aqua, orange, blue, green, and yellow—to an endless horizon.

I have been so fortunate. Now I can look back and see that I dragged heavy bags around with me for most of my life, bags packed with old hurts and lies, with masks and uniforms, all the trappings I thought necessary to disguise myself. I have been taking a long trip around and around my world as I thought I knew it. Now I am coming home, home to a house I built myself to share with people who love me and whom I love, to fill with the things I have gathered on my journey. Another antique Japanese vase, the Amari pottery, the joyful life-sized wooden otter holding a red fish, carved in Maine, and beside it the accidental carving by Baxter the beaver who chugged around the little pond at the farm when he wasn't chomping down trees, my diploma from the doctoral program at Boston University, my ivory goddess. This time, as I come home, I will leave my old bags on the airport carousel to turn and turn until someone throws them away for me. I am going to buy new clothes and pack a new bag with only the things I really want. And I will travel lighter.

ABOUT THE AUTHOR

Barbara Kent Lawrence received a B.A. from Bennington College in 1965, an M.A. from New York University in 1969, and an Ed.D. from the Boston University School of Education in 1998, where her dissertation won the National Rural Education Association Award. She has taught anthropology, sociology, and history at schools in Washington, D.C., Connecticut, and Maine; co-founded and ran a real-estate-and-construction firm; and worked as a real-estate agent in Boston. She now directs the Initiative on Infrastructure and Facilities for the Annenberg Rural Challenge Policy Group. She lives in Cambridge, Massachusetts.

ABOUT THE TYPE

This book is set in Bembo, which is considered one of the first old-style typefaces, along with the highly popular Garamond. Bembo is based on the roman types cut by Francesco Griffo and used by Aldus Manutius in Venice in 1495 to print Cardinal Bembo's tract *DeAetna*. There were no italics at that time. *Bembo Italic* is based on an original print from the writing master Giovanni Tagliente, Venice, 1524. The modern version of Bembo was designed in 1929 by the Monotype Type Drawing Office, supervised by Stanley Morison.

Bembo has been widely used in books, advertising, and display work over the last sixty years. One reason for its popularity is its functional serifs, which help provide readability and guarantee an easy reading experience. Books and other texts set in Bembo can encompass a wide variety of subjects and formats because of its quiet, classical beauty.